GW01375237

MEDIUM ÆVUM MONOGRAPHS
EDITORIAL COMMITTEE

K.P. CLARKE, G. DAVIES, A.J. LAPPIN,
S. MOSSMAN, P. RUSSELL, C. SAUNDERS

Responsible Editor
A.J. LAPPIN

MEDIUM ÆVUM MONOGRAPHS
XLVI

GUTIERRE DE PALMA

BREUE REPREHENSORIUM AD QUOSDAM FRATRES RELIGIOSOS

Edited by
Bernhard Holl

The Society for the Study of Medieval Languages and Literature

OXFORD · MMXXIV

THE SOCIETY FOR THE STUDY OF MEDIEVAL LANGUAGES AND LITERATURE

https://aevum.space/monographs

© Bernhard Holl, 2024

British Library Cataloguing in Publication Data
A catalogue record for this book is available from the British Library

ISBN-13:

978-1-911694-21-2 (pb)
978-1-911694-22-9 (hb)
978-1-911694-23-6 (pdf)

CONTENTS

List of Abbreviations VII
Introduction XI
   Scholarly Context XII
   Historical Background XV
      Place of Composition: Toledo XIX
      Time of Composition: 1465 XXI
      The Author: Gutierra de Palma? XXIV
      Comparable Texts and Authors XXIX
   The Treatise: Style and Contents XXXIV
      Language and References XXXV
      Rhetoric and Intended Audience XXXVII
      Main Sections and Themes XXXIX
         A Scandal in Toledo (preface and article 1) XL
         Basic Principles: Birth, Faith, Sin and Unity (articles 2–4) XLI
         The History of Salvation (articles 5–8) XLIV
         Lessons to be Learned (articles 9–12) XLVIII
         Call to Action (articles 13–14) LI
   The Edition LV
      The Manuscript, Ms. 23-7 LV
      The Present Edition LVII
      English Translation LVIII

Breue reprehensorium ad quosdam fratres religiosos 1
   Primus articulus 7
   Secundus et tercius articulus 9

Quartus articulus 27
Quintus articulus 33
Sextus articulus 39
Septimus articulus 43
Octauus articulus 65
Nonus articulus 71
Decimus articulus 77
Undecimus articulus 91
Duodecimus articulus 99
Tercius decimus articulus 107
Quartus decimus articulus... 119

Bibliography 133

LIST OF ABBREVIATIONS

Biblical (Vulgata iuxta LXX)

Gn	Liber Genesis
Ex	Liber Exodi
Lv	Liber Levitici
Nm	Liber Numerorum
Dt	Liber Deuteronomii
Ios	Liber Iosue
Idc	Liber Iudicum
Rt	Liber Ruth
I Sm	Liber Samuhelis (Regum Primus)
II Sm	Liber Samuhelis (Regum Secundus)
III Reg	Liber Malachim (Regum Tertius)
IV Reg	Liber Malachim (Regum Quartus)
I Par	Verba Dierum (Paralipomenon I)
II Par	Verba Dierum (Paralipomenon II)
I Esr	Liber Ezrae
II Esr	Liber Ezrae Secundus (Neemiae)
III Esr	Liber Ezrae Tertius
IV Esr	Liber Ezrae Quartus
Tb	Liber Tobiae
Jdt	Liber Iudith
Est	Liber Hester
Iob	Liber Iob
Ps	Psalmi
Prv	Liber Proverbiorum
Ecl	Liber Ecclesiastes
Ct	Canticum Canticorum
Sap	Liber Sapientiae
Sir	Liber Iesu Filii Sirach (Ecclesiastici)
Is	Liber Isaiae Prophetae
Ier	Liber Hieremiae Prophetae
Lam	Lamentationes (Threni)
Bar	Liber Baruch
Ez	Liber Hiezechielis Prophetae

Dn	Liber Danihelis Prophetae
Os	Osee Propheta
Ioel	Iohel Propheta
Am	Amos Propheta
Abd	Abdias Propheta
Ion	Ionas Propheta
Mi	Micha Propheta
Na	Naum Propheta
Hab	Abacuc Propheta
So	Sofonias Propheta
Agg	Aggeus Propheta
Za	Zaccharias Propheta
Mal	Malachi Propheta
I Mcc	Liber Primus Macchabeorum
II Mcc	Liber Secundus Macchabeorum
Mt	Evangelium secundum Mattheum
Mc	Evangelium secundum Marcum
Lc	Evangelium secundum Lucam
Io	Evangelium secundum Iohannem
Act	Liber Actuum Apostolorum
Rm	Epistula ad Romanos
I Cor	Epistula ad Corinthios Prima
II Cor	Epistula ad Corinthios Secunda
Gal	Epistula ad Galatas
Eph	Epistula ad Ephesios
Phil	Epistula ad Philippenses
Col	Epistula ad Colossenses
I Th	Epistula ad Thessalonicenses Prima
II Th	Epistula ad Thessalonicenses Secunda
I Tim	Epistula ad Thimotheum Prima
II Tim	Epistula ad Thimotheum Secunda
Tit	Epistula ad Titum
Phlm	Epistula ad Philemonem
Hbr	Epistula ad Hebraeos
Iac	Epistula Iacobi
I Pt	Epistula Petri Prima
II Pt	Epistula Petri Secunda

I Io   Epistula Iohannis Prima
II Io   Epistula Iohannis Secunda
III Io   Epistula Iohannis Tertia
Iud   Epistula Iudae
Apc   Apocapsis Iohannis Apostoli

Legal and Canonical

C.   Causa *(Decretum Gratini)*
c.   caput *(Decretum Gratiani)*
Clem   *Liber Septimus (Constitutiones Clementis V)*
Cod.   *Corpus Iuris Civilis, Codex Iustinianus*
D.   Distinctio *(Decretum Gratiani)*
de cons.   *Decretum Gratiani*, Pars III *(Tractatus de consecratione)*
de poen.   *Decretum Gratiani, Tractatus de poenitentia*
Inst.   *Corpus Iuris Civilis, Institutiones*
Dig.   *Corpus Iuris Civilis, Digesta (Pandectae)*
Nov.   *Corpus Iuris Civilis, Novellae*
q.   Quaestio *(Decretum Gratiani)*
VI   *Liber Sextus Decretalium Bonifacii VIII*
X   *Liber Extra Decretalium Gregorii IX*

INTRODUCTION

Some fifty years ago the eminent Spanish scholar Ramón Gonzálvez Ruiz (1928-2019) discovered an until-then forgotten manuscript in the cathedral archives of Toledo. He went on to publish two short studies of his find, but did not finish the critical edition he had planned and announced.[1] Undoubtedly even a simple transcript of those twenty folios would have been much appreciated given its pertinence to the extensively studied field of *converso* history. Even so, a number of international scholars have since referred to the *Breue reprehensorium ad quosdam fratres religiosos* and its presumed author Gutierre de Palma, albeit only in passing given that the text itself was not available.[2]

With this edition and translation of the full text that has until now only been accessible in manuscript, I hope to contribute a small facet to the ever growing picture we have of the *converso* phenomenon – or more precisely: of the theological debate surrounding Jewish conversion to the Catholic faith in late medieval Iberia. The following introductory remarks are intended to situate the treatise both in terms of its historical origin and its significance for modern research.

---

[1] Ramón Gonzálvez Ruiz, 'El bachiller Palma, autor de una obra desconocida en favor de los conversos', in *Simposio "Toledo Judaico"*, vol. 2 (Toledo, 1973), 31-48; id., 'El Bachiller Palma y su obra de polémica proconversa', in *"Qu'un sang impur..."*. *Les conversos et le pouvoir en Espagne à la fin du moyen âge*, ed. Jeanne Battesti Pelegrin (Aix-en-Provence, 1997), 47–59.

[2] Cf. e.g. Carlos Gilly, 'The Council of Basel's "De Neophytis" Decree as Immediate Cause of and Permanent Antidote to the Racial Purity Statutes', in *The Conversos and Moriscos in Late Medieval Spain and Beyond*, vol. IV: *Resistance and Reform*, ed. Kevin Ingram (Leiden, 2021), 13–44; Carmen C. Gil Ortega, 'Alfonso Carrillo de Acuña: un arzobispo proconverso en el siglo XV castellano', *eHumanista/conversos*, 3 (2015), 138–55, pp. 139–41; Juan Hernández Franco, 'El pecado de los padres: construcción de la identidad conversa en Castilla a partir de los discursos sobre limpieza de sangre', *Hispania*, 64 (2004), 515–42; Julio Valdeón Baruque, *Cristianos, judíos y musulmanes* (Barcelona, 2006), p. 120.

Scholarly Context

By the time the *Breue reprehensorium* was discovered, research about religious conversion, *limpieza de sangre* and the Spanish Inquisition in late medieval and early modern Spain was already well established. Among the first modern publications on these topics were the works of José Amador de los Ríos who in the nineteenth century began to restore the country's conscious memory of its Jewish heritage and was followed in this effort by Francisco Cantera Burgos, Américo Castro and others in the twentieth century.[3] At the same time a significant portion of Spanish historians remained almost completely oblivious to the sufferings and contributions of New Christians in the history of their homeland. This included highly influential figures like Ramón Menéndez Pidal and Claudio Sánchez-Albornoz and coincided by and large with the ideological bias of the Franco era.[4] Consequently, the most important contributions to our field of study were subsequently made by authors of different national backgrounds, including (but not limited to) Yitzhak Baer, Haim Beinart and Albert Sicroff.[5] The latter also pioneered comparative research into pro- and anti-converso theological and canonical writing.

Ever since, the study of Iberian Jewish and *converso* history has remained very much an international concern with publications in

---

[3] Cf. i.a. José L. Lacave, 'Los estudios hebraicos y judaicos en España, desde Amador de los Ríos hasta nuestros días', in *Los judíos en la España contemporánea: historia y visiones, 1898–1998*, ed. Ricardo Izquierdo Benito *et al.* (Ciudad Real, 2000), 115–20; José Amador de los Ríos, *Historia social, política y religiosa de los judíos en España y Portugal* (Madrid, 1875); Francisco Cantera Burgos, *Álvar García de Santa María y su familia de conversos: historia de la judería de Burgos y de sus conversos más egregios* (Madrid, 1952); Américo Castro, *España en su historia: cristianos, moros y judíos* (Buenos Aires, 1948).

[4] Cf. Ramón Menéndez Pidal, *Los españoles en la historia: cimas y depresiones en la curva de su vida política* (Madrid, 1947); Claudio Sánchez-Albornoz, *España: un enigma histórico* (Buenos Aires, 1956). For historiography under Franco, cf. Anna L. Menny, *Spanien und Sepharad: über den offiziellen Umgang mit dem Judentum im Franquismus und in der Demokratie* (Göttingen, 2013).

[5] Cf. e.g. Yitzhak (Fritz) Baer, *Die Juden im mittelalterlichen Spanien* (Berlin, 1936); Albert A. Sicroff, *Les controverses des statuts de 'pureté de sang' en Espagne du 15e au 17e siècle* (Paris, 1960); Haim Beinart, *Conversos on Trial: the Inquisition in Ciudad Real* (Jerusalem, 1981).

Introduction   XIII

English increasingly at the forefront. A milestone in the retelling of the emergence and institutionalisation of anti-*converso* resentment, Benzion Netanyahu's study on the origin of the Spanish Inquisition remains a work of reference down to today.[6] As opposed to most authors before him, Netanyahu made a strong case for the possibility that the vast majority of New Christians were in fact sincere in their religious affiliation and that allegations of heresy against them were motivated by racist prejudice alone. The question of *converso* religious identity has since been commented on in a more balanced way. The hightened sense for ambiguity is exemplified by the comprehensive overview works of Norman Roth and David Gitlitz as well as by the numerous insightful studies by David Nirenberg.[7]

The further quest for authentic expressions of converso identities (often designated as the "*converso* voice"), has been advanced by Bruce Rosenstock, Gregory Kaplan, Claude B. Stuczynski, Ryan Szpiech, Elaine Wertheimer and John Edwards, to name only a few.[8] What it

[6] Benzion Netanyahu, *The Origins of the Inquisition in Fifteenth-Century Spain* (New York, ²2001).

[7] Norman Roth, *Conversos, Inquisition and the Expulsion of the Jews from Spain* (Madison, Wisconsin, ²2002); David M. Gitlitz, *Secrecy and Deceit: the religion of the Crypto-Jews* (Albuquerque, 2002). David Nirenberg, *Anti-Judaism: the western tradition* (New York, 2013); idem, 'Was there Race before Modernity? The example of "Jewish" blood in late medieval Spain', in *The Origins of Racism in the West*, ed. Miriam Eliav-Feldon *et al.* (Cambridge, 2009), 232–64; idem, 'Discourses of Judaizing and Judaism in Medieval Spain', *La Corónica*, 41 (2012), 207–33; idem, 'Poetics and Politics in an Age of Mass Conversion', in *Cultures of Conversions*, ed. Jan N. Bremmer *et al.* (Leuven, 2006), 31–51; idem, 'Figures of Thought and Figures of Flesh: "Jews" and "Judaism" in late-medieval Spanish poetry and politics', *Speculum*, 81 (2006), 398–426; idem, 'Conversion, Sex and Segregation: Jews and Christians in medieval Spain', *American Historical Review*, 107 (2002), 1065–93; idem, 'Mass Conversion and Genealogical Mentalities: Jews and Christians in fifteenth-century Spain', *Past and Present*, 174 (2002), 3–41.

[8] Cf. i.a. Bruce Rosenstock, *New Men: conversos, Christian theology and society in fifteenth-century Castile* (London, 2002); Gregory B. Kaplan, *The Evolution of Converso Literature: the writings of the converted Jews of medieval Spain* (Gainesville, 2002); Claude B. Stuczynski, 'Pro-Converso Apologetics and Biblical Exegesis', in *The Hebrew Bible in Fifteenth-Century Spain: exegesis, literature, philosophy, and the arts*, ed. Jonathan Decter, Arturo Prats (Leiden, 2012), 151–76, and idem, 'Converso Paulinism and Residual Jewishness:

is, exactly, that constitutes this elusive *converso* voice and whether it can be found in some or all of the learned apologetic source texts in favour of the New Christians (such as the *Breue reprehensorium*) is an ongoing debate.

On the side of Spanish-speaking authors numerous studies by Eloy Benito Ruano, Juan Hernández Franco, Juan Gil and others have continued to do expand and evaluate the corpus of available sources and shed light on a range of aspects regarding *converso* history.[9] Since at times there seems to have been a notable rift between the anglosphere and the hispanosphere of historical research, all the more credit goes to academics like Rosa Vidal Doval, Moisés Orfali, Rica Amrán and the aforementioned David Nirenberg whose publishing and lecturing careers have been key to connecting the two initially somewhat separate scientific communities.[10] The topic has furthermore continued to spark interest with a considerable number

---

conversion from Judaism to Christianity as a theologico-political problem', in *Bastards and Believers: Jewish converts and conversion from the Bible to the present*, ed. Theodor Dunkelgrün & Paweł Maciejko (Philadelphia, 2020), 112–33; Ryan Szpiech, *Conversion and Narrative: reading and religious authority in medieval polemic* (Philadelphia, 2013); Elaine Wertheimer, 'Converso "Voices" in Fifteenth- and Sixteenth-Century Spanish Literature', in *The Conversos and Moriscos in Late Medieval Spain and Beyond*, vol. 1: *Departures and Change*, ed. Kevin Ingram (Leiden, 2009), 97–119; John Edwards, 'New Light on the Converso Debate? The Jewish Christianity of Alonso de Cartagena and Juan de Torquemada', in *Cross, Crescent and Conversion: studies on medieval Spain and Christendom in memory of Richard Fletcher*, ed. Simon Barton & Peter Linehan (Leiden, 2008), 311–26.

[9] Cf. Eloy Benito Ruano, *Los orígines del problema converso* (Madrid, ²2001); Juan Hernández Franco, *Sangre limpia, sangre española: el debate de los estatutos de limpieza (siglos XV-XVII)* (Madrid, 2011); Juan Gil, *Los conversos y la inquisición sevillana* (Sevilla, 2000).

[10] Cf. Rosa Vidal Doval, *Misera Hispania: Jews and Conversos in Alonso de Espina's 'Fortalitium fidei'* (Oxford, 2013); Moisés Orfali, 'Jews and Conversos in Fifteenth-Century Spain: Christian apologia and polemic', in *From Witness to Witchcraft: Jews and Judaism in medieval Christian thought*, ed. Jeremy Cohen (Wiesbaden, 1996), 337–60; Rica Amrán, *Judíos y conversos en el reino de Castilla: propaganda y mensajes políticos, sociales y religiosos (siglos XIV-XVI)* (Valladolid, 2009); eadem, 'Judíos y conversos en las crónicas de los reyes de Castilla (desde finales del siglo XIV hasta la expulsión)', *Espacio, Tiempo y Forma*, 9 (1996), 257–75.

of French historians of whom Maurice Kriegel, Sophie Coussemacker, Michel Jonin and Adeline Rucquoi are only the most widely recognized.[11] Also academics of Italian (S. Pastore, F. Accorsi) and German (U. Horst, M. S. Hering Torres) backgrounds have presented a number of noteworthy contributions, making the Iberian pure-blood controversy one of the most intensely studied phenomena in international historical research.[12]

Historical Background

It would certainly not be wrong to describe Castile under Henry IV (1454-1474) as marked by conflict, crisis and poor government – it would, however, be also rather commonplace and lay perhaps undue blame at the feet of this particular monarch.[13] Indeed, one would be hard pressed to point to a period of overall order and stability at any time since the Trastámara dynasty first seized the throne – or even before.

---

[11] Cf. e.g. Maurice Kriegel, 'Entre "Question" des nouveaux-chrétiens et expulsion des Juifs: la double modernité des procés d'exclusion dans l'Espagne du XVe siècle', in *Xudeus e conversos na historia*, vol. 1, ed. Carlos Barros (Santiago de Compostela, 1994), 171–94; Sophie Coussemacker, 'Convertis et judaïsants dans l'Ordre de Saint-Jérôme: un état de la question', *Mélanges de la casa de Velázquez*, 27 (1991), 5–27; Michel Jonin, 'Transformations discursives et stratégies indentitaires: le cas des nouveaux chrétiens (Espagne XVe siècle)', *Cahiers d'études romanes*, 4 (2000), 99–113; Adeline Rucquoi, 'Les juifs dans les écrits castillans: peuple, genre ou nation?', *Revue de l'histoire des religions*, 234 (2017), 359–84.

[12] Cf. Stefania Pastore, *Un'eresia spagnola: spiritualità conversa, alumbradismo e inquisizione (1449–1559)* (Firenze, 2004); Federica Accorsi, '*El espejo de verdadera nobleza* y la cuestión de los conversos', in *Mosén Diego de Valera: entre las armas y las letras*, ed Cristina Moya García (Rochester, 2014), 21–52; Max S. Hering Torres, *Rassismus in der Vormoderne: die "Reinheit des Blutes" im Spanien der Frühen Neuzeit* (Frankfurt, 2006); Ulrich Horst, 'Kardinal Juan de Torquemada und sein Traktat zur Verteidigung der Neuchristen', in *Dominikaner und Juden: Personen, Konflikte und Perspektiven vom 13. bis zum 20. Jahrhundert* ed. Elias H. Füllenbach & Gianfranco Miletto (Berlin, 2015), 251–72 and idem, 'Die spanischen Dominikaner und das Problem der Judenchristen ("conversos")', ibid., 273–98.

[13] Cf. i.a. Luis Suárez Fernández, *Enrique IV de Castilla: la difamación como arma política* (Barcelona, 2001).

Putting aside for a moment the massive religious unrest of the era, late medieval societies on the Iberian Peninsula (and elsewhere) were under immense strain:[14] The demographic decline in the wake of the Black Death in the middle of the fourteenth century as well as the climatic effects of the transition from the Medieval Warm Period to the Little Ice Age threatened to throw agricultural production off balance and were often interpreted as signs of divine wrath.[15] Doubts have been raised recently as to how much the Iberian Peninsula was really affected by the the plague of 1348–50 given the lack of hard and fast evidence, but even so, fear of the Black Death was certainly a factor.[16]

By comparison, the fifteenth century can be described more as a period of slow overall economic recovery. Nevertheless the strain of social, religious and military conflict continued unabatedly. Developments in economics and warfare undermined the power of the feudal elites and called the traditional social order into question. While common foot soldiers with pikes and firearms took the place of armoured knights on the battle fields, merchants and creditors easily surpassed the lower nobility in terms of wealth and prosperity – a shift in power especially upsetting for the Spanish realms where the percentage of denizens claiming noble birth was higher than in any other region of Europe.[17] Moreover, wars to facilitate this redistribution of power were frequent in late medieval Iberia, be it

---

[14] Cf. Peter Schuster, 'Die Krise des Spätmittelalters: zur Evidenz eines sozial- und wirtschaftsgeschichtlichen Paradigmas in der Geschichtsschreibung des 20. Jahrhunderts', *Historische Zeitschrift*, 269 (2001), 19–55; Philippe Wolff, 'The 1391 Pogrom in Spain: social crisis or not?', *Past and Present*, 50 (1971), 4–18; Stefania Pastore, 'Doubt in Fifteenth-Century Iberia', in *After Conversion: Iberia and the emergence of modernity*, ed. by Mercedes García-Arenal (Leiden, 2016), 283–303.

[15] Cf. Mariano Barriendos & Josep Barriendos, 'Los inicios de la Pequeña Edad del Hielo en España: aportaciones de la climatología histórica al clima del siglo XIV', *Geographicalia*, 73 (2021), 55–79.

[16] Guillermo Castán Lanaspa, 'La gran mortandad de 1348: sobre el mito y la realidad (conocida) de la Peste Negra en España', *Nuestra Historia*, 9 (2020), 73–94; Ricardo Izquierdo Benito, 'Edad Media', in *Historia de Toledo*, ed. Julio de la Cruz Muñoz (Toledo, 1997), 115–256, pp. 189–90.

[17] Cf. Teofilo F. Ruiz, *Spanish Society, 1400-1600* (Harlow 2001), pp. 68–80.

against the Muslims of Al-Andalus, be it against neighbouring Christian kingdoms or against rivalling factions and pretenders of the same crown. In particular the civil war between Henry IV and the supporters of his younger half-brother Alfonso dominated the political scenery at the time the *Breue reprehensorium* was written. The Mediterranean slave trade, to name one final factor, was expanding vastly near the end of the Middle Ages, displacing tens of thousands of people and causing immeasurable suffering.[18]

Faith and religion may at times have played a silent role to mollify social frictions and ease overall anxiety, but all too often tended to aggravate, if not create, conflicts. Even before the great rifts of the Reformation, bitter controversies separated Conciliarists and Papalists, Nominalists and Realists, radicals and moderates over the question of poverty, and more generally church authorities and heterodox believers. The Iberian realms were affected little less than other parts of Latin Christianity by these doctrinal struggles, but still more by interreligious confrontation. The proximity of the Islamic world and a relatively great number of Muslim and Jewish inhabitants inevitably posed a challenge to a Catholic community that regarded eternal salvation as an existential matter and its own faith and practice as indispensable for it.

After centuries of relative tolerance towards Jews and Muslims, the Iberian kingdoms counted a significant number of non-Christian denizens. In particular the Jewish presence was notable in comparison to other parts of the Latin West, where Jews had been banned from England, expelled from French territories on several occasions and subjected to pogroms and massacres in countless German cities, often in connection with ongoing crusades, popular uprisings and epidemics. Although the Mediterranean world in general seems to have been less prone to anti-Jewish violence, religious tolerance in the Christian realms of the Iberian Peninsula experienced a sharp decline

---

[18] Cf. i.a. William D. Phillips, *Slavery in Medieval and Early Modern Iberia* (Philadelphia, 2014); idem, 'La historia de la esclavitud y la historia medieval de la Península Ibérica', *Espacio, Tiempo y Forma*, 23 (2010), 149–65; Alfonso Franco Silva, 'La esclavitud en Andalucía a fines de la edad media: problemas metodológicos y perspectivas de investigación', *Studia*, 47 (1989), 147–67.

near the end of the fourteenth century.[19] Especially in Castile and Aragon (initially less so in Navarre and Portugal) the periodically renewed pressure on non-Christians to convert was combined with a growing reluctance to fully accept the converts as true Christians. This paradox created a spiral of religiously fuelled hostility that resulted in ever more frequent and violent riots and pogroms. As the Jewish population decreased in size and significance, religious zeal and general discontent targeted more and more Christians of known or suspected Jewish descent. The prejudice that had been held so long against the Jews was transferred rather effortlessly on the so called New Christians or *conversos*.[20]

Even though exaggerared enormously by the courtly propaganda of Henry's successors, their relative progress in strengthening royal government is undeniable. Whether indeed owing to a decadent and feeble character, as contemporary critics would have it, or due to political circumstances, Henry "the Impotent" often changed alliances, failed to rein in the powerful families of the realm and was ultimately perceived as a weak and morally questionable ruler. From a Jewish or *converso* perspective though, his often ineffective and wavering policies were still a lesser evil compared to the determination with which Isabella and Ferdinand established the Inquisition to persecute the slightest trace of heresy among New Christians and expelled their remaining Jewish subjects under pain of death.[21]

---

[19] For possible reasons of this turn towards intolerance cf. e.g. Jeremy Cohen, *The Friars and the Jews: the evolution of medieval anti-Judaism* (Ithaca, 1982); José M. Monsalvo Antón, 'Mentalidad antijudía en la Castilla medieval (ss. XII–XV)', in *Xudeus e Conversos na Historia*, vol. 1: *Mentalidades e cultura*, ed. by Carlos Barros (Santiago de Compostela, 1994), 21–84.

[20] Cf. Albert A. Sicroff, *Los estatutos de limpieza de sangre: controversias entre los siglos XV y XVII* (Madrid, 1985), p. 85; Luis Suárez Fernández, *Monarquía hispana y revolución trastámara* (Madrid, 1994), pp. 108–09; Eloy Benito Ruano, 'Del problema judío al problema converso', in *Los orígines del problema converso* (Madrid, 2001), 15–38.

[21] Cf. Óscar Perea Rodríguez, 'Enrique IV de Castilla y los conversos: testimonios poéticos de una evolución histórica', *Revista de poética medieval*, 19 (2007), 131–75.

In the grand scheme of things then, the *converso* crisis, or rather the disastrous failure of the Spanish Christian majority to accept and include in the long run the converts it had so urgently demanded, can be regarded as a self-imposed detriment on top of and cross-related with other ongoing social conflicts. As such it stands out as something like an Iberian peculiarity. Certainly other Jewish communities in Europe had suffered their share of persecution, and individual conversions to Christianity were not unheard of in German and Italian principalities. But it was only in the Spanish realms that tens of thousands were baptised under the pressure of stifling anti-Jewish legislation and taxation, zealous missionising campaigns, physical violence and finally the threat of exile or death in the expulsions 1492-1498.

Place of Composition: Toledo

Social problems, political conflict and religious tensions certainly had a tendency towards mutual aggravation. As indicated above, the relevant aspects have been extensively studied over the last years and decades: late medieval Iberian mass conversions, the resulting social crisis and creation of a *converso* caste, the phenomenon (real and imagined) of crypto-Judaism and the responses of the Old Christian majority – inquisition, expulsion and statutes of blood purity.[22] In light of the aforementioned studies it would be superfluous to add here yet another rundown of the relevant dates and events. Instead I intend to confine myself to recalling only a few key circumstances with direct impact on the situation in the Toledo of the 1460s, where the *Breue reprehensorium* was composed.

The city of Toledo had been at the centre of the *converso* controversy from the start and continued to be so long after the lifetime of our author: in 1391 it had seen the same brutal riots and forced conversions as many other Castilian cities. The once thriving Jewish community had been drastically diminished, though the exact

---

[22] For an insightful and very concise summary of the origins and development of the *converso* controversy cf. e.g. the first two chapters of Vidal Doval, *Misera Hispania*.

numbers of those murdered and forcibly baptized can only be guessed today.[23]

In 1449 the Old Christian inhabitants of Toledo rose up in open revolt against the king's minister, Álvaro de Luna, lynched a number of *conversos* associated with him, and subjected others to show trials for their alleged judaizing heresy. As the rebel junta tightened its grip over the city, it infamously tried to pass a law that would prevent anyone of Jewish descent to ever again hold office or power in the city.[24] Although the so-called *sentencia-estatuto* was condemned by both the pope and the king of Castile and was then quickly rescinded, it went on to later serve as a model for numerous institutions that sought to declare themselves exclusively Old Christian: university colleges, cathedral chapters, religious and military orders, guilds, pious fraternities and other corporations adopted similar statutes beginning in the 1480s. It is indeed hard to imagine a greater impact for legislation that never formally came into effect.

Behind this unrelenting discrimination was the (sincere or tactical) suspicion of heresy that followed New Christians generation after generation. Perhaps in an effort to settle the question once and for all, Archbishop Alonso Carrillo allowed a diocesan inquistion to be held under his authority.[25] The appointment of the Hieronymite friar Alonso de Oropesa for this delicate mission meant that the proceedings were indeed not designed to entrap and convict suspects by all means but rather to disprove the generalised belief that all *conversos* were really secret Jews. However fair and impartial this tribunal of 1461-2 may or may not have been, it was not able to pacify the Toledan urban community. Deadly riots broke out again in 1467, with a *converso* militia even putting up a rugged defence before being overcome and subjected to murder and pillage. In 1485 Toledo

---

[23] Cf. Izquierdo Benito, 'Edad Media', pp. 192–95.

[24] Cf. Linde M. Brocato, 'Toledo 1449: the complex political space(s) and dynamics of civil violence', in *A Companion to Medieval Toledo*, ed. Yasmine Beal-Rivaya & Jason Busic (Leiden, 2018), 164–94.

[25] Cf. Francisco Bautista, 'Predicación anticonversa, inquisición y tolerancia en un discurso de 1461–1462: en torno a Alonso de Oropesa y Alonso de Espina', *Medieval Encounters*, 28 (2022), 377–446; Ricardo García Cárcel & Doris Moreno Martínez, *Inquisición: historia crítica* (Madrid, 2000), p. 30.

became one of the first Castilian cities to host a permanent tribunal of the Spanish Inquisition, which this time worked purposefully and effectively against the New Christians.

In 1547, almost a century after the first failed attempt to put anti-*converso* resentment into law, like-minded efforts finally succeeded. The cathedral chapter adopted an official statute excluding from its ranks anyone of Jewish lineage. For at least those roughly hundred years since 1449 the same chapter must have been itself a fiercely contested battle ground for *converso* clerics and their enemies, and its fall to the pure-blood-ideology must have sounded like a death knell to the hopes and aspirations of Spanish New Christians. After all, the archdiocese of Toledo was the seat of the primate of all of Spain, ancient centre of the glorified Visigoth Empire, site of eighteen venerable councils, home to a number of national saints and scene of some of the most famous historic battles between Muslims and Christians. Its importance in setting legal and moral precedents could hardly be overrated.

Time of Composition: 1465

At the time the *Breue reprehensorium* was written, the forces hostile to the New Christians within the cathedral chapter were still reined in by the aforementioned archbishop Alonso Carrillo de Acuña (1410-1482). Descendant of a Portuguese noble family, he himself had no known genealogical connection to the Jewish people but apparently felt no sympathy for the advocates of Old Christian superiority either. Quite remarkably indeed for a prelate well versed in political power play and not at all above a certain opportunism in the dynastic struggles of the era, his conviction in favour of the *conversos* never seems to have faltered in his 36 years as primate of Spain – or at least he never thought it advantageous to alter his stance in this question.

Thus in a diocesan synod in 1481 Alonso Carrillo was still insisting on legal measures to end the separation of Old and New Christians by outlawing the exclusion of either from pious fraternities and cemeteries. "Reborn through baptism, we are made new men", he argued, "out of which follows how guilty those are who – forgetting the purity of the law about the nations – call themselves Old Christians and others New Christians or *conversos* thereby causing a

schism between the faithful".[26] Bearing this in mind, the *Breue reprehensorium* might even be a commissioned work to provide the archbishop with the needed theological and canonistic arguments to defend the case of the *conversos*. Mention of the author working "at the feet" (preface) of the Spanish primate and his praise as "a second Saint Ildefonsus" (article 13) indicate a relationship of employment or patronage. On the other hand, Alonso Carrillo may have just been the most promising addressee for the author's complaint against the anti-*converso* propaganda of the Dominicans.

The presence of this mendicant order in Toledo dates back to even slightly before the formal foundation of its Spanish province in 1221, the first settlement being based on a donation by king Fernando III: Saint Paul outside the city walls.[27] In 1364 the Dominican community of Toledo was joined by a monastery of its female branch. This famous convent of Santo Domingo el Real counted from the beginning with the support of several noble families and with the considerable donations it received greatly enhanced the Dominicans' economic resources. The monastery referred to by the *Breue reprehensorium*, however, is the one donated to the order in 1407 and dedicated to Saint Peter Martyr.[28]

The historical building, situated in the much more prestigious centre of the city, is today part of the *Universidad de Castilla-La Mancha*. In the 1420s it was headed by the famous theologian and defender of the *conversos*, Juan de Torquemada (1388-1468), who

---

[26] "[...] por el bautismo regenerados, somos fechos nuevos homes, de que se sigue quanto son culpables los que olvidada la limpieza de la ley de gentes, unos llamandose christianos viejos e otros llamandose christianos nuevos o conversos, induciendo cisma entre los fieles" – José Sánchez Herrero, *Concilios provinciales y sínodos toledanos de los siglos XIV y XV: la religiosidad cristiana del clero y pueblo* (La Laguna, 1976), p. 336.

[27] Cf. Eugenio Serrano Rodríguez, '*Laudare, benedicere, praedicare*: Toledo y la Orden de Predicadores', *Anuario de historia de la Iglesia*, 30 (2021), 65–102; Francisco García-Serrano, 'Ambiguity, Friendship and Pragmatism: medieval friars in Iberia and beyond' in *Conflict and Collaboration in Medieval Iberia*, ed. Kim Bergqvist, Kurt Villads Jensen & Anthony John Lappin (Newcastle, 2020), 181-206.

[28] Cf. Donald Prudlo, *Thomas Agni da Lentini: Vita Sancti Petri Martiris* (Oxford, 2022).

then went on to serve as cardinal and advisor to the pope. Some time after his term as prior, the community's attitude towards the New Christians must have changed somewhat for the worse. And yet the individual relationship between the convent and the author of the *Breue reprehensorium* was perhaps not unequivocally bad: as some evidence found by Gonzálvez Ruiz indicates, he not only owned a house in the friars' vicinity but he (or a homonymous relative of his) also obtained in 1484 the degree of a licentiate in canon law under their authority.[29] These somewhat contradictory findings are not so odd considering that the whole Dominican order's stance in the *converso* question and regarding the so-called purity of blood was rather complicated.[30] If the convent in Toledo indeed allowed an open display of adversity to New Christians in its own church, whatever friars with Jewish ancestors or allies they once had had in the priory must have been considerably marginalized by the time the *Breue reprehensorium* was written. But when was that, exactly?

Gonzálvez Ruiz dated the manuscript between 1455 and 1465, drawing upon the biographical dates of king John II and pope Nicolas V (both referred to as being already deceased) and what seems to be a subsequent note in Castilian on the back of the manuscript.[31] However, a more precise guess can be made based on a margin note on fol. 16v. Without this addition, the text would simply refer to Alonso Carrillo and Henry IV, comparing them in a panegyric manner to the revered Saint Ildefonsus and King Recceswinth respectively. The addendum then modifies the portrayal of king Henry, declaring him to have been rejected by God in favour of his younger brother.

This notable alteration clearly mirrors a shift in allegiance by archbishop Alonso Carrillo, who in June 1465 openly joined a coalition of nobles in support of Henry's younger half-brother

---

[29] Cf. Gonzálvez Ruiz, 'Obra de polémica', pp. 49–50.

[30] Cf. Horst, 'Kardinal Juan de Torquemada' and idem, 'Die spanischen Dominikaner'.

[31] Cf. Gonzálvez Ruiz, 'Obra desconocida', pp. 39–40.

Alfonso of Castile.[32] In a symbolic public spectacle later known as the "Farce of Avila" (*farsa de Ávila*), he and other rebel leaders dethroned the king in effigy and declared the prince his successor. It is then no stretch of the imagination to assume that the *Breue reprehensorium* (lauding king Henry) was almost finished and ready to be presented to the archbishop when his political coup suddenly called for this last minute edit in favour of the emerging pretender to the throne. This concession to the political demands of the day being made, the author would certainly have concluded and submitted his work at the next possible opportunity, most likely that same year of 1465. The remaining blank spaces after very few of the quotes in the manuscript lead one to believe that the author sought and found this opportunity sooner than he was able or could be bothered to verify and fill in the corresponding sources. Likewise the somewhat premature dismissal of Henry IV, although certainly inopportune after his half-brother died in 1468, is left unaltered.

The Author: Gutierre de Palma?

The author of the *Breue reprehensorium* introduces himself in the preface as "Palma" by means of a play on words referring to a bent palm tree – most likely a reference to the family's origin on the Balearic Islands or in Andalusia turned into a surname. Gonzálvez Ruiz was all but certain that he must be the same person as one "bachiller Palma", author of another treatise called *Diuina rretribuçion sobre la cayda d'Espanna*.[33] This vernacular work composed in about 1479 has also been interpreted as a defence of the Spanish *conversos*,[34] although it is foremost an unabashed glorification of the Catholic Monarchs Isabella and Ferdinand and their victory (actually more of a

---

[32] Cf. Nicolás López Martínez, 'El Arzobispo Carrillo y la política de su tiempo', in *Miscelánea José Zunzunegui*, vol. 1 (Vitoria, 1975), 247–67.

[33] Gonzálvez Ruiz, 'Obra desconocida', pp. 40–41; cf. discussion in Scott Ward, *Historiography, Prophecy, and Literature: "Divina retribución" and its underlying ideological agenda* (Bloomington, 2009), pp. 17–27; J. M. Escudero de la Peña, *Divina retribución sobre la caida de España en tiempo del noble rey Don Juan el primero, compuesta por el Bachiller Palma* (Madrid, 1879), p. 26.

[34] Cf. Maria L. Giordano, *Apologetas de la fe: elites conversas entre inquisición y patronazgo en Espana (siglos XV y XVI)* (Madrid, 2004), pp. 75–76.

stalemate) against Portugal. While a similar play on words and hint to his surname in both works may well point to the author being one and the same, it is certainly no hard-and-fast proof. However, the diligent research done by Gonzálvez Ruiz in the cathedral archive of Toledo brought to light other contemporary documents (albeit more mundane in nature) bearing witness to a certain bachelor Gutierre de Palma and thus providing us with a possible full name.[35] Considering that these testimonies of various property deals speak to a considerable level of wealth and income, this would definitely place his family in the upper strata of the city's patriciate.

As the author himself tells the reader in article 11 of his treatise, he studied at the university of Salamanca. If he is indeed identical with the *bachiller* Palma (who wrote the *Diuina rretribuçion*) one would assume that he graduated there as bachelor of canon law, as his comprehensive use of the legal sources seems way too advanced for a mere bachelor of the liberal arts. A throwaway remark about his education also gives us the best clue as to the year of his birth. He reports having witnessed there in Salamanca an eclipse of the sun around the year, when an anti-*converso* uprising took place in Toledo – almost certainly 1449. Being still a "young boy" *(paruulus)*, yet old enough to have enrolled into university would make him about 14 years of age at the time, his year of birth therefore being 1435, give or take a few years. In his later days, as mentioned above, he may have earned the higher academic degree of a licentiate, doing business under that very title. This kind of prolonged academic career interrupted by many years of mundane obligations and engagements was in fact not uncommon in the world of late medieval European universities.[36]

Though again there is no direct information, everything points to the author being a layman, neither ordained as a priest nor member of a religious order. As such he is often "occupied by worldly business" *(secularibus occupatus negotiis*, preface) and demands the proper distinction between right and wrong doctrine from "you churchmen" *(uos ecclesiasticos*, article 14). If the additional archival

---

[35] Cf. Gonzálvez Ruiz, 'Obra desconocida', pp. 43–46.
[36] Cf. Robert Gramsch-Stehfest, *Bildung, Schule und Universität im Mittelalter* (Berlin, 2019), pp. 181–96.

evidence unearthed by Gonzálvez Ruiz is indeed linked to the same man named Palma, this would also mean that he had two legitimate sons, virtually ruling out that he was ever ordained a priest or took perpetual vows.[37] Therefore, although the historical person Gutierre de Palma, apologetic author, canonist and well-to-do Toledan resident, remains elusive, the sources collected still seem strong enough to favor this preliminary sketch until further evidence contradicts it.

Finally, a time-honoured question in historical studies concerning pro-*converso* authors (or indeed any notable person of late medieval and early modern Spain) goes: Were they themselves *conversos*? It is fair to say that almost every known clergyman, friar, jurist, chronicler and poet who so much as made a sympathetic comment towards Jews or converts or a wary remark about the Spanish Inquisition has been suspected of being of Jewish descent by at least some modern researchers. This includes authors of whom the historical record shows otherwise no indication at all of a Jewish family background, such as Alonso Díaz de Montalvo, Lope de Barrientos or Alonso de Oropesa. The reasoning at its core seems to be, that anyone who ever spoke up for Christians of Jewish descent must necessarily be one of them – an evidently highly problematic assumption which especially when applied to the putative characteristics of *converso* thought, voice and identity all too easily becomes a way of begging the question.

But there is another problem besides the uncertainty of determining lineages from a distance of more than five hundred years: these same lineages were blurred concepts already in their own time, socially constructed labels with only ambiguous connections to how someone saw themselves, how they were perceived by others and even who their ancestors had in fact been. Especially before the sixteenth century, the so-called impurity of blood was still not much more than a hazy notion of resentment against anything Jewish, and it was all but unclear what exact degree of genealogical relation constituted it. It was not until a century after the rebellion of Toledo that a single Jewish ancestor would be generally judged a detrimental flaw in an

---

[37] Cf. Gonzálvez Ruiz, 'Obra desconocida', pp. 46–47.

otherwise Old Christian lineage.³⁸ "Jewishness" as a disqualifying accusation in theological disputes as well as in the rhetorical feuds between poets could be virtually unrelated to the facts of one's family and creed.³⁹

Therefore, one person might be labelled a *converso* by the social conventions of their time but reject that category in their own theological understanding and renounce all connections to Judaism. Another could have Jewish ancestors but be publicly cleared of all negative associations with them. Another who had no Jewish family background at all might nevertheless be suspected of "judaizing" if they associated too closely with Jews or New Christians. Thus, oddly enough, Juan de Torquemada was believed at least by some to be of Jewish descent, while his nephew, Tomás, was not.⁴⁰ King Ferdinand's great-grandmother was probably a Jewess, yet no one in their right mind would dispute his purity of blood (at least not to his face).⁴¹ The descendants of Pablo de Santa María, the most famous convert of his time, could not possibly deny their Jewish heritage, yet nothing short of a royal decree granted them *limpieza de sangre* on the grounds that they were said to belong to the same lineage as the Virgin Mary.⁴² Despite all these and many more ambiguous cases, being or not being *converso* is treated almost like an essential quality by some of today's researchers. And while no doubt the impact of any social stigma is only too real for those suffering under it, its true nature as an artificial

---

³⁸⁾ Cf. Juan Hernández Franco, 'Construcción y deconstrucción del converso a través de los memoriales de limpieza de sangre durante el reinado de Felipe III', *Sefarad*, 72 (2012), 325–50; id., *Sangre limpia*, pp. 144–54.

³⁹⁾ Cf. Nirenberg, *Anti-Judaism*, pp. 236–44; idem, 'Poetics and Politics'; idem, 'Figures of Thought'.

⁴⁰⁾ See the discussion in Vidal Doval, *Misera Hispania*, pp. 37–38; Joseph A. Levi, *Hernando del Pulgar: Los Claros Varones de España (ca. 1483). A semi-paleographic edition* (New York 1996), p. 91; Bruce Rosenstock, *New Men: conversos, Christian theology and society in fifteenth-century Castile* (London 2002), p. 14, and Netanyahu, *Origins*, pp. 432–44.

⁴¹⁾ Cf. Roth, *Conversos*, p. 320.

⁴²⁾ Cf. Francisco Cantera Burgos, *Álvar García de Santa María y su familia de conversos: historia de la judería de Burgos y de sus conversos más egregios* (Madrid, 1952), pp. 280–84.

and protean construct should not be forgotten and the extent of its negotiability not be overlooked.

Bearing all this in mind, to determine if the author of the *Breue reprehensorium* was (in any sense of the word) a *converso* is mostly guesswork. Conflating the subjective, social and factual side of things, Gonzálvez Ruiz was rather convinced of this possibility despite having to lean on nothing but circumstantial evidence. Thus he explained Gutierre's failure to name his parentage in business contracts as an attempt to conceal his Jewish origins, connected him with a pious fraternity favoured by New Christians and (quite appallingly, really) pointed to his "mercantile attitude" *(actitud mercantil)* as further proof. According to Gonzálvez Ruiz therefore we are meant to believe that our author Gutierre tried to hide his *converso* background from business partners while at the same time openly joining a New Christian brotherhood that would give away the very fact even centuries later. Setting aside the self-contradictory nature of this supposed evidence it is obvious that all of these supposed clues could have entirely different explanations and that even their coincidence was hardly exclusive to *converso* Castilians at the time.

In conclusion, it is certainly possible that Gutierre counted among his parents or more distant ancestors at least some Jewish relations – as countless of his contemporaries did. However, if his social environment indeed tended to label him as a New Christian, this had to do at least as much with his personal associations and the stance he obviously took against the pure-blood-ideology. As a learned man and devout Christian he might really have felt that there was no essential significance to a Jewish or non-Jewish lineage and therefore rejected those very categories for himself. In his treatise at least, he never overtly identifies as a *converso* as did Alonso de Cartagena, Fernán Díaz de Toledo or Fernando de Pulgar in their respective works, nor does he explicitly claim to be of Old Christian stock like Alonso de Oropesa, Juan de Corrales or Antonio de Ferrariis. And although he makes a remarkable show of being offended by an inscription that he takes to mock the *converso* victims of 1449, this could well be a purely moral stance and not an expression of familial consternation. It is therefore by all means possible to search for an authentic *converso* voice in the *Breue reprehensorium*, but one should be aware that it is a

concept the author himself declared and probably genuinely believed to be meaningless.

Comparable Texts and Authors

The "Brief Reprehension" is one of numerous apologetic texts in favour of the *conversos* that has come down to our times. Even more, no doubt, were written before the expulsions of 1492-1498 but have been lost. Together, these treatises, sermons, letters and legal opinions constitute a school of thought that can be described as "Indistinctionist" in so far as it was directed against any distinction being made between Christians according to their genealogy. Essentially conservative in nature and rooted deep in the scholastic tradition, the basic tenets of this spiritual and academic school continued to inform criticism of the Spanish obsession with *limpieza de sangre* in the sixteenth and seventeenth century.[43]

The earliest works that are by now well known and published in modern editions answer directly to the rebellion of Toledo in 1449 and the until then unheard-of anti-*converso* actions of its partisans. As such, the "Sermon on the day of Saint Augustine" is a homily preached before the royal court in that very summer of 1449 and composed by an unnamed cleric.[44] Soon to follow was the "Instruction of the Relator" by Fernán Díaz de Toledo,[45] a royal official who prepared this text for Lope de Barrientos, bishop of Cuenca and once tutor to the crown prince. Bishop Lope in turn adapted the short but pugnant condemnation of the rebels to write his own polemic "Against some Sowers of Discord" with only slight

---

[43] Cf. Bernhard Holl, *Die Conversos: christliche Gegner und Verteidiger der iberischen Neuchristen in den Jahren vor 1492* (Baden-Baden, 2022), pp. 272–74.

[44] The latest critical edition of the *Sermo in die beati Augustini* can be found in Tomás González Rolán and Pilar Saquero Suárez-Somonte, *De la sentencia-estatuto de Pero Sarmiento a la Instrucción del Relator: estudio introductorio, edición crítica y notas de los textos contrarios y favorables a los judeoconversos a raíz de la rebelión de Toledo de 1449* (Madrid, 2012), pp. 33–56.

[45] *Instrucción del relator para Don Lope de Barrientos, obispo de Cuenca, sobre la çiçaña de Toledo contra Pero Sarmieno y el bachiller Marcos Garçia de Mora*. Text in González Rolán/Saquero Suárez-Somonte, *De la sentencia-estatuto*, pp. 95–120.

alterations to the original.[46] Some years later, however, he redacted the "Response to a Question by a Certain Bachelor", an original in-depth analysis of one particular church law concerning the *converso* question.[47] Likewise from before the death of John II in 1454 dates the "Mirror of True Nobility", a treatise on the nature of the noble estate by Diego de Valera.[48] It argues in one chapter that converts to Christianity retain all honours and dignities that they had (potentially) possessed in their former community; the important point being that no one was to be barred from noble titles or church offices simply on account of being a *converso*.

Still in the wake of the Toledo crisis, Alonso Díaz de Montalvo, another royal official and in the decades to come one of the most notable jurists of the kingdom, prepared "A Certain Thin Treatise about the Events in Toledo" which he included many years later as an extensive footnote in his annotated collection of Castilian laws.[49] Finally, two heavyweights both in terms of academic and ecclesiastical standing joined the apologists. Cardinal Juan de Torquemada, probably the most influential Castilian of the time at the papal curia, penned the treatise "Against the Midianites and Ismaelites".[50] This

---

[46] *Contra algunos çiçañadores de la nación de convertidos del pueblo de Israel.* Text in González Rolán/Saquero Suárez-Somonte, *De la sentencia-estatuto*, pp. 122–41.

[47] *Quaesitum a domino Lupo de Barriento, espicopo Conchensi, illustrissimi domini nostri domini Enrici Castellae Legionisque confessore, cancellarioque maiore ac eiusdem regiae maiestatis consiliario, per quendam bacalarium eiusdem paternitatis familiarem et devotum – Responsio praedicti domini episcopi.* Text in González Rolán/Saquero Suárez-Somonte, *De la sentencia-estatuto*, pp. 144–65.

[48] *Espejo de verdadera nobleza.* Text in Federica Accorsi, *Estudio del 'Espejo de verdadera nobleza' de Diego de Valera con edición crítica de la obra* (Pisa, 2011), pp. 289–351.

[49] *Tractatus quidam levis, quem de mandato Illustrissimi Domini nostri Regis Ioannis II. super factis Toleti contingentibus invalide compilavi (also: Glosa a la palabra tornadizo).* Text in Matilde Conde Salazar, Antonio Pérez Martín & Carlos del Valle Rodríguez, *Alonso Díaz de Montalvo. La causa conversa* (Madrid, 2008), pp. 103–45.

[50] *Tractatus contra madianitas et ismaelitas adversarios et detractores fidelium qui de populo israelitico originem traxerunt.* Text in Carlos del Valle Rodríguez, *Tratado contra los madianitas e ismaelitas de Juan de Torquemada (contra la discriminación conversa)* (Madrid, 2002), pp. 125–239.

relentless denunciation of the rebels as enemies of Christ's lineage and by extension of Christ himself constituted the theological groundwork of Pope Nicholas V's authoritative response in favour of the *conversos*. Finally, Alonso de Cartagena's "Defence of Christian Unity", dedicated to King John II, can be regarded as an early pinnacle of pro-*converso* theology both in scope and theological proficiency.[51]

A very recent study has unearthed an until-recently forgotten discourse that was held around 1462 during the proceedings of an episcopal inquisition (prior to the later Spanish Inquisition) in Toledo.[52] This vernacular text contains the denunciation of a Franciscan preaching campaign against the New Christians and as an admonition of certain anti-*converso* mendicants is rather akin to our *Breue reprehensorium*. The unnamed author reasons also on a more general note against any distinction between Old and New Christians. Chairing the tribunal where the discourse was pronounced was the Hieronymite friar Alonso de Oropesa. In all likelihood the episcopal inquisitor was himself determined to use the trials to the eventual advantage of the New Christians by proving at least the general suspicion against them false. Three years later he finished his own treatise "Light to the Revelation of the Gentiles", a lengthy and somewhat repetitive work in favour of *converso* equality.[53] His order apparently had a significant number of New Christian members and was implicated early on as an alleged safe haven for those who secretly reverted to the faith of their Jewish ancestors and were thus in the eyes of the church guilty of "Judaizing". This bad reputation probably accounts for many of the polemical passages against Judaism in

---

[51] *Defensorium unitatis christianae*. Text in Manuel Alonso, *Don Alfonso de Cartagena: Defensorium unitatis christianae. Tratado en favor de los judíos conversos. Edición, prólogo y notas* (Madrid, 1943), pp. 61–370.

[52] *Discurso sobre la predicación anticonversa*. Text in Bautista, 'Predicación anticonversa', pp. 420–46.

[53] *Lumen ad revelationem gentium*. A Spanish translation was published by Luis A. Díaz y Díaz, *Luz para conocimiento de los gentiles. Alonso de Oropesa. Estudio, traducción y edición* (Salamanca, 1979). A transcript of the Latin original can be consulted online at http://www.cervantesvirtual.com/obra-visor-din/luz-para-conocimiento-de-los-gentiles--o/html).

Alonso's work, as he was anxious to distance himself and the order from any accusation of suspicious sympathy towards Jewish beliefs. His own and the work of Gutierre de Palma, both from 1465, basically mark (as far as we know) the end of fully-fledged pro-*converso* treatises before the expulsions.

In the last third of the 15th century literary activity in defence of the New Christians was much less outspoken and much less confident. As such, the "Catholic Refutation of a Heretical Pamphlet" by Hernando de Talavera,[54] another Hieronymite, can be called a defence of the *conversos* only on account of its underlying intention. For the heretical pamphlet in question was an anonymous profession of judaizing beliefs that had been disseminated in and around Seville and had provoked enormous scandal. Though in reality very probably a forgery designed to foment fears of a crypto-Jewish conspiracy,[55] Hernando took it very much at face value and meticulously disproved its doctrinal errors while at the same time insisting again and again that it was in no way representative of the pious and devout Andalusian New Christians in general.

The controversy that raged also within the Hieronymite order came to a head in the 1480s when one faction tried to implement a statute of *limpieza de sangre*. Of the ensuing struggle only the outlines can be reconstructed today from the account a later chronicler of the order provides:[56] On one side were friars who advocated in favour of the statute, like Juan de Corrales and Gonzalo de Toro; on the other those who defended the rights of the New Christians, such as Rodrigo de Orense and García de Madrid. The original pleas, very likely once set down in writting, are lost today, as no doubt an unknown number of likeminded sermons, letters, treatises and legal comments are.

---

[54] *Católica impugnación del herético libelo maldito y descomulgado que en el año pasado del nacimiento de nuestro Señor Jesucristo de mil cuatrocientos y ochenta años fue divulgado en la ciudad de Sevilla*. Text in Stefania Pastore, *Católica impugnación* (Córdoba, 2012), pp. 3–181.

[55] Cf. Bernhard Holl, 'Antijüdische Polemik unter falscher Flagge: das vorgebliche Pamphlet eines anonymen Judaisierers 1480 in Sevilla', *Zeitschrift für Religions- und Geistesgeschichte*, 72 (2020), 412–24.

[56] Cf. Juan C. García López, *José de Sigüenza. Historia de la Orden de San Jerónimo* (Madrid, 1907).

Other statements opposed to the prejudices against *conversos* can be found in the more private (or semi-public) frame of personal letters. The royal scribe Fernando de Pulgar for one expressed in various communications to friends, relatives and benefactors what he only hinted at in his chronicles and biographies: a deep concern for his fellow New Christians who were being progressively excluded from the rest of society and relentlessly targeted by inquisition tribunals.[57] The *converso* question seems to have gained pertinence even in Aragonese ruled Southern Italy, where the Apulian physician and humanist Antonio de Ferrariis composed a letter to a noble friend encouraging him not to turn away a potential daughter-in-law for having Jewish ancestors.[58] If nothing else his advice shows that the concern for a "pure" genealogical lineage was spreading throughout the Spanish Mediterranean sphere of influence, and scholarly reasoning continued to oppose it.

After the expulsion of the Jews from Castile, Aragon, Navarre and Portugal the New Christian controversy in theory could have been considered settled – with no Jews left to convert, the population of literal converts would naturally fade away over time. However, the genealogical prejudice against anyone with so much as a remote Jewish ancestor continued to trouble Spanish society for centuries. Treatises in favour of the New Christians on the other hand became increasingly rare and, above all, more deliberative and reserved. The theological arguments put forward by authors like Domingo de Valtanás, Agustín Salucio and Gaspar de Uceda in opposition to the ideology of *limpieza de sangre* were by and large the same as they had been in the fifteenth century, but their overall tone was notably less resolute. Some authors indeed preferred not to attach their names to pro-*converso* treatises that were certain to attract the attention of the Inquisition and at the very least would have an unpredictable bearing on one's reputation and career.[59]

---

[57] Cf. Jesús Domínguez Bordona, *Fernando del Pulgar: Letras* (Madrid, 1929).

[58] *Ad Belisarium Aquevivum, de neophytis.* Text in Antonio Altamura, *Antonio de Ferrariis Galateo: Epistole. Edizione critica* (Lecce, 1959), pp. 220–25.

[59] Cf. Tarsicio de Azcona, 'Dictamen en defensa de los judíos conversos de la Orden de San Jerónimo a principios del siglo XVI', in *Studia Hieronymiana*, vol. 2, ed. Pedro Sainz Rodríguez (Madrid, 1973), 347–80.

In comparison to all available sources, the *Breue reprehensorium* appears prima facie to be rather representative of contemporary pro-*converso* thought. Less systematic than Alonso de Cartagena, not as concise as Juan de Torquemada, and yet less comprehensive than Alonso de Oropesa, Gutierre de Palma still proved his worth as a well educated defender of the New Christian cause. Indeed, the survival of his *Breue reprehensorium* can be regarded as an extraordinary stroke of luck for today's researchers, since many more texts like it were probably written but have not come down to us. One important frame of reference for the next section of this short study will be how Gutierre's work compares to those of like-minded jurists and theologians of his time: how accurately does it fall into the established patterns of pro-*converso* apologetic texts? Or how much indeed might it rather change our perception of what the accepted exegetical and canonistic arguments were at the time?

The Treatise: Style and Contents

The genre of the *Breue reprehensorium* is that of a scholastic *tractatus*, which of course is a rather broad category. As opposed to texts that are closer to the academic tradition of the *disputatio*, the question at hand here is not designed as an open deliberation with arguments for both sides. Indeed, almost no room at all is given to the refutation or even presentation of possible reasons why a different treatment of New and Old Christians could hypothetically be legitimate. Instead the exclusion and disregard of the *conversos* is treated from the start as a dangerous heresy and the argumentation aims basically to compile the scriptural and legal evidence for this and urge the authorities to take action. While other academically minded authors like Alonso Díaz de Montalvo, Alonso de Cartagena and Juan de Torquemada had made reference to at least some arguments of the Toledan insurgents of 1449, Gutierre de Palma contents himself with summing up anti-*converso* sentiment in a rather sweeping way, making out his adversaries as "those who call others confesos" (Art. 11), "they who do not want unity" (Art. 12) or "they who want division" (Art. 14). This could well be because his treatise does not respond to an elaborate polemic but to a comparatively simple public insult. Although general resentment of the New Christians was

Introduction

omnipresent in 1460s Castile, it had only just begun to take literary form.[60] Proper learned defences of pur-blood statutes and like-minded texts on an academic level were yet to be penned and did not appear before the turn of the century.

Language and References

By and large the *Breue reprehensorium* is written in simple but sound medieval church Latin, drawing heavily from the Vulgate and the *Corpus iuris canonici*. The very few short passages and single words in the vernacular are worked seamlessly into the Latin.[61] While the author's skills do not reach the highest level of scholastic (not to mention humanist) eloquence, neither would they have caused him embarrassment in any ecclesiastical or academic context of the time.

Every now and again an explicit quote from the Latin bible differs to a noticeable degree from the canonical text for reasons that cannot be determined beyond doubt in each case. In some instances, the author may have copied a verse from another manuscript containing a less common version of the passage. It bears repeating in this context that even the relatively authoritative Vulgate counted with numerous variations in the fifteenth century and versions of the *Vetus Latina* were also still in use.[62] In other cases the author may have quoted from memory without double checking the exact phrase. At yet other times he was possibly consciously paraphrasing to emphasize a certain meaning.

Though columns after columns are filled with perfectly plain – not to say dull – sequences of biblical and legal quotations, other passages are full of character and fancy. Regarding the former, one cannot help but notice that some parts of the scriptural evidence presented in favour of Gutierre's arguments are more ornate than compelling in character. In more than one instance it seems that the author merely

---

[60] Cf. Holl, *Die Conversos*, pp. 57–61.

[61] Cf. Carmen Kämmerer, *Codeswitching in Predigten des 15. Jahrhunderts: Mittellatein-Frühneuhochdeutsch, Mittellatein-Altitalienisch/Altspanisch* (Berlin, 2006).

[62] Cf. Cornelia Linde, *How to Correct the Sacra Scriptura?: textual criticism of the Latin Bible between the twelfth and fifteenth century* (Oxford, 2012), pp. 81–104.

compiled a litany of biblical verses that share a common keyword regardless of context. Likewise he regularly quotes canons and chapters of church law that contain a biblical passage of interest to him despite their rather tangential legal relation to the question at hand. Possibly using a verbal concordance of some sort, these exercises seem intended to bolster the semblance of learning and orthodoxy that was expected from a scholastic treatise.[63] Thus, many citations of the Church Fathers and other references are more likely taken from the *Decretum Gratiani* rather than from the original source – a technique that was quite common at the time and added the weight of continuous tradition to that of the original authority.

When it comes to the validity of the legal argumentation, some citations, as mentioned above, serve more as a general show of learnedness than anything else. Other references, however, are diligently researched illustrations of how biblical and doctrinal maxims actually translate into church law. As conclusive as these connections are, Gutierre's adversaries would probably maintain that the canonical norms (say, about the administration and consequences of baptism) did still not equate to the full equality of all *conversos* whom they summarily regarded as heretics. Where the author's expertise once again shines is when he meticulously lays out the particulars of his case against the Dominicans, explaining, for instance, how a seemingly innocuous inscription can still amount to a punishable insult, depending on the circumstances and intent (Art. 9).

In his practical use of biblical and other sources, Gutierre de Palma's treatise is in many regards quite the example of late medieval scholarship. The appeal to authority forms the basic structure of any given reasoning. A telling example of his understanding of attribution and authorship is his use of Alonso Díaz de Montalvo's legal comment on the *converso* question.[64] While copying entire passages word by word, the author of the *Breue reprehensorium* never even once mentions the name of his colleague or indicates that he avails himself of his work. Even several quotations of the Church Fathers and other

---

[63] Cf. Michel Albaric, 'Hugues de Saint-Cher et les concordances bibliques latines (XIIIe–XVIIIe siècles)', in *Hugues de Saint-Cher († 1263), bibliste et théologien: études réunies*, ed. Louis-Jacques Bataillon *et al.* (Turnhout, 2004), 467–79.

[64] Cf. Matilde Conde Salazar *et al.*, *La causa conversa*.

sources are simply copied straight from Alonso's *Tractatus*. The result is a number of quasi third-hand quotes passed down from, say, John Chrysostom to Gratian to Alonso Díaz to Gutierre de Palma.

What would be regarded blatant plagiarism in later ages was in fact completely acceptable by the standard of our author's time. The only reason for citing another author by name, be it Aristotle, Saint Paul or even relatively recent canonists like Nicolaus de Tudeschis or John of Imola, was to add the weight of their fame to the argument. Alonso Díaz on the other hand, a contemporary of reputable but still modest academic standing, was simply not regarded as an author *(auctor)* in the sense of a source imbued with authority *(auctoritas)*,[65] but simply as a competent scholar who had already done some of the work Gutierre himself was going to undertake. He did not so much claim Alonso's ideas as his own (after all, he never even gives his own name in the entire text baring one playful allusion), but rather saw them as part of the objective truth he himself was defending. His declared aim was not to come up with a particularly inventive take on the controversy, but to convey the most obvious and plausible proof possible of what he claimed was basically self-evident. This disregard (at least in demeanour) for originality and creativity was, too, an almost indispensable part of the pre-modern academic sensibility.

Rhetoric and Intended Audience

As opposed to the rather dry catenae of biblical and canonist quotes, the passages in which the author directly addresses other persons are more original and personal. Yet even at times when these dialogical elements appear slightly quirky, they nevertheless follow certain conventions of the time. There are basically two entities Gutierre explicitly addresses his arguments at: the parts directed towards the archbishop of Toledo were very likely meant literally for the principal intended reader; the admonitions aimed at the titular "certain friars" on the other hand seem to be more of a rhetorical gesture to underscore the passion and seriousness of the argument, which is not to say that Gutierre did not mean for the Dominicans to learn of his

[65] Cf. Seraina Plotke, *Die Stimme des Erzählens: mittelalterliche Buchkultur und moderne Narratologie* (Göttingen, 2017), pp. 86-92.

accusations eventually. Both techniques – the straightforward as well as the affectuated address – were common in late medieval treatise literature.[66]

A certain amount of flagrant adulation and professed humility was obviously expected in the typical dedication to a reader of superior standing. Thus Diego de Valera presented his mirror of nobility to "you, the very high and very illustrious prince and lord Don John, by divine grace king of Castile and Leon to whom it pertains more than to any other as much because of the great nobility of the royal line you come from as because of the many virtues with which our Lord has willed to endow you".[67] And dedicating his treatise to the same archbishop of Toledo as Gutierre de Palma, Alonso de Oropesa feels it necessary to write "to the most revered father in Christ and most illustrious lord, Don Alonso Carrillo, archbishop of Toledo and most noble Primate of Spain" introducing himself as "Brother Alonso de Oropesa, his unworthy petitioner, deservedly his servant and helpless son".[68]

Likewise directing one's reprimand with almost theatrical emphasis at the perceived wrongdoers was a popular literary device. "Listen, dearest Marcus, and turn your mind not out of spite to the shell of the letter understood by corrupt envy",[69] demands Alonso de

---

[66] Cf. Karl Kohut, 'Der Beitrag der Theologie zum Literaturbegriff in der Zeit Juans II. von Kastilien. Alonso de Cartagena (1384-1456) und Alonso de Madrigal, genannt El Tostado (1400?-1455)', *Romanische Forschungen*, 89 (1977), 183–226; Nicholas G. Round, '"Perdóneme Séneca": the translational practices of Alonso de Cartagena', *Bulletin of Hispanic Studies*, 75 (1998), 17–29.

[67] "a vos, el muy alto e muy esclaresçido prínçipe e señor don Iohan, por la divinal graçia rey de Castilla e de León, [...] a quien mayormente pertenesçe que a otro, así por la mucha nobleza de la real estirpe donde venís como por las muchas virtudes de que nuestro Señor dotar vos quiso [...]." – Diego de Valera, *Espejo de verdadera nobleza*, ed. Federica Accorsi, pp. 291–92.

[68] "Reverendissimo in Christo patri ac domino illustrissimo domino Alfonso Carrillo, archiepiscopo Toletano, ac Hispaniarum primati nobilissimo. Frater Alfonsus de Oropeza, suus orator indignus, ac merito servus et inutilis filius [...]." – Alonso de Oropesa, *Lumen ad revelationem*, preface.

[69] "Audi, marche carissime, et non cortici littere per livorem invidie prava interpretatione intellecte [...] mentem appone [...]." – Alonso de Cartagena, *Defensorium unitatis christianae*, ed. Manuel Alonso, p. 225.

Cartagena of his adversary Marcos de Mora, and Hernando de Talavera attacks an anonymous pamphleteer: "May our Lord cut you in half, as the holy boy Daniel said to the elder judge, for like a schismatic and sower of discord you divide and drive apart New and Old Christians!"[70] By this standard even Gutierre's harsher admonitions seem perfectly in line.

At two points in particular the *Breue reprehensorium* combines the direct speach towards friend or foe with digressions into topics of contemporary piety. The outward appearance of Jesus Christ as described by the "Letter of Lentulus" serves as an apropos to chastise those who would disregard the Saviour's Jewish heritage, whereas the legend of Saint Leocadia's resurrection witnessed by Saint Ildefonsus and king Rekkared precedes an appeal to the spiritual and secular authorities of the author's present day. Both passages will be looked at in greater detail below.

Main Sections and Themes

The *Breue reprehensorium* is laid out in fourteen chapters or "articles", the headings of which are listed at the beginning after a short preamble (some minor inconsistencies will be addressed in the manuscript description). Although in great part meandering and excursive, its line of thought can roughly be divided into five main parts:

(1) an anecdotal introduction blaming the Dominicans of Toledo for an instant of anti-*converso* propaganda;
(2) a discussion of the theological principles speaking for the equal treatment of Old and New Christians;
(3) a contemplation on the history of salvation to the same effect; and
(4) a lengthy consideration of what is to be concluded, morally and legally, about the offence given by the friars of Saint Peter Martyr. This last part proceeds subtly from a general summation of the arguments to

---

[70] "[...] divídate nuestro Señor por medio, como dizo el santo mozo Daniel, al más juez viejo, porque, como escismático y sembrador de discordias, haces división y apartamiento entre los cristianos nuevos y viejos [...]." – Hernando de Talavera, *Catolica impugnación*, ed. Stefania Pastore, p. 163.

(5) an urgent appeal to the authorities to intervene and set things right.

A Scandal in Toledo (preface and article 1)

The author begins his treatise relating how he noticed a certain inscription next to an altar piece in the church belonging to the Dominican friary of Toledo. This inscription mentions the year the retable was finished by citing the insurrection of Toledo in 1449 and the ensuing infamous pillage of *converso* households. The author judges this to be a mockery of the victims, whom the inscription calls *confesos* (confessed sinners or Christians by lip-service only) – a slur on a par with *marrano* (swine) or *tornadizo* (traitor) slandering Christians of Jewish origin with the implication of them being untrustworthy opportunists or even heretics secretly still practising the Jewish rites of their ancestors.

Explicitly despite his young age (about 30 by our estimate), the author affirms his resolve to speak out against this perceived public insult and confides in his patron's "kindness and holiness". In the course of his treatise, Gutierre will come back again and again to his demand of erasing the offensive inscription, so one can assume that this is not only a pretence for him but a real issue. Although such a case of public slander was hardly singular at the time, this one leads to a sequence of theological reasoning that goes far beyond questions of churchly decorum.

The first article then serves as a transition to more general questions of faith and morals by denouncing the inscription and its allusion to the anti-*converso* violence some sixteen years ago as gloating and boastful, ascertaining that it is wrong to take pride in evil deeds. Employing an *argumentum a fortiori* Gutierre cites among other examples the disciples of Jesus who were told not to rejoice in their successful working of miracles but in their eternal salvation (Lc 10:20). Therefore, he argues, if boastfulness is objectionable even in regard to good things – how much more is it to be avoided in regard to evil deeds?

Basic Principles: Birth, Faith, Sin and Unity (articles 2–4)

The next three articles provide the dogmatic groundwork on which the distinction between Old and New Christians is rejected. Still lingering on the insult made against the *conversos* in general the section opens with the emphatic affirmation that there is no shame in being converted. To proof this, the author compiles a long catena of biblical citations some of which bear little more than a semantic proximity to the notion of conversion. Slightly more to the point he continues by giving various scriptural evidence of the idea that the Israelite lineage is chosen by God and must therefore not be held in contempt by the Christian community. His line of thought then culminates in the argument that Jesus Christ himself was born by a Jewish mother, rendering absurd the contention that there could be anything disrespectful about a Jewish ancestry per se.

While no like-minded scholar before Gutierre had failed to make this exact point, our author then adds a peculiar piece of evidence to his reasoning: a complete transcript of the apocryphal "Letter of Lentulus".[71] Allegedly written by a Roman prefect of Judea who preceded Pontius Pilate, this detailed description of Jesus's appearance surfaced in western Europe at some point in the first half of the fifteenth century and was then believed to be authentic. It seems plausible that this figment answers to the Christian desire to know for certain what the Son of God actually looked like. An evolving concern for the visual aspects of the faith was notable in late medieval piety all over Europe,[72] and after all, curiosity about the historical person of Jesus is not uncommon even today. While parts of the description may come from older (though not necessarily more

---

[71] Cf. Marianna Cerno, 'Jesus' New Face: a newly discovered version of the "Epistula Lentuli"', *Apocrypha*, 32 (2022), 9–49; Cora E. Lutz, 'The Letter of Lentulus Describing Christ', *The Yale University Library Gazette*, 50 (1975), 91–97.

[72] Cf. e.g. Matilde Miquel Juan, 'Sentimientos pintados y contemplaciones mentales: espiritualidad visual y literatura medieval hispana a finales del siglo XV', in *Isabel de Villena i l'espiritualitat europea tardomedieval*, ed. Anna Isabel Peirats Navarro (Valencia, 2022), 357–86; Kathleen Kamerick, *Popular Piety and Art in the Late Middle Ages: image worship and idolatry in England 1350–1500* (New York, 2002).

reliable) sources, the precise circumstances of its composition remain still unknown.

As part of our pro-*converso* treatise the *epistola Lentuli* serves no immediately clear purpose, since the urgent demand "Look into the face of your Christ!" in the direction of his adversaries does not really explain the necessity for the lengthy digression. Given the popularity and relative novelty of the letter at Gutierre's time, he might just have presumed or known readers like the archbishop to enjoy a complete citation for its own sake. It does in any case lead to one of his boldest and thereby most notable statements, claiming that the Jewish ancestry of Jesus Christ is proof "that they who are from God according to flesh and spirit are more so than those who are so according to the spirit alone". The affirmation that Jewish Christians, by being both carnally and spiritually related to Jesus Christ, were in and of themselves "more from God" *(magis ex Deo)* than their Gentile brethren goes decidedly beyond the demand for equality. It was, however, not unheard of at the time but can be found to some extent in the works of Alonso de Cartagena and Juan de Torquemada some fifteen years earlier.[73] In a first excursion into the history of salvation (later to be explored in more detail), the *Reprehensorium* then goes on to enumerate various saintly figures connected with the Jewish heritage both from biblical sources and church history.

By somewhat conflating the idea of Israel as the Chosen People and the Augustinian notion of an *ecclesia ab Abel* (potentially encompassing all peoples), Gutierre lays the ground for his second important point: that the proclamations of Old Testament prophets and New Testament apostles mirror each other and are in essence manifestations of the same faith. The baseline for this argument is of course not new. From very early on, Christians had read the Torah and the Prophets as the "Old Testament" and had drawn connections to the apostolic letters and gospels that were to become the "New Testament". One key reasoning in the anti-Jewish apologetic tradition was the exegetical proof that Jesus of Nazareth was indeed the messiah promised by God through the words of his prophets. However, in the context of the *converso* controversy this traditional paradigm takes a new and different turn. Insisting that everything prophetised in the

---

[73] Cf. Rosenstock, *New Men*.

Tanakh had been fulfilled by Jesus as the Christ (anointed one) of God meant no longer urging the Jews to accept this belief. It was now proving to self-styled Old Christians that their Jewish brethren were in fact called and disposed to join the *verus Israel* which was the church. This general discursive technique of "repurposing" traditional arguments to adapt them to new apologetic needs was of course not an invention of pro-*converso* apologists, but had been in use for centuries.

In order to elaborate the idea of covenantal continuity,[74] the treatise juxtaposes the Apostles' Creed with Old Testament prophecies (more or less) traditionally associated with the individual articles of faith. While there is a long tradition in Christian art of depicting the twelve parts of the creed being pronounced by the twelve apostles respectively, the assignation of prophets and their corresponding verses is much less common, although not unheard-of.[75] The order of the apostles in the *Breue reprehensorium* corresponds to the Eucharistic prayer of the *canon romanus* (as opposed to, say, the order in one of the gospels or the acts of the apostles), whereas the four major prophets with the addition of the psalmist king, David, and seven of the minor prophets are listed according to the contents of their cited verses. The result is a poignant display of how every key belief of Christianity is already present in the Old Testament, provided of course, one shares the often allegorical Christian interpretation thereof. In any case the contrast could not be starker to contemporary authors like Pedro de la Cavallería or Jaime Pérez de Valencia, who dedicated long passages of their writing to explaining

---

[74] Cf. Jennifer Harris, 'Enduring Covenant in the Christian Middle Ages', *Journal of Ecumenical Studies*, 44 (2009), 563–86.

[75] Cf. James D. Gordon, 'The Articles of the Creed and the Apostles', *Speculum*, 40 (1965), 634–40; Gertrude Townsend, 'Prophets and Apostles in the Creed Tapestry', *Bulletin of the Museum of Fine Arts*, 26, (1928), 64–70.

how the Mosaic covenant was irredeemably deficient, obsolete and if anything destracted the Jews from the true Christian faith.[76]

The third major idea to be subsequently introduced is again a favourite of pro-*converso* apologists. Derived from the book of Ezekiel, the assurance that "a son shall not bear the iniquity of the father" carries considerable weight in shorter comments like the ones by Diego de Valera, Fernán Díaz de Toledo and Lope de Barrientos as well as in the more copious works of Alonso de Cartagena, Juan de Torquemada and Alonso de Oropesa. The need to emphasise this principle of divine justice arose in great part from Christianity's deeply rooted resentment of the Jewish people, blaming its entirety for the rejection and crucifixion of the true messiah even after countless generations. In general Christian pro-*converso* authors employed a twofold strategy to contest this age old anti-Jewish tradition so detrimental to their cause. One way was to downplay the supposed collective Jewish guilt and correlate it with the sins committed by Gentiles according to the Bible and church history. The other – exemplified by the quote from Ezekiel – was to deny altogether any pertinence of the faults of past generations on the individual faithful in the present.

Both lines of thought are also present in the *Breue reprehensorium*, but in this introductory part Gutierre de Palma relies exclusively on the latter and even expands the argument others had made before him (Art. 4): all men "the Lord made from one mud", he cites from canon law and church fathers, and therefore neither pride nor shame are due in regard to one's bodily origin. In the feudal society of late medieval Iberia, a polity the hierarchical organisation of which depended heavily on inherited claims on power and status, this may sound like a radical statement – and at the same time it is not. In a purely spiritual frame of reference Christian theology was all but expected to hold true that all men were equal before God, high birth and worldly

---

[76] Cf. i.a. Justo Formentín Ibáñez & María José Villegas Sanz, *Jaime Pérez de Valencia: Tratado contra los judíos* (Madrid, 1998); Núria Gómez Llauger, 'Radicalism and Pauline Thought in Pedro de la Cavallería's *Zelus Christi contra iudaeos, sarracenos et infideles*' in *Propaganda and (Un)Covered Identities in Treatises and Sermons: Christians, Jews, and Muslims in the premodern Mediterranean* ed. Cándida Ferrero Hernández & Linda G. Jones (Barcelona, 2020), 71–82.

goods accounted for nothing in comparison to sincere faith, and true honour could only ever be gained from a life righteously lived. At the same time this theological equality obviously did not translate directly to the functional composition of the realm that distinguished fundamentally the position of its members as nobles or commoners, free or unfree, clergy or laity, male or female. The crucial divide in the development of the *converso* question was in fact in how far the Christian community was ready to honour the primarily spiritual ideal of equality in terms of actual social acceptance. Apparently it was one thing to enter into the kingdom of God and quite another to enter into an Old Christian dominated cathedral chapter, university college or military order.

The History of Salvation (articles 5–8)

Once more, similar to other treatises written in favour of the *conversos*, Gutierre goes on to explain the unity and equality of all Christians further as providential result of the entire history of salvation. However, different from Alonso de Cartagena, he does not present a chronological rundown of events but starts with the incarnation and then explores the state of human kind before and after this all important turning point, ending with an evaluation of his present day. Within this meditation the entire fifth article is basically one vast compilation of biblical quotes referring to the Incarnation; the verses taken from the Old Testament of course doing so only in terms of a specifically Christian interpretation.

Article six then elaborates more on the desolate state of the world before the coming of Christ. In an approach very similar to the *Lumen ad revelationem* by Alonso de Oropesa (finished the same year as the *Breue reprehensorium*), the precarious situation of Jews and Gentiles are seen as analogous. Modern-day researchers have often quoted Alonso's obviously harsh accusations against the Jewish people as undeniable proof that he and other apologists of the New Christians were die-hard Jew-haters. However, the evidence looks a lot less compelling as soon as one takes into account the purpose it served as a parallel to the equally relentless indictment of pre-Christian Gentiles. Along the same lines Gutierre de Palma cites several passages of the Bible that were traditionally used in anti-Jewish

polemical works but complements them with quotations critical of the gentile peoples to show that both groups were equally in need of salvation. To that end he even reads the song of Moses (Dtn 32) in a rather bold exegetical move as lamenting Hebrew and Gentile worshippers of idols alike. Consequently, the death of Christ on the cross is also explained as a responsibility shared by Jews and Gentiles: "Jews accused him unjustly, Gentiles however condemned Jesus to death". This exact argumentation dates back at least to Alonso Díaz de Montalvo from whose writing entire paragraphs are copied word-for-word, and it was also popular with other pro-*converso* writers.

Gutierre's narration of the history of salvation then takes a positive turn with article seven regarding the formation of the One Holy Church. The following discourse again touches on a theme that was omnipresent in pro-*converso* literature: the unity of the church. Even before the great confessional divide brought about by the reformation two generations later, ecclesiastical unity was one of the most serious concerns in Western Christianity. From the Great Occidental Schism to the conflicts with Hussites and other heterodox believers to the failed reunification attempts with the Eastern churches at the council of Ferrara and Florence, the pain of division was felt deeply. The accusation of sectarianism and discord was therefore certain to raise the alarm, and consequently the advocates of the Iberian New Christians made extensive use of it against their opponents.

Likewise the affirmation that the sacrament of baptism unfailingly lets its recipient be reborn as a child of God and member of the Church washed clean from all sins is more than a theological commonplace. Gutierre de Palma and others highlighted very consciously the potential heresy of denying equal rights to the newly converted as this seemed to call into question the general effectiveness of holy baptism. The abundance of scriptural and canonical evidence given in support of the proposition that, yes indeed, the Church is to be one and united, is of course not meant to persuade a hypothetical reader whose opinion might differ, but rather to emphasise the importance of the issue and the error of those opposed to treating the *conversos* as equals.

Leaping forward in his meditation of the history of salvation the *Breue reprehensorium* next takes a glimpse at the end-times. This will be, according to the author, when "all men will be united in Christ";

a slight overgeneralisation of the Christian believe that before the end of all times the remaining Jews will be converted to Christianity. Based on Augustine's reading of Paul's letter to the Romans (Rm 11), this expectation was generally popular with the advocates of the New Christians. Different from some chiliastic enthusiasts who hoped for the second coming to occur in their lifetime, for the defenders of the *conversos* since Pablo de Santa María it proved one simple point: if God's unfailing plan was for all Jews to be converted ultimately, then the refusal to accept Jewish converts amounted to doubting the divine intent and wisdom.

Finally the chapter concludes with two more references to Pauline theology: the assurance that "there is no respect of persons with God" (Rm 2) and the image of the mystical body of Christ made up of all members of the church. Both were tested items of pro-*converso* apologetic writing from the beginning, although both did not unequivocally work in its favour. The insistence that each and every Christian would ultimately be judged by God not according to their ancestry but by their individual faith and charity was as such a sound argument. However, it seemed to contradict at least to some degree the effort made by Gutierre and others to vindicate the Jewish lineage with regard to the genealogy of Christ, the role of the prophets and the part Jews played in the Passion. If indeed the Jewish (or for that matter any) origin accounted for nothing, why was it necessary to reimagine it as ideally suited for a Christian believer? Both lines of thought are not logically incompatible, but they do seem to mutually leave each other less pertinent and compelling. The allegory of all faithful as one mystical body on the other hand is in itself ambivalent. It does convey strong notions of unity and harmony, but at the same time it allows for almost any amount of functional and hierarchical difference. Even if the most zealous Old Christian may have been opposed to the idea of belonging to the same "body" as the New Christians, most would probably have been content as long as they themselves were guaranteed to hold the most prestigious and powerful positions within it.

Both as an afterthought to this discourse on the history of salvation and a transition into the following conclusions, article eight deals with the author's present time. At first glance the demand that "the sinners must not be separated from the righteous" seems to

contradict the overall reasoning of the rest of the treatise. If those who are not to be separated and excluded are meant to be the *conversos*, why would the author suddenly admit to their being sinners, the kind of sweeping allegation that he so passionately opposed before? If on the other hand he refers to the Old Christian agitators by calling them sinners, why would he plead for lenience here and for severe punishment later on? The reasoning becomes slightly clearer thanks to the biblical verses and examples Gutierre cites in its support: the cockle among the wheat is not to be weeded out before the time (Mt 13:29-30) – this classic scriptural proof in favour of tolerance together with other similar passages is basically intended to convey a simple warning: not to judge rashly nor by outer appearance those who are in God's good graces and those who are not. So whilst the author would most certainly have proven heretics and criminals be sentenced and punished, he objects to the distinction between sinner and righteous to be made according to superficial criteria such as genealogy.

Lessons to be Learned (articles 9–12)

The following articles until the end of the treatise propose to draw the practical consequences out of the theological argumentation that came before. This part comprises roughly half of the entire work and contains everything one would expect – harsh criticism of the author's adversaries coupled with threats of severe punishment in this life and the next, stern warnings against idly standing by and unabashed pandering to the authorities expected to lead the charge against the unruly friars.

In article nine Gutierre returns to his original concern: the offensive inscription he found next to an altarpiece in the Dominicans' church. Knowing or expecting the friars to deny its abusive character, the author takes great care to make his case. The affront does not lie in the literal meaning of the word "confesos" but in the malign intent in which it is used, according to several legal sources and comments which the author diligently provides. After this, his line of thought trails off slightly as he explains that converts especially are to be protected from insults so as not to make them

waver in their faith. On the contrary, he argues, they should even be rewarded in order to incentivise more conversions.

Slightly different in tone, article 10 deals with the misfortune of the just, the purpose of this meditation not being immediately obvious: why dwell on the hardship that the righteous have to endure in this valley of tears, if the intention is to better their lot, at least where unjustly persecuted *conversos* are concerned? While no doubt posing an eternal philosophical and theological conundrum, the suffering of the just seems to have consternated the *converso* community from the later half of the fifteenth century on in a more than general way. The fictional deathbed colloquium of the Marqués de Santillana by Pedro Díaz de Toledo, Juan de Lucena's philosophical dialogue about happines as well as countless poetic laments in the *cancionero* tradition, speak of profound despair in the face of injustice and adversity.[77] For many, whatever had been their motivation, conversion had simply failed to make good on its promise: personal safety for those forcibly baptised, social betterment for those seeking opportunities and – probably most heartbreakingly – true acceptance into the Christian community of faith for those who had genuinely embraced their new creed. Meanwhile the second, third and fourth generation of so called New Christians, born and raised in the Catholic faith, could not possibly understand what they had done to deserve the scorn of their self-styled Old Christian brethren. It is no wonder then, that many *conversos* were cast into doubt about their faith in a just and loving God. The poets' answer to this was more often than not bitter sarcasm, the philosophers' and theologians' the kind of consolatory reflection that we also find here in the *Breue reprehensorium*.

---

[77] The *Diálogo y razonamiento en la muerte del marqués de Santillana* is edited in Antonio Paz y Melia, *Opúsculos literarios de las siglos XIV á XVI* (Madrid, 1892), 245–360; see also Jerónimo Miguel, *Juan de Lucena: Diálogo sobre la vida feliz; Epístola exhortatoria a las letras. Edición, estudio y notas* (Madrid, 2014); Óscar Perea Rodríguez, '"Quebrantar la jura de mis abuelos": los conversos en los cancioneros castellanos del tardío medievo (1454–1504)', *La Corónica*, 40 (2011), 183–225; Julio Rodríguez Puértolas, 'Jews and Conversos in Fifteenth-Century Castilian Cancioneros: texts and contexts', in *Poetry at Court in Trastamaran Spain: from the Cancionero de Baena to the Cancionero General*, ed. E. Michael Gerli & Julian Weiss (Tempe, 1998), 187–97.

The chapter begins, however, with a careful discernment, whether it might in fact be legitimate to commit theft or not. The Israelites, Gutierre argues, were justified when they robbed the Egyptians during the exodus, because God had directly ordered them to do so. A thief acting of his own volition on the other hand is always in the wrong despite any good intentions he might have. The following condemnation of anyone who commits crimes under the guise of a noble purpose is clearly an indictment of the insurgents of 1449 who had looted *converso* homes under the pretence of carrying out justice against heretics.

Only after this does the article turn to the victims of robbery and abuse: they are called to accept their hardship as coming from God who chastises them like a stern but loving father and to expect justice and eternal consolation in the hereafter. Persecuted faithful like the New Christians, Gutierre argues, are only tested by God to reveal their trustworthiness and will receive their full reward in heaven; fortune or misfortune in this world can never account for all the good or evil someone does, but only slightly alter the balance of what will be due to each in eternity. Lest anyone should doubt this reasoning, the article closes with an example that would be equally hard to refute for any self-respecting Old Christian as for any New Christian with at least some faith left in them: the Muslims (called Saracens and Hagarenes here) also seem to thrive and prosper in this world, even ruling over the Holy Land and as of late over Constantinople – but surely this temporary success hardly means that they are in the right?

If there was any risk for the last chapter to be read as a proposal to suffer injustice impassively, article 11 is anxious to rectify this impression. The demand to erase the offensive inscription by the Dominicans' altar is repeated with renewed urgency. After a lengthy appeal to the friars and their better judgment Gutierre finally brings into play the possibility of concrete legal action. Since the present king's predecessor explicitly forbade discrimination against the *conversos*, their mistreatment could even be judged as a crime against the crown and high treason. Similarly going back and forth between the aspect of ultimate responsibility before God and the very mundane threat of worldly justice article 12 explains the moral hazard of even standing idly by in the face of a crime like the one at hand. Bolstered with a collection of authoritative quotes Gutierre insists that

not opposing a misdeed equals condoning it, and the act of condoning it equals being an accessory and thus as guilty and punishable as the perpetrator.

Call to Action (articles 13–14)

As if having exhausted his efforts to convince the unruly friars by way of moral encouragement the author finally takes his case to the authorities. In this sense the article's heading "that the power of the pope and the Church is great" is less a disputed thesis than a reminder to the powers that be of their responsibility. The final portion of the treatise thus begins with a lament in the style of an Old Testament prophet. If Gutierre is to be believed, the Dominicans' offence in slighting the *conversos* bodes no less ill for Toledo than the rejection of the true messiah did for Jerusalem. Feeling perhaps that he himself lacks the standing to pronounce such a grave judgment, the author then recounts a famous legend involving two of the most prominent local saints: Leocadia, a fabled martyr under the Diocletianic persecution, and Ildefonsus, an archbishop in the Visigothic kingdom. According to this legend, Leocadia, already a revered saint for over three centuries, mysteriously rose from her tomb in the presence of Ildefonsus and the royal court. King Recceswinth then desired a relic of the famous virgin martyr and Ildefonsus complied by cutting off a piece of her veil before she returned to her resting place.

This miraculous episode (besides perhaps invoking some local patriotism) transitions more or less smoothly to the demand for intervention directed at the ecclesiastical and secular authorities. By fulfilling their sacred duty and reigning in the troublesome friars, the present archbishop and king are to become a second Ildefonsus and a second Recceswinth respectively. While clearly Alonso Carrillo is to take the place of his saintly predecessor, the king in question is not as unambiguously designated. The original manuscript casts Henry IV in this role, whereas a secondary amendment declares him to have been rejected by God in favour of his younger brother – no doubt a reflection of the dynastic struggle breaking out in June 1465.

From the mouth of the saints then follows another short rundown of the history of salvation, this time concerned with the origin of the

power held by the church and its prelates: God delegated the right to rule and judge first to Noah and his offspring, later to Moses and the priests and kings of Israel and finally transferred that authority on Saint Peter and his successors. The purpose of this explanation is not entirely clear, but it may have some relation to the dogmatic questions raised by the whole *converso* crisis about the exact relationship of the so-called Old and New Covenant. By and large the defenders of the New Christians usually emphasised a certain continuity in this respect (as Gutierre did already in article 3), anti-Jewish and anti-*converso* writers would typically highlight the rupture that had supposedly been effected by the coming of the Christ. In this respect, the salient point of the treatise's account of spiritual authority is not so much that it had supposedly been taken away from the Jews but that it had been held by them legitimately for a long time to be ultimately passed on to the Church.

Other than that, the power of the pope and the Church was hardly up for debate. There were certainly those among the author's contemporaries who saw things differently – advocates of the conciliar movement would no doubt object to the strong emphasis that the *Breue reprehensorium* puts on the fullness of power vested in the papacy. And even more radical thinkers in the vein of John Wycliffe or Marsilius of Padua might not even have accepted the institution of the Church as a whole to hold such authority. However, the Dominicans of Toledo are not likely to have upheld strong beliefs to that effect and neither are the enemies of the *conversos* in general. The ideology of *limpieza de sangre* did have certain subversive implications in that it put the supposed "purity of blood" above all traditional criteria for one's standing within the Christian community. But this does not seem to be the concern here.

Most likely Gutierre is on one hand simply trying to win favour with the dignitaries he means to rally to his cause by recognizing their claim to power in the most unmistakeable way. On the other hand his aim quite explicitly is to invoke a sense of duty and responsibility in those he has reassured so loyally of their power. In a perhaps even genuine gesture of conciliatoriness he admits that it would first be the Dominicans' own obligation to regulate their affairs and assure unity with the rest of the church. However, if they fail to do so, dignitaries higher up the church hierarchy cannot but intervene. Ultimately even

force administered by the secular powers may be legitimate and necessary, as the treatise explains at length in the fourteenth and final article.

THE EDITION

As far as we know the manuscript discovered by Ramón Gonzálvez Ruiz is the only existing material source for the *Breue reprehensorium*. Although nothing certain can ultimately be known, it seems likely that the text, possibly an autograph, after its completion in 1465 was then filed in the cathedral archives not to be noticed much for the next five centuries. In 1808 the cathedral chapter had the treatise listed in its catalogue of manuscripts without paying much attention to its contents.[1]

The Manuscript, Ms. 23-7

The surviving copy of the *Breue reprehensorium* consists of 20 parchment folios, filled on both sides with two columns of gothic minuscule script. The generous margin space is broad enough to allow for subsequent corrections and additions, which can be found on about one third of the pages. The capital letters of each of the fourteen headlines are illuminated and decorated with flowery motifs. The headlines themselves as well as some punctuation is in red. The binding most likely dates from a later age than the folios it contains but has still done very well in preserving the centuries-old writing.

For the most part the manuscript looks like a fair copy by the author, possibly made from previous drafts – with only a few notable exceptions: one being the change made to the role of king Henry IV (explained above). Another is a more technical error where the author (or scribe) accidentally wrote down the text of the second and third article without including the heading of the latter or at least visibly setting apart one from the other. He amended this slip of the pen by expanding the caption to read "Second and third article [...]". At the beginning of the fourth chapter, the heading "third article [...]" in turn is stroked trough and amended by the correct caption "fourth article [...]". Other corrections can be found in the margin notes or between the lines, though not in great number. A rather obvious but uncorrected error can be found on fol. 3v where the verse Eph 1:4

---

[1] Cf. Gonzálvez Ruiz, 'Obra desconocida', p. 36.

appears word-for-word twice in a row. Besides a mere oversight on the part of the author, this could be an indication that in fact a scribe less comprehending of the contents had been hired for the manual writing work. Another possibility is that either of them was copying the quote from a breviary (where the words would in fact be echoed as part of a responsory verse) and unwittingly reproduced the reduplication.

Somewhat curious is the verso of the last folio where the author made what seems to be a postscript, albeit with no direct connection to the main text. The fact that it is written in the vernacular (where it does not quote from the Latin Bible) makes it probably more of a private afterthought than a proper addendum. It reads as follows:

They will look with sadness upon him whom they pierced (John, chapter 19); Originally Zechariah, chapter 12: They shall regard me whom they have pierced. [The wisdom] that I learned without pretence, I tell without envy and I do not hide her righteousness (Wisdom, Chapter 7). 21st July in the year [14]65: Sunday morning on the eve of Saint Mary Magdalene, I saw the battlements of the great tower of the bridge of Saint Martin of Toledo burn, and how everything came tumbling down, a famous thing to see – a time to scatter stones, as in Ecclesiastes, chapter 3. Isaiah, chapter 5: You who justify the wicked for bribes and take the justice of the just away from him.[2]

While the first two quotations (Io 19:37; Za 12:10) could be meant to relate the afflicted *converso* population with Jesus Christ suffering on the cross, the last one (Is 5:23) seems to be along the lines of the allegations put forward against Old Christian bigotry and the Dominicans of Saint Peter Martyr in particular. If the episode related in between these verses – a burning bridge tower on the eve of Saint

---

[2] ¶ Videbunt in quem transfixerunt tristicie iohannis XIX° originaliter zacharie XII° // aspicient ad me quem confixerunt //· ¶ quam sine fictione didisci ¶ sine inuidia comunico ¶ et honestatem illius non abscondo //· sapiencie VII° capitulo // XXI de iullio de LXV annos //· ¶ domingo de manana vispera de santa maria madalena vi arder los cuencos de la grande torre de la puente de sant martin de toledo e de commo arryo toda por suelo cosa famossa de ver tiempo de piedras derramar ut ecclesiastici III° capitulo //· ysaie V° capitulo ¶ qui iustificatis impium pro muneribus et iusticiam iusti aufertis ab eo

Mary Magdalene's day – is to bear any relevance to the rest, one would have to assume that it is connected with some sort of public violence against the *converso* population. As such it would eerily mirror the infamous *fuego de la Magdalena*, since this anti-*converso* riot on the eve of the same feast day (22nd July) caused a fire that destroyed entire neighbourhoods and visited death and destruction on the New Christians of Toledo. That incident, however, took place two years later in 1467.[3]

Since the 21st July of the Julian Calendar fell indeed on a Sunday in 1465 but not in 1467, the most likely conclusion seems to be that despite all commonalities we are looking at two different events. After all, tensions between Old and New Christians had never really been resolved since the uprising of 1449. Certainly not every single clash between local gangs and neighbourhood militias and not even every resulting fire is reported in the chronicles at our disposal today. As the enmity against the *conversos* was building up more and more, manifestations of hostility might very well have broken out regularly on similar dates from year to year, each one seeking to outdo the previous one and taking revenge for perceived insults and injuries of the past. Much like the regular violence surrounding modern day Drumcree parades or May Day protests, the late medieval denizens of Toledo could well have developed a habit of having at each other on certain Christian holidays until things finally came to a head in the devastating pogrom of 1467.

The Present Edition

Since we have only the one surviving manuscript of the *Breue reprehensorium* the transcript mirrors the source's spelling as closely as possible, inconsistent as it partly is. This includes the scribe's varying use of **v** and **u**, whereas the often very slight difference between long and short **i** is neglected. Probable copying mistakes in comparison

---

[3] Cf. Eloy Benito Ruano, 'El fuego de la Magdalena: un pogrom contra los conversos de Toledo en 1467', in *Los orígines del problema converso*, ed. E. Benito Ruano, 141–58; Ricardo Izquierdo Benito, 'Edad media', in *Historia de Toledo*, ed. Julio de la Cruz Moñoz (Toledo, 1997), pp. 199–200; Carmen C. Gil Ortega, 'Alfonso Carrillo de Acuña: un arzobispo proconverso en el siglo XV castellano', *eHumanista/conversos*, 3 (2015), 139–41.

with a cited source are pointed out in the apparatus in cases where they potentially alter the meaning of the original. Abbreviations are expanded in accordance with the scribe's apparent preferences (e.g. **c** instead of **t** before **io**, **ia** etc.; **e** instead of **æ**). Punctuation and capitalisation follow the manuscript text using ʳ to represent the simple paragraphus (marking sentence partitions) and ¶ for the more accentuated capitulum (used to start a new section of the text).

Margin notes have been inserted into the running text and marked as such in the apparatus. Where the author refers to the titles of canon laws and glosses these are italicised in the edition as a reading help. Since numerous citations of biblical or legal sources are seemingly not exact, the source most likely intended in each case is annotated in the apparatus. All references use modern citation conventions, such as:

Cod. 4,13,5	*Corpus Iuris Civilis, Codex Iustinianus*, book 4, title 13, constitution 5
Inst. 1,4,1	*Corpus Iuris Civilis, Institutiones*, book 1, title 4, section 1
Dig. 33,6,16	*Corpus Iuris Civilis, Digesta*, book 33, title 6, law 16
Nov. 18,5	*Corpus Iuris Civilis, Novellae*, book 18, chapter 5
D.81, c.23	*Decretum Gratiani*, Pars I, distinction 81, chapter 23
C.8, q.1, c.9	*Decretum Gratiani*, Pars II, case 8, question 1, chapter 9
D.1, c.87 de poen.	*Decretum Gratiani*, Tractatus de poenitentia, distinction 1, chapter 87
D.4, c.1 de cons.	*Decretum Gratiani*, Pars III, distinction 4, chapter 1
X 5.31.9	*Liber Extra*, book 5, title 31, chapter 9
VI 5.4.1	*Liber Sextus*, book 5, title 4, chapter 1
Clem 5.2.1	*Liber Septimus*, book 5, title 2, chapter 1.

English Translation

The annotated translation is designed to provide the reader with an immediately usable interpretation of the *Reprehensorium*'s text in English. It stays mostly close to the Latin original and only

occasionally simplifies syntax and grammar for greater clarity where this is possible without altering the meaning. For convenience and better readability references to biblical passages are given in the format used in current editions of the Vulgate with verse numbers added (where applicable) to the original quotation of chapters only. References to canonical and legal sources are shortened and partly amended to modern standardized abbreviations (see above). Other than that I have only added some basic information about persons and works referred to as well as some explanatory comments on dates and context that readers other than the most professed experts might otherwise feel the need to look up.

BREUE REPREHENSORIUM
AD
QUOSDAM FRATRES RELIGIOSOS

A BRIEF REPREHENSION

OF CERTAIN FRIARS

Here begins a brief reprehension of certain friars.

For in our times, they who are filled with the advice of a malign spirit carry the burden of the accusation that they had madly come to dismember the Christian faith and make infidels out of Christ's faithful, employing devious sophisms, songs and subtleness. And they were not ashamed to strike the inseparable Christian unity with a sacrilegious schism by producing an indeed most truly heretical discord between those Christian believers recently converted to the true faith in Christ and the old ones, and afflicting them with insults. To this sect adhere those who in the monastery of Saint Peter Martyr of this city of Toledo[1] wrote such words near a certain altar:

"This altar screen was finished on the eve of Assumption Day 1449, the year when the *confessos*[2] of Toledo were robbed"[3]

As I read them, indeed, I thought [at first] to pass by in silence such utterly hostile words of old, and as though I had not read them abandon the intention to write [this treatise], and to excuse myself saying with Jeremiah: *ah, Lord! I don't know how to speak, because I am a youth* (C.8, q.1, c.9 and Ier 1:6).

---

[1] The Dominican Convent Saint Peter Martyr, named after Peter of Verona (c. 1205–52), was founded 1407 in Toledo. See the introduction to this edition for more details.

[2] The term *confeso* or *confesso*, phonetically and semantically close to *converso*, referred to someone who had converted to Christianity by avowing their faith and as a slur possibly also alluded to a convict, i.e. someone confessing their guilt in a forensic context. It was a common insult used to imply that New Christians were newcomers whose profession of faith was only superficial or even feinted. The author then goes on to attribute a positive meaning to the word, e.g. in the sense of giving testimony of one's genuine faith.

[3] This citation as opposed to the rest of the Latin manuscript is in the vernacular. The Solemnity of the Assumption of Mary is celebrated on August 15th. Whether the subject of the altar piece in question is related to this holiday, to the veneration of Mary in general or to something else entirely can only be guessed.

¶ Incipit breue reprehensorium ad quosdam fratres religiosos ·

¶ cum quidam nostris temporibus maligni spiritus consilio replecti reatus pondera tradidissent ut ad demembrandum xpistianam fidem et de xpisti fidelibus facere infidelibus insana mente per deuia sophismata canticas et cauilaciones accesisent ʳ et sacrilego scismate vnitatem xpistianam colidere non erubuissent indiscretam ymo verius hereticam discordiam inter xpisti fideles ad veram xpisti fidem nouiter conuersos cum antiquiis faciendo et contumeliis aficiendo ʳ hanc sunt secuti sectam qui in monasterio santi petri martiris huius toletane vrbis talia circa quodam altare descripsere verba

Este retablo se acabo vispera de santa maria de agosto era de mill e CCCC e XL·IX· annos el anno que se rrobaron los confessos en toledo

quibus quidem lectis cogitaui tam infesta opido ab antiquo verba sub silencio preterire et quasi · si non legisem ab scribendi proposito discedere · meque scusandum cum ieremia dicere · a · a · a · domine nescio loqui quia puer ego sum ·VIII· quescione ·I· capite *in scripturis* et ieremie ·Iᵒ·

---

16 a¹ ... **17** sum Ier 1:6.

---

17 in scripturis C.8, q.1, c.9.

But because it is bad to desist from an intention and even worse to purport an intention (C.13, q.1, c.18), and because the aforementioned statement *is not one that calls forth compassion but rather incites anger and arouses rage* (Idt 8:12), I must not keep silent about what I am saying with sadness and bitterness of mind (D.81, c.23).

Behold, it was recently the spirit of God who uttered such a call in my ears: do not cease to speak, because I will teach you *what you shall say* (Lc 12:12). Therefore, trusting in the Saviour's mercy, I directed my hand to the reed pen. Although I am occupied by worldly business, by this way I have addressed to the friars of said monastery this very short summary of the unity of the Christian faithful.

I only wish that my imperfection may be amended by the pastoral kindness and holiness of your most famous person,[4] at whose feet I, like the palm tree I am named after,[5] incline my head, not to be washed alone out of your deep fount, but also hands and feet, so that I may be cleansed from all error and ignorance, if there are any in this short summary, which I, who am unworthy and ignorant of your greatness and bright rosy brilliance, am arranging to reach your hands, and which is expressed in these fourteen parts:

1. That boasting with something evil is condemned.
2. That no one is to be scolded for his origin, if he has faith.
3. That the faith of the apostles and of the prophets were the same.
4. That a son shall not be punished for the sin of the father nor the other way around.
5. That the Saviour came to this world.
6. That before the incarnation of the Saviour all were divided in errors, Jews as much as Gentiles.
7. That the Saviour brought together his Church out of Jews and Gentiles.

---

[4] Though not in name, the author very probably refers to Alonso Carrillo de Acuña, born 1412, who was archbishop of Toledo 1446–82. As the primate of Spain Alonso was vastly powerful and brought the weight of his position to various political power struggles of the era. Though generally not above a certain opportunism when choosing sides, his support for the *converso* cause was consistent and probably genuine.

[5] This play on words is the only indication of the author's name: *Palma*.

ʳ Sed quia malum est cadere de proposito sed peius est simulare propositum in capite *certe ego sum* ·XIII· quescione ·I· ʳ et quia predictus sermo non est qui misericordiam prouocet sed pocius iram excitet et furorem acendat iudit ·VIIIº· capitulo ʳ nec enim hoc silere debeo quod cum animi tristicia et amaritudine dico in capite *oportet* ·LXXXI· distincione ·

¶ Ecce recens dei spiritus qui in auribus meis talem emisit clamorem ʳ ne ceses loqui quia ego docebo te quod loquaris ʳ igitur confisus de misericordia saluatoris manum ad calamum direxi · licet secularibus occupatus negotiis in hunc modum fratribus dicti monasterii hoc breuisimam compendium vnionis xpistifidelium destinaui ·

¶ Sed ut inperfectum meum benignitas et santitas pastoralis vestre tan celeberrime persone suppleat ʳ sub cuius pedibus laboriosus · Ego ut palma de qua nucupor inclino capud ut non solum lauer ex vestro alto fonte sed manus et pedes ut mundus sim ab omni errore et ignorancia si que sint in hoc breui compendio ʳ quod indignus et ignotus magnitudinis roseoque candore prefulgencie vestre manus peruenire procuro · per has quatuordecim particulas articulatum

·1º· ¶ quod mali gloriacio dampnatur

·2º· ¶ quod propter originem non est quis vituperandus si fidem habet

·3º· ¶ quod eadem fuit fides apostolorum et prophetarum

·4º· ¶ quod filius non punietur propter pecatum patris nec e contra

·5º· ¶ quod saluator uenit in hunc mundum

·6º· ¶ quod ante incarnacionem saluatoris omnes tam iudei quam gentes erant in erroribus diuisi

·7º· ¶ quod saluator ex iudeis et gentibus in vnum congregauit suam ecclesiam

---

21 sermo...**22** acendat Idt 8:12.   **26** quia...loquaris Lc 12:12.

---

20 certe...sum C.13, q.1, c.18.   **23** oportet D.81, c.23.

8. That in the present age the sinners must not be separated from the just.

9. That frivolous words, from which scandal may arise, are to be cut short.

10. That in this age the good suffer and the reprobate pride themselves.

11. That for many reasons misdeeds must be set right.

12. That one who tolerates seditious evil is severely punished.

13. That the power of the pope and the Church is great.

14. That those who err in faith are to be corrected first by the Church and her pastors and finally by the secular princes.

First article: that boasting with something evil is condemned

Can it be, brothers, servants of God, that you turn your eyes to said letters, where among other things is said "the year when the confesos of Toledo were robbed"? Oh, how grievous is it to boast with a crime! (X 5.31.9). And a sentence from the book of virtues:[6] it shall be as sad for you to be praised by disgraceful people as when you are praised because of a disgrace.

Similarly what is written in Idt 6:15: because *you do not abandon those who rely on you, and you humiliate those who rely on themselves and boast with their strength.* And Ps 51:3: *why do you glory in malice?* Ier 9:23-24: *the wise man shall not glory in his wisdom, and the rich man not in his riches, and the strong man not in his strength. But let him who glories glory in knowing and understanding me, for I am the Lord and I exercise mercy and justice.* And since it is not allowed to glory in one's own virtues, how much less in one's vices that cannot be committed by any good man, such as thefts and blasphemies and the like (X 5.41.2).

And if you do not believe me, believe the gospel (Lc 10:17.20)! For the disciples of our Lord Jesus Christ came back after they had gained the power to drive out demons and said with joy: *Lord, behold, for the demons are subject to us!* And Jesus replied: *do not rejoice in that, but because your names*

---

[6] Martin of Braga (c. 520–580), originally from the central European province of Pannonia, became archbishop of Bracara Augusta, today Braga in Portugal. Among his many writings is the *Formula vitae honestae* here quoted, also known as *De differentiis quatuor virtutum*. What was then believed to be the Christian reading of a work by the Roman philosopher Seneca was in fact probably a mostly original composition by Martin himself.

·8º· ¶ quod in presenti seculo pecatores non debent separari a iustis

·9º· ¶ quod leuia verba ex quibus nascitur scandalum sunt rresecanda

·10º· ¶ quod in hoc seculo boni paciuntur et reprobi gloriantur

·11º· ¶ quod multis ex causis maleficia sunt corrigenda

·12º· ¶ quod valde punitur qui tolerat malum sediciosum   50

·13º· ¶ quod magna est pottestas pape et ecclesie

·14º· ¶ errantes in fide quod sunt corrigendi prius per ecclesiam et eius pastores et finaliter per principes seculares

primus articulus quod mali gloriacio dampnatur

Numquid aduertistis oculos vestros fratres serui dei ad predictas literas · ubi inter alia dicitur el anno que se rrobaron los confesos en toledo · O · quam graue est gloriari de delicto in capitulo *quam sit graue de excesibus prelatorum* ʳ et sentencia in libro de virtutibus tam tibi triste   5
sit laudari a turpibus quam lauderis ob turpia

ʳ iuxta id quod scribitur iudit ·VIº· capitulo · quoniam non derelinquis presumentes de te et presumentes de se et de sua virtute gloriantes humilias et in psalmo · quid gloriaris in malicia ʳ ieremie ·IXº· capitulo ad finem · ne glorietur sapiens in sapiencia sua · nec   10
diues in diuitiis suis · nec fortis in fortidudine sua · sed qui gloriatur in hoc glorietur scire et nose me quia ego sum dominus qui facio misericordiam et iusticiam ʳ et si de propria virtute gloriari non licet quantominus de viciis · que non posunt bono aliquo fieri ut furta et blasfemie et similia in capitulo *estote de regulis iuris*   15

ʳ et si michi non creditis euangelio credite luce ·Xº· capitulo discipuli enim domini nostri ihesu xpisti accepta potestate eiciendi demonia reversi sunt cum gaudio dicentes · domine ecce quia demonia subiciuntur nobis et ihesus rrespondit in hoc nolite gaudere sed quia nomina vestra scripta sunt in celis · numquid credebant potestatem   20

---

7 quoniam...9 humilias Idt 6:15.   9 quid...malicia Ps 51:3.   10 ne...13 iusticiam Ier 9:23-24.   18 reversi...20 celis Lc 10:17.20.

---

4 quam²...graue² X 5.31.9.   5 tam...6 turpia Martin of Braga, *Formula vitae honestae*, 4.   15 estote X 5.41.2.

are written in heaven! Can it be that they believed in the power to work miracles out of themselves and not out of God? By their own merits and not by grace? Surely they did not arrogantly pretend to have what they did not have and rather confessed Christ so as to leave gratitude to God?

So why are they blamed, if not because they preferred to pride themselves in other things, accepting these gifts before others and usurp the praise that is primarily owed to God? And it is written: *God who creates evil* (Is 45:7 and C.24, q.3, c.39). And: *there is no evil in the city that I did not make, says the Lord* (Amos 3:6 and C.24, q.3, c.38). This is understood of the evil of punishment, not of fault. And in the gospel (Mt 18:7): *it is necessary that scandals come.* And Io 19:11: *if it had not been given to you from above, you would have no power against me.* Therefore this boasting with evil is reprobate and against the law of Christ. For Jesus said: *if someone calls his brother a fool* – like a *tornadiso*[7] – *he will be liable to hell* (Mt 5:22).

Second and third article: that the faith of the apostles and of the prophets were the same, and that no one is to be scolded for his origin, if he has faith

Can it possibly be disgraceful to be converted? God forbid! For in the psalm (Ps 84:2.7) we read about the true God: *you blessed [your land], Lord, after turning around you will bring us to life; rising from on high* (Lc 1:78). And elsewhere he threatens the inveterate, saying: *unless you will be converted, he will brandish his sword and he has bent his bow and prepared tools of death in it* (Ps 7:13-14 and D.1, c.87 de poen.). *I praise with all my heart* (Ps 9:2). And: *give glory to the Lord, for he is good* (Ps 105:1). And: *I will confess against myself* (Ps 31:5). And: *convert us, God, our salvation* (Ps 84:5)! And: *when the*

---

7) The Spanish slur *tornadizo* or *tornadiso* roughly translates to "turncoat", "renegade" or "traitor" and was commonly used as insult referring to New Christians. It implied that converts had turned their back on their old religion for purely opportunistic reasons and would likewise betray their new faith happily at any moment.

faciendi miracula ex se ipsis · non sed ex deo · numquid pro meritis suis · non sed gratis · numquid iactanter menciebantur · se habere quod non habuerunt · non sed pocius xpistum confitentes quasi gracias cedebant deo ·

₰ Cur ergo rreprehensi nisi quia preferebant se ceteris inaniter gloriantes se hec dona pro aliis accepisse gloriam deo debitam principaliter usurpantes ͬ et quia scriptum est deus creans malum et non est malum in ciuitate quod ego non faciam dicit dominus ysaie ·XLVº· capitulo et in capite *cum quidam* § *coliciani* et ·XXIIII· quescio ·III· *deus* ͬ quod intelegitur de malo pene non culpe ͬ et in euangelio necesse est ut scandala ueniant mathei ·XVIIIº· capitulo ͬ et iohannis ·XIXº· nisi datum esset tibi desuper non haberes potestatem in me ͬ ergo ista mali gloriacio est reprobata et contra legem xpisti · dixit enim ihesus si quis dixerit fratri suo rracha ut tornadiso reus erit iehenne mathei ·Vº· capitulo

Secundus et tercius articulus quod eadem fuit fides apostolorum et prophetarum ͬ et propter originem non est quis vituperandus si fidem habet

Nonne esse conuersum est innominiosum · absit legitur enim de deo vero in psalmo benedixisti · domine tu conversus uiuificabis nos oriens ex alto. ͬ et alibi minatur inconvertibiles dicendo nisi conversi fueritis gladium suum vibrabit et archum suum tetendit et in eo parabit vasa mortis ͬ ad idem *de penitencia* distincione ·I· confitebor tibi in toto corde meo ͬ et confitemini domino quoniam bonus ͬ et confitebor aduersum me ͬ et conuerte nos deus salutaris noster ͬ et cum conuersus ingemuerit tunc saluus erit ezechielis ·XXXIIIº· et

---

27 deus...malum Is 45:7. **28** non[1]...dominus Amos 3:6. **31** necesse... ueniant Mt 18:7. **32** nisi...me Io 19:11. **34** si...**35** iehenne Mt 5:22. **5** benedixisti...nos Ps 84:2.7 **6** oriens...alto Lc 1:78. | nisi...**8** mortis Ps 7:13-14. **8** confitebor...**9** meo Ps 9:2. **9** confitemini...bonus Ps 105:1 par. **10** confitebor...me Ps 31:5. | conuerte...noster Ps 84:5. **11** cum... erit Ez 33:14-15.

---

29 cum quidam C.24, q.3, c.39. **30** deus C.24, q.3, c.38. **8** distincione ·I· D.1, c.87 de poen.

converted cries out in regret, he will be saved (Ez 33:14-15 and D.1, c.32 de poen. and C.26, q.6, c.13). And again: *do not deliver those who trust in you to a people that does not know you!* (Idt 7:20) And so we must not only be converted – that is to say turned in heart – but also confess with the mouth our Saviour Jesus Christ (D.1, c.34 de poen.).

Similarly: *with the heart one believes unto justice – confession is made unto salvation* (Rm 10:10). Because of this the gloss to C.11, q.3, c.85 notes: it says that he who denies Christ with the mouth though not with the heart commits a mortal sin, because even if he does not want to deny Christ, he still wants more that for which he denies him, namely: the safety of his mortal body.

And because it is known that our Saviour took flesh from this shoot, in this he placated himself saying: *and I took root in an honourable people* (Sir 24:16). And: *he has not done likewise to every nation* (Ps 147:9). And: *a light for the revelation to the Gentiles and glory of your people Israel* (Lc 2:32), on which Nicholas of Lyra[8] struck his lute, saying that in the birth of the Saviour there was bestowed great glory to those coming from that lineage from which the Saviour himself took flesh.

And: *again Judea was made his sanctuary* (Ps 113:2). And: *in Judea God is known* (Ps 75:2). And: *he has received Israel his servant* (Lc 1:54). This Jesus, our Lord, saviour and messiah is [called] by a prophetic voice true God, true man (X 5.7.7). *For he is our flesh and our brother* (Gn 37:27). *For the Lord raised for us a prophet from our brothers, like me. You shall listen to everything whatsoever he will say to you. But if someone refuses his word which he will speak in my name, I will take vengeance on him* (Act 3:22; Dt 18:18-19). And thus we read about the shoot of David in Ier 23:5-6: *behold, days will come, says the Lord, when I will raise David a righteous shoot and he will reign as*

---

[8] Nicholas of Lyra (c. 1270–1349) was a Franciscan theologian from Normandy in France. He was and is best known for his *Postillae perpetuae*, a comprehensive work of exegetical annotations to the Bible. Since he seems to have had some knowledge of Hebrew and rabbinical teaching, he is thought by some to have been of Jewish descent. A play on words refers here to "lyra" as both a musical instrument and Nicholas's place of birth.

capite *is qui* et capite *cognouimus* ·XXXI· quescio ·VI· ʳ et iterum noli tradere confitentes te populo qui ignorat te iudit ·4°· capitulo et sic non tantum conversi · quasi corde versi · sed eciam ore confessi debemus esse ad saluatorem nostrum ihesum xpistum ut in capite *convertimini de penitencia* distincione ·I·

ʳ iuxta id corde creditur ad iusticiam confessio fit ad salutem ad rromanos ·X°· ʳ ex quo notante glossa in caput *non solum* ·XI· quescio ·III· dicit quod negans xpistum ore et non corde pecat mortaliter nam etsi noluit negare xpistum plus tamen vult illud propter quod negat scilicet mortalis sui corporis tutellam

ʳ Et cum notum sit saluatorem nostrum de hoc germine asumpsise carnem in eo sibi conplacuit dicendo ʳ et rradicaui in populo honorificato ʳ et non fecit taliter omni nacioni ʳ et lumen ad reuelacionem gencium et gloriam plebis tue israel ʳ super quo nicholas de lira pulsat liram suam dicens quod in natiuitate saluatoris fuit magna gloria venientibus ex illa stirpe ex qua ipse saluator carnem asumpsit

ʳ et iterum facta est iudea santificacio eius ʳ et notus in iudea deus israel ʳ et suscepit israel puerum suum ʳ hic ihesus dominus noster saluator mixias voce prophetica uerus deus verus homo est in capite *cum xpistus de hereticis* ʳ quia caro et frater noster est genesis ·XXXVII°· capitulo ʳ quoniam prophetam suscitauit nobis dominus de fratribus nostris tamquam me ipsum audietis omnia quecumque locutus fuerit uobis ʳ qui autem uerba eius que loquetur in nomine meo noluerit ego ultor existam · devteronomii ·XVIII°· capitulo actuum ·III°· capitulo et sic de germine dauid ʳ legitur enim geremie

---

12 noli...**13** te² Idt 7:20. **17** corde...**17** salutem Rm 10:10. **23** et...**24** honorificato Sir 24:16. **24** non...nacioni Ps 147:9. | lumen...**25** israel Lc 2:32. **29** iterum...eius Ps 113:2. | notus...**30** israel¹ Ps 75:2. **30** suscepit...suum Lc 1:54. **32** quia...noster Gn 37:27. **33** quoniam... **35** uobis Act 3:22, Dt 18:18. **35** qui...**36** existam Dt 18:19.

---

12 is qui D.1, c.32 de poen. | cognouimus C.26, q.6, c.13. **16** convertimini D.1, c.34 de poen. **18** non solum C.11, q.3, c.85. **26** in...**28** asumpsit Nicolaus de Lyra, *Postilla seu expositio super evangelium Lucae*. **32** cum xpistus X 5.7.7.

king. He will be wise. He will execute judgment and justice in the land. And it is added below: *in those days Judah will be saved and Israel will dwell confidently.* And it follows: *this is the name that they will call him: the Lord is our just one.*

And in the book of the begetting of our Lord Jesus Christ he is called son of David, son of Abraham. For God promised him (Gn 12:3 and 26:4) that *in his seed* – that is, in the Saviour Jesus Christ – *all peoples should be blessed.* And elsewhere: *a child is born to us, a son is given us, dominion is placed upon his shoulder, and his name will be called: wonderful counsellor, mighty God, father of the coming age, prince of peace* (Is 9:6).

And: *you, Bethlehem Ephrata, are very small among the thousands of Juda; but the one who will be ruler over Israel will come out of you for me. His going forth is as from the beginning, from the days of eternity* (Micha 5:2). Also: *come out, daughters of Zion, and see King Solomon in the diadem his mother crowned him with* (Ct 3:11). And also: *rejoice greatly, daughter Zion! Cheer, daughter Jerusalem! Behold, your king will come to you, a holy saviour, he is poor and riding on a she-ass* (Za 9:9). And: *his generation – who shall declare it?* (Is 53:8).

By all this is splendidly proven, that the Saviour took flesh from the Israelites out of Mary, ever virgin, begotten by the work of the Holy Spirit, made true man incarnate through the whole Trinity equally (VI 1.1.1 and VI 5.4.1). Hence Hab 3:18 says in order to explain the name of God and of our saviour: *I rejoice in the Lord and will cheer in God, my Jesus.*

Hence we read, that in times of the emperor Octavian [Augustus], when those who where in charge of the provinces for the senate and the people of

·XXIII°· capitulo ecce dies ueniunt dicit dominus suscitabo dauid germen iustum et regnabit rex sapiens erit faciet iudicium et iusticiam in terra et ibi subditur ʳ in diebus illis saluabitur iuda et israel habitabit confidenter et sequitur hoc est nomen quod uocabunt eum dominus iustus noster

ʳ et in libro generacionis domini nostri ihesu xpisti dicitur filius dauid filii habraham ʳ promiserat enim deus genesis ·XII°· capitulo quod in semine eius id est in ihesu xpisto saluatore benedicerentur omnes gentes ʳ et alibi paruulus natus est nobis filius datus est nobis factum est principatum eius super humerum eius et uocabitur nomen eius admirabilis consiliarius deus fortis pater futuri seculi princeps pacis ysaie ·IX°· capitulo

ʳ et tu belem efrata paruulus est in milibus iuda ex te enim michi egredietur qui sit dominator in israel · egresus eius sicut ab inicio a diebus eternitatis michee ·V°· capitulo ʳ item egredimini filie sion et videte regem salomonem in diademate qua coronauit eum mater sua canticorum ·IIII°· ʳ ad idem exulta satis filia syon iubila filia iherusalem ecce rex tuus veniet tibi santus saluator ipse pauper et ascendens super asinam zacharie ·IX°· ʳ et generacionem eius quis enarrabit ysaie ·LIII°·

ʳ ex quibus loculenter probatum de israelitis saluatorem carnem asumpsisse ex maria semper virgine spiritu santi cohoperacione conceptus verus homo factus a tota trinitate pariter incarnatus ut in capitulo ·I· *de suma trinitate* et in capitulo *pro humani de homicidio* libro sexto ʳ vnde abachuc ·III°· capitulo in fine in exposicio de nomine dei et saluatoris nostri ait ʳ ego autem in domino gaudeo et exultabo in deo ihesu meo

¶ Vnde legitur quod temporibus octauiani cesaris cum ex diuersi mundi partibus hii qui pro senatu populoque rromano preerant

---

38 ecce...**42** noster Ier 23:5-6. **43** filius...**44** habraham Mt 1:1.
45 benedicerentur...**46** gentes Gn 12:3, 26:4. **46** paruulus...**48** pacis Is 9:6. **50** tu...**52** eternitatis Micha 5:2. **52** egredimini...**53** sua Ct 3:11.
54 exulta...**56** asinam Za 9:9. **56** generacionem...**57** enarrabit Is 53:8.
63 ego...**64** meo Hab 3:18.

---

61 de[1]...trinitate VI 1.1.1. | pro humani VI 5.4.1.

Rome wrote from different parts of the world news that occurred throughout the climes of the world to the senators who were in Rome, Publius Lentulus, governor for the Roman senate and people in Judea, sent a letter whose words are these:[9]

There appeared in our times, and still is present, a man of great virtue whose name is Christ Jesus, who is said by the people to be a prophet of truth, whom his disciples call son of God. He raises dead and heals infirmities. He is a man of truly tall and handsome figure and has a venerable face, which those who look at it can love and fear. He has hair of the colour of unripe hazelnut, straight nearly unto the ears, but from the ears on curly, falling a little bit more blueish and shiny over the shoulders; the parting being in the middle of the head after the custom of the Nazarenes. His forehead is level and very serene with a face without any wrinkle or stain, adorned with a mild rosiness. There is no fault at all in his nose and mouth. He has an abundant beard the same color as the hair, not long, but divided in the middle. He has a simple and mature gaze with gray colored and bright eyes, terrible when chiding, in his advice gentle and pleasant. Cheerful while conserving dignity, he has never been seen laughing, but weeping indeed. In bodily stature he is upright and straight, has hands and arms that are lovely to behold, and in conversation he is grave, deliberate and modest – magnificent among the children of man. This is only written in the annals of the Romans.

And also [Titus Flavius] Josephus,[10] a great history-writer of the Jews says in the eighteenth books of the Jewish Antiquities about Jesus the Nazarene: There was in these times a man, Jesus the Nazarene, if it is even possible to call him a [mere] man. For he was a worker of miracles and a teacher to those who willingly listen to what is true. Indeed, he gathered a lot of the Jews and many from the Gentiles to himself. He was the One. He was

---

[9] The following "Letter of Lentulus" *(epistula Lentuli)* is a somewhat curious text that appeared in the middle of the 15th century first in Italy and was eagerly received throughout Europe. Detailing the appearance of Jesus of Nazareth it seems to be rather an inventive answer to the then growing visually inspired piety than an authentic document from antiquity.

[10] Flavius Josephus (c. 37-100) was a Jewish-Roman historian. Medieval scholars would have known his *Antiquitates Iudaicae*, composed originally in Greek, only through later Latin translations. His mention of Jesus of Nazareth *(testimonium Flavianum)* is probably heavily redacted (if not entirely inserted) by Christian copyists to up-play its reverence of Jesus.

prouinciis scribebant senatoribus qui erant rrome nouitates que ocurrebant per mundi climata · publius lentulus in iudea preses senatui populoque rromano epistolam misit cuius verba sunt hec

ʳ apparuit temporibus nostris adhuc est homo magne virtutis cui nomen est xpistus ihesus qui dicitur a gentibus propheta veritatis quem eius discipuli vocant filium dei · suscitans mortuos et sanans langores homo quidem statura procerus et spectabilis vultum habens venerabilem quem intuentes posunt diligere et formidare · capilos habens coloris nucis auellane prematuræ et planos fere usque ad aures ab auribus uero crispos aliquantulum ceruliores et fulgidiores ab humeris ventilantes · discrimen habens in medio capitis iuxta morem nazarenorum · frontem planam et serenissimam cum facie sine rruga et macula aliqua quam moderatus rubor uenustat · nasi et oris nulla prorsus est reprehensio · barbam habens copiosam et capilis concolorem non longam sed in medio bifurcatam · aspectum habens simplicem et maturum · occulis glaucis variis et claris existentibus · increpacione terribilis · in admonicione placidus et amabilis illaris seruata grauitate · cui numquam visus est ridere flere autem sic · in statura corporis propagatus et rectus manus habens et brachia visu delectabilia · et in colloquio grauis rarus et modestus speciosus inter filios hominum hec sola in annalibus rromanorum scripta est

¶ ad idem iosephus magnus ystoriographus iudeorum ·XVIII· libro antiquitatis iudaice ait de ihesu nazareno fuit hiisdem temporibus ihesus nazarenus vir · si tamen eum virum nominare fas est · erat einm mirabilium operum efector et doctor eorum hominum qui libenter ea que vera sunt audiunt · multos quidem iudeorum multos ex gentilibus sibi adiunxit hic erat ʳ hunc acusauerunt primorum nostre

---

70 apparuit...87 hominum *Epistula Lentuli.*   89 fuit...97 predixerunt Josephus Flavius, *Antiquitates Judaicae*, XVIII,3,3.

accused by some of the leading men of our nation, and when [Pontius] Pilate ordered him to be crucified, those who loved him from the beginning did not desert him. For he appeared to them again alive according to what divinely inspired prophets had foreseen about this and innumerable future miracles of his.

So now for the proposition: look into the face of your Christ, you who are dull, who doubt that they who are from God according to [both] flesh and spirit are more so than those who are so according to the spirit alone. For *a threefold cord is hard to break* (Ecl 4:12 and X 1.34.1). And: they must not be disdained because they trace their origin from the people of the Jews (X 1.3.7). For the holy mother Church was founded out of converted Jews (D.21, c.2; C.32, q.4, c.2 and D.61, c.8).

Hence we read in Dt 33:29: *blessed are you, Israel! Who is like you, people that is saved by the Lord, the shield of your help and sword of your glory? Your enemies will deny you, and you will tread their neck.* And also Dt 26:19, confirmed by Is 60:21 who says: *your people are all just, forever shall they inherit the land.* Likewise Paul (Rm 11:1) says of himself: *I am an Israelite of the people of Abraham from the tribe of Benjamin.* And in Rm 7:6 he says: *we are all in the newness of faith servants of Jesus Christ.*

Likewise Jerome says about the letter of Paul (Act 16:1, Gal 2:3, II Tim 1:5) to Timothy,[11] that Timothy was a son of a Gentile and the apostle raised him in the law of Moses and circumcised him so that he might be more apt to receive the faith in our Lord Jesus Christ. And Paul consecrated him as bishop in order to give to understand that the crossing from the written law of Moses to the law of grace of our Lord Jesus Christ is easier than to be newly converted without knowledge of any law.

---

[11] The passage from Galatians refers in fact to Titus, not Timothy.

gentis virorum · cum pilatus in cruce agendum esse decreuisset non
deseruerunt eum hii qui ab inicio dilexerunt apparuit enim iterum eis
viuus secundum quod divinitus inspirati prophete hec et alia innume-
rant de eo futura miracula predixerunt ʳ

ʳ Ergo nunc ad propositum respice in faciem xpisti tui quis es ebes qui
dubitat non esse magis ex deo qui sunt secundum carnem et spiritum
quam illi qui sunt secundum spiritum solum quia funiculus triplex
dificile rumpitur ecclesiastici ·IIIIº· capitulo et in capitulo ·I· *de treuga
et pace* ʳ et quia de gente iudeorum originem ducunt dedignari non
debent in capitulo *eam te de rescriptis* quia de iudeis conversis fundata
fuit santa mater ecclesia ·XXI· distincione capite *in nouo* ·XXXII·
quescione ·IIII· capite *recurrat* pulcher textus in § *econtra* ·LXI·
distincione

ʳ vnde legitur deuteronomii ·XXXIIIº· in fine beatus tu israel quis
similis tui popule qui saluaris in domino scutum auxilii tui et gladius
glorie tue negabunt te inimici tui et tu eorum cola calcabis ʳ ad idem
devteronomii ·XXVIº· circa finem quod aserit ysaie ·LX· circa finem
inquiens populus autem tuus omnes iusti in perpetuum hereditabunt
terram ʳ item paulus ad rromanos ·Xº· ait de se ipso ego israelita sum
de gente habraham ex tribu beniamin ʳ et ad rromanos ·VIIIº·
capitulo ait omnes sumus in nouitate fidei servi ihesu xpisti

ʳ item ieronimus super epistula pauli ad timotheum actuum ·XVIº· et
ad galatas ·IIº· capitulo ait quod timotheus fuit filius gentilis et
apostolus nutriuit eum in lege moysi et eum circumcidit ut habilior
esset ad fidem domini nostri ihesu xpisti suscipiendam et paulus eum
in episcopum consecrauit ad dandum intelligi faciliorem esse transi-
tum de lege moysi scripta ad legem gracie domini nostri ihesu xpisti
quam de nouo conuerti sine alicuius legis cognicione

---

100 quia...101 rumpitur Ecl 4:12.   107 beatus...109 calcabis Dt 33:29.
111 populus...112 terram Dt 26:19; Is 60:21.   112 ego...113 beniamin
Rm 11:1.   114 omnes...xpisti Rm 7:6.   116 timotheus...117 circumcidit
Act 16:1, Gal 2:3, II Tim 1:5.

101 de...102 pace X 1.34.1.   103 eam te X 1.3.7.   104 in nouo D.21, c.2.
105 recurrat C.32, q.4, c.2. | econtra D.61, c.8.

Likewise Apc 14:1: *hundred forty-four thousand* – according to the number of the redeemed that he heard – *with the signs of servants of God on their forehead are found amongst the twelve tribes of Israel. For they are the ones who came out of great tribulation and washed their garments in the blood of the lamb* (Apc 7:14). Likewise Elijah complained to God, saying against Israel: *Lord, they killed your prophets and removed your altars, and I alone escaped, and they seek my life* (III Rg 19:10). And the Lord answered him: *I will leave in Israel seven thousand of those who did not bend their knees before Baal* (III Rg 19:18), that is, the idol that was thus called.

Likewise in the Martinian[12] accounts of the Holy Fathers we read that Evaristus,[13] a Greek by nation whose father was a Jew by the name of Judah from the city of Bethlehem, was a Roman pontiff in the Church of God. On account of writing the truth he was crowned with martyrdom and was buried next to blessed Peter in the time of the emperors Trajan and Hadrian. He is mentioned in the title of the decrees C.1, q.7, c.1; C.1, q.7, c.17 and C.1, q.7, c.21.

And also in the chronicle that was composed by Rodrigo,[14] the Archbishop of Toledo, we read that Julianus Pomerius[15] of the Jewish people was so

---

[12] Martin of Opova (?–1278), also known as Martinus Polonus, was a Dominican friar, head of the papal penitentiary and author of various scholarly and pious works. His *Chronicon pontificum et imperatorum* was translated into many vernacular languages and even into Persian and Armenian.

[13] Of Evaristus (Bishop of Rome c. 99-107) little more is known than what is written here. Since the sources specifically mention his Jewish heritage, he was often cited in pro-*converso* literature as a positive example and proof that a Jewish lineage was no obstacle to high church offices or indeed holiness even after the time of the apostles.

[14] Rodrigo Jiménez de Rada (c. 1170–1247) served as Archbishop of Toledo from c. 1209 until his death. He was one of the most influential medieval writers of Spanish history and an important early promoter of Castilian "Goticismo", a narrative that puts Germanic tribes in the centre of Spanish Christian historiography. The mention of Julianus Pomerius here refers to his *Historia gótica*, III,13, also known under various titles such as *De rebus Hispaniae* and *Historia de los hechos de España*.

[15] Probably originally from Northern Africa, Julianus Pomerius (5th century) fled before the Vandals to Gaul and settled down in Arles. The book in three parts mentioned here would be his *De vita contemplativa*, a guide to an ascetic and virtuous life. The author of our manuscript, however, seems to conflate his

ʳ item apochalipsis ·XVIIIº· centum et quadraginta et quatuor milia secundum numerum saluorum quam audiuit sigantorum in frontibus eorum pro seruis dei per ·XII· tribus israel sunt reperti ʳ hii enim sunt qui uenerunt ex magna tribulacione et lauerunt stolas suas in sanguine agni apocalipsis ·VIº· ʳ item elias conquestus fuit domino dicens aduersus israel domine prophetas tuos interfecerunt et altaria tua exterminauerunt et ego euasi solus et querunt animam meam ʳ et rrespondit ei dominus Ego relinquam in israel septem mille ex hiis qui genua sua non flexerunt bahali id est idolo sic uocato ʳ

ʳ item in martiniana santorum patrum legitur quod euaristus nacione grecus ex patre iudeo nomine iuda de ciuitate bethlehem · fuit pontifex romaus in ecclesia dei propter stillum veritatis martirio coronatus sepultus est iuxta beatum petrum tempore imperatorum traiani et adriani de quo fit mencio in decretis in suprascripcione capite ·I· et capite *si qui sunt* et capite *sunt nonnulli* ·II· quescione ·VII·

ʳ ad idem in coronica per rrodericum archiepiscopum toletanum composita legitur quod iullianus pomerius de gente iudeorum tantum

---

122 centum...**124** eorum Apc 14:1. **124** hii...**126** agni Apc 7:14. **127** domine...**128** meam III Rg 19:10. **129** Ego...**130** uocato III Rg 19:18.

---

131 in...**141** substancie Alonso Díaz de Montalvo, *Tractatus quidam levis*, 15. **135** capite ·I· C.1, q.7, c.1. **136** si...sunt[1] C.1, q.7, c.17. | sunt nonnulli C.1, q.7, c.21.

famous in the teaching of the Lord, that for his virtue and wisdom he was named archbishop and composed a book in three parts in favour of the faith. Likewise Peter says: *but you are a chosen stock, a royal priesthood, a holy nation, a people of [God's] acquisition, so that you may announce the virtues of him who called you out of the shadows into his marvellous light: who once were no people, but are now the people of God; and who had not obtained mercy, but have now obtained mercy* (I Pt 2:9-10).

For and in fact the new just like the old are made *contemporaries in the faith* (II Pt 1:1). Likewise: *the foundations* of the church militant *are in the holy mountains*. As mountains the prophet understands apostles and preachers (VI 1.6.17 and Ps 86:1). And also Jesus the Saviour chose from this lineage the holy apostles. Hence Paul (Eph 1:3-5): *blessed be the father of our Lord Jesus Christ, who blessed us with every spiritual blessing in the heavens in Christ. He thus chose us before the foundation of the world, so that we might be holy and immaculate in his sight in charity, that predestined us to an adoption as children through Jesus Christ* (D.4, c.9 de poen. and D.4, c.11 de poen.).

Whom he predestined, them he called (Rm 8:30 and D.4, c.11 de poen.). And: *you are the light of the world* (Mt 5:14 and C.24, q.1, c.25). Likewise: *once you were darkness, but now light in the Lord* (Eph 5:8 and D.4, c.12 de poen.).

Similarly we read about the fathers of the Old Testament, who were elevated to sainthood by the voice of God in Sir 44:1-2, where it is said: *let us praise the glorious men, our fathers in their generation! God created much glory, his magnificence from the beginning*; which is [also] declared by Pope Innocent

person with that of the archbishop Julian of Toledo (642–690) who is revered as a saint and believed to have had Jewish ancestors.

fuit in doctrina domini preclarus quod sua virtute et prudencia fuit in
archiepiscopum decoratus et in fidei fauorem librum composuit trine
substancie ʳ item petrus ait vos autem genus electum regale sacerdocium gens santa populus acquisicionis ut virtutes anuncietis eius qui
de tenebris uocauit vos in admirabile lumen suum qui aliquando non
populus nunc autem populus dei et qui non consecuti misericordiam
nunc autem misericordiam consecuti ·Iᵃ· petri ·IIº· capitulo

ʳ coequales namque fidei noui sicut et veteres efecti sunt ·IIᵃ· petri in
principio ʳ item fundamenta militantis ecclesic in montibus santis per
montes inteligit propheta apostolos et predicatores in capitulo
fundamenta de elleccione libro sexto et psalmo ·LXXXVIº· ʳ ad idem
ihesus saluator de hac prosapia santos apostolos elegit vnde paulus ad
ephesios ·Iº· benedictus pater domini nostri ihesu xpisti · qui
benedixit nos in omni benedicione spirituali in celestibus in xpisto sic
elegit nos ante mundi constitucionem ut essemus santi et inmaculati ·
in conspectu eius in caritate que predestinauit nos in apdopcione
filiorum per ihesum xpistum *de penitencia* distincione ·IIII· capite
benedictus et capite *in domo* § *itaque*

ʳ quos predestinauit hos et uocauit iohannis ·VIIIº· capitulo *de penitencia* distincione ·IIII· *in domo* ʳ et vos estis lux mundi mathei ·Vº·
capitulo ·XXIIII· quescione ·I· capite *quoniam vetus* ʳ item fuistis
aliquando tenebre nunc autem lux in domino ad ephesios ·Vº· *de
penitencia* distincione ·IIII· § *hanc societatem*

ʳ similiter patres veteris testamenti canonizatos voce dei legimus in
ecclesiastico ·XLIIIIº· capitulo ubi dicitur laudemus viros gloriosos
parentes nostros in generacione sua multam gloriam fecit deus sua
magnificencia a seculo quod declarat innocencius in capitulo

---

141 vos...145 consecuti I Pt 2:9–10.   146 coequales II Pt 1:1.
147 fundamenta...santis Ps 86:1.   151 benedictus...157 xpistum Eph
1:3–5.   157 quos...uocauit Rm 8:30.   158 vos...mundi Mt 5:14.
159 fuistis...162 domino Eph 5:8.   163 laudemus...167 seculo Sir 44:1–2.

---

149 fundamenta VI 1.6.17.   156 benedictus D.4, c.9 de poen. | in domo
D.4, c.11 de poen.   158 in domo D.4, c.11 de poen.   159 quoniam vetus
C.24, q.1, c.25.   161 hanc societatem D.4, c.12 de poen.

[III] in X 4.45.1. By saying *glorious* he shows that they had been elevated to sainthood. Otherwise the Church would not be told to praise them. By saying *our fathers* he says that no one is elevated to sainthood but one who has faith. For only those of his fathers (who where Jews) who at that time had faith were to be elevated to sainthood. About this canonization Moses said to God (Ex 32:31-32): *forgive the people this trespass or strike me out of the book in which you have written me!* – that is: canonized me (D.45, c.9).

Hence Augustine [wrote]: the same church that gave birth to Abel and Enoch and Noah and Abraham also gave birth to Moses and the prophets in the time of the law [and] to the later good men in the time before the advent of the Lord; and she herself gave birth to the apostles and many martyrs and to all good Christians she gave birth; one may know: at the time of grace. For she gave birth to all who at different times were born and appeared, but are gathered as society of a single people and citizens of the same community, as is expressed in C.32, q.4, c.2.

And also Paul: *I want you to know, brethren, our fathers were all under the cloud and all crossed the sea and all were in Moses baptized in the cloud and in the sea* (I Cor 10:1 and D.4, c.127 de cons.).

These most holy apostles and prophets were indeed pictured by the twelve stones over which *the children of Israel carried the Ark of the Lord* when *they passed over the Jordan* (Ios 3:13-14). Implicitly and explicitly they made manifest the faith, as it is right according to [Pope] Innocent [III] (X 1.1.1). And various things that the prophets alluded to earlier, the apostles preached more clearly.

audiuimus de reliquiis et veneracione santorum in eo quod dicit gloriosos ostendit quod canonizati erant aliter non mandaretur ecclesie quod eos laudaret per id quod dicit parentes nostros dicit quod nullus canonizatus est nisi qui fidem habet soli enim parentes eius qui erant iudei penes quos erat fides tunc canonizandi erant ʳ de hac enim canonizacione exodi ·XXXII· moyses ad dominus ait dimite populo noxiam hanc aut dele me de libro in quo me scripsisti id est canonizasti ut in capite *disciplina* ·XLV· distincione 170

ʳ vnde agustinus super iohanncm ecclesia que peperit abel et enoch et noe et habraham ipsa peperit tempore legis moysem et prophetas bonos tempore posteriores ante domini aduentum et que istos ipsa et apostolos et martires numerosos et omnes bonos xpistianos peperit scilicet tempore gracie · omnes enim peperit qui diuersis temporibus nati aparuerunt sed societate vnius populi continentur et eiusdem ciuitatis ciues ut est expresum in capite *recurrat* ·XXXII· quescione ·IIII· 175 180

ʳ ad idem paulus nolo vos ignorare fratres quoniam patres nostri omnes sub nube fuerunt et omnes mare transierunt et omnes in moyse baptizati sunt in nube et in mari ·Iᵃ· ad corinthios ·Xº· *de consecracione* distincione ·IIII· *nec quemquam* 185

ʳ isti quidem santissimi apostoli et prophete figurati per duodecim lapides super quos filii israel habuerunt archam domini cum transierunt iordan · iosue ·IIIº· capitulo implicite et explicite fidem propalarunt ut decet secundum innocencium in capitulo ·I· in fine *de suma trinitate et fide catolica* · et permixta quod perprius prophete predixerant apostoli clarius predicarunt // 190

---

171 dimite...**174** scripsisti Ex 32:31–32.   **182** nolo...**186** mari I Cor 10:1-2.   **187** filii...**188** iordan Ios 3:13-14.

---

166 audiuimus X 4.45.1.   **173** disciplina D.45, c.9.   **174** ecclesia...**179** peperit Augustine, *De baptismo contra Donatistas*, I,25.   **180** recurrat C.32, q.4, c.2.   **185** nec quemquam D.4, c.127 de cons.   **189** capitulo ·I· X 1.1.1.

Jeremiah said (Ier 3:19): *you will call me father and you will not cease to walk after me*. And: *is he not your father who possessed you and made you* (Dt 32:6)? Peter: I believe in God, the almighty father.

David said (Ps 2:7): *the Lord said to me: you are my son, today I have begotten you*. And II Sm 7:12-14: *I will confirm his kingdom. He will build a house for my name. I will be a father for him, he will be a son for me*. Andrew: and in Jesus Christ, his only son, our Lord.

Isaiah said (Is 7:14): *behold, a virgin will conceive and bear a son. A rod will come forth from the root of Jesse and a flower will rise from its root* (Is 11:1). James: who was conceived from the virgin Mary.

Zachariah said (Za 13:6-7): *what are these wounds in the middle of your hands? And he will say: with these I was wounded in the house of them who loved me. Sword, rise against my shepherd and against the man close to me, says the Lord of hosts*. And: *they stabbed my hands and my feet and counted all of my bones* (Ps 21:17-18). John the Evangelist: he suffered under Pontius Pilate, was crucified, died and was buried.

Hosea said (Os 13:14): *o death, I will be your death! I will be your bite, hell! I will bite you for I will crush you*. And III Rg 22:35: *although victorious, the king is dead and blood runs from his chariot*. Thomas: he descended to hell, on the third day he rose from the dead.

Amos said to wit (Amos 9:6): *he built his ascension in heaven*. James the Less: he ascended to heaven, he sits at the right hand of God the father.

Malachi said (Mal 3:5): *I will come to you in judgment and will be a swift witness*. Philip: thereupon he is to come to judge the living and the dead.

Joel said (Ioel 2:28): *I will pour out my spirit over all flesh*. Bartholomew: I believe in the Holy Spirit.

¶ dixit enim ieremia ·III°· patrem uocabis me et post me ingredi non cesabis et numquid non ipse est pater tuus qui posedit te et creauit te deuteronomii ·XXXII°· capitulo ʳ petrus credo in deum patrem omnipotentem

¶ dixit dauid psalmo ·II°· dominus dixit ad me filius meus es tu ego hodie genui te et ·II°· regum ·VI°· capitulo firmabo regnum eius ipse edificabit domum nomini meo ego ero ei in patrem ipse erit mi in filium ʳ andreas et in ihesum xpistum filium eius vnicum dominum nostrum

¶ dixit ysaias ·VII°· capitulo ecce virgo concipiet et pariet filium ʳ egredietur virga de radice iese et flos de rradice eius ascendet ysaias ·XI°· ʳ iacobus qui conceptus est ex maria virgine

¶ dixit zacharias ·XIII°· capitulo que sunt plage iste in medio manuum tuarum et dicet hiis plagatus sum in domo eorum qui diligebant me framea suscitare super pastorem meum et super virum coherentem mi dixit dominus exercituum ʳ et foderunt manus meas et pedes meos et dinumerauerunt omnia osa mea psalmo ʳ iohannes evangelista pasus sub poncio pilato crucifixus mortuus et sepultus

¶ dixit osee ·XIII°· capitulo o mors ero mors tua morsus tuus ero inferne ego mordebo te quia frangam te ʳ et ·III°· regum ultimo licet victor mortuus est rex et currit sanguis de curru eius ʳ thomas descendit ad inferos tercia die resurrexit a mortuis

¶ dixit enim amos ·IX°· capitulo qui edificauit in celo ascensionem suam ʳ iacobus minor ascendit ad celos sedet ad desteram dei patris

¶ dixit malachias ·III°· capitulo ascendam ad uos in iudicio et ero testis uelox ʳ philipus inde venturus est iudicare uiuos et mortuos

¶ dixit ioel ·II°· capitulo efundam de spiritu meo super omnem carnem ʳ bartolomeus credo in spiritum santum

---

192 patrem...193 cesabis Ier 3:19. 193 numquid...te² Dt 32:6.
196 dominus...199 te Ps 2:7. 197 firmabo...201 filium¹ II Sm 7:12–14.
201 ecce...filium Is 7:14. 202 egredietur...ascendet Is 11:1. 204 que...
207 exercituum Za 13:6–7. 207 foderunt...210 mea Ps 21:17–18.
210 capitulo...213 te² Os 13:14. 211 licet...214 eius III Rg 22:35.
214 qui...217 suam Amos 9:6. 216 ascendam...219 uelox Mal 3:5.
218 efundam...221 carnem Ioel 2:28.

Zephaniah said (Zef 3:9): *all will call upon the name of the Lord our God and serve him.* Matthew: *the holy Catholic Church, the communion of saints.*

Micah foretold (Micha 7:19): *the Lord will put away all our iniquities.* Simon: the forgiveness of sins.

Ezekiel said (Ez 37:12): *I will bring you out of your graves, my people.* Jude Thaddeus: the resurrection of the flesh.

Daniel said (Dn 12:2): *all will wake, some to live, some to reproach.* Matthias: the life everlasting. Amen.

Fourth article: that a son shall not be punished for the sin of the father nor the other way around

Those indeed who trust abidingly in this orthodox faith trace their origin from the Jews, because the Lord chose [them as] apostles, that is, bishops of the Jewish law (Mt 4; Lc 6; Io 6; D.23, c.1; C.35, q.1, c.1). But to arbitrate according to birth is of dirt and foulness, for *the earth is the Lord's and its fullness* (Ps 23:1 and C.13, q.2, c.26). *Earth*, that is: the bodies of men. Like Gn 2:7: *God formed man from mud of the earth. Fullness*, that is: the souls that fill the bodies. For *it is the spirit that brings to life, but the flesh is not useful for anything* (Io 6:64; II Cor, 3:6 and D.4, c.8 de poen.).

Poor and rich men the Lord made from one mud, and one earth carries poor and rich men (D.8, c.1). And: wherever they come from, called by divine grace, so long as they do their duty in a way worthy of praise, their nation is not to be called into question (X 2.1.16). Likewise Augustine says: wherever

⁋ dixit sophonias inuocabunt omnes nominem domini dei nostri et seruient ei ʳ matheus santam ecclesiam catolicam santorum comunionem

⁋ micheas ·VII°· capitulo predixit deponet dominus omnes iniquitates nostras ʳ symon remisionem pecatorum

⁋ dixit ezechiel ·XXXVII°· capitulo educam vos de sepulchris vestris popule meus ʳ iudas thadeus carnis resurreccionem

⁋ dixit daniel ·XII°· capitulo vigilabunt omnes alii ad vitam alii obprobrum ʳ mathias vitam eternam amen

quartus articulus quod filius non punietur propter pecatum patris nec econtra

Isti quidem fidem hanc orthodoxiam fideliter confitentes de iudeis traxerunt originem ʳ nam dominus elegit apostolos id est episcopos de lege iudaica matheus ·IIII°· luce ·VI°· iohannis ·VI°· XXIII· distincione *deus noster* ·XXV· quescione ·I· § *hanc* ʳ Sed diceptare de genere est de luto et putredine quia domini est terra et plenitudo eius in capite *ubicumque* ·XIII· quescio finalis · terra id est corpora hominum iuxta id genesis ·I°· formauit deus hominem de limo terre plenitudo id est anime que replent corpora ʳ quia spiritus est qui uiuificat caro autem non prodest quidquam ad corinthios ·III°· capitulo in capite *ex bono de penitencia* distincione ·IIII· circa finem

ʳ pauperes et diuites de vno limo fecit dominus et pauperes et diuites vna terra suportat in capite *quo iur* ·VIII· distincione ʳ et vndecumque venerint gracia diuina uocati dum tantum suum officium laudabiliter exerceant non est querenda sua nocio nacionis in capitulo *cum*

---

220 inuocabunt...223 ei Zef 3:9. 223 deponet...226 nostras Micha 7:19. 225 educam...228 meus Ez 37:12. 227 vigilabunt...230 obprobrum Dn 12:2. 4 dominus...apostolos Mt 4:18-22, Lc 6:13, Io 6:68–70. 7 domini...eius Ps 23:1 par. 9 formauit...terre Gn 2:7. 10 spiritus...11 quidquam Io 6:64; II Cor 3:6.

---

6 deus noster D.23, c.1. | hanc C.35, q.1, c.1. 8 ubicumque C.13, q.2, c.26. 12 ex bono D.4, c.8 de poen. 14 quo iur D.8, c.1. 16 cum...17 deputati X 2.1.16.

men are born, if they do not follow the vices of their parents, they will be honest and saved. For the seed of man, whatever a man is like, is a creature of God (D.56, c.3).

Hence John Chrysostom in his fourth homily about Matthew: let us never be ashamed of the vices of [our] parents, but seek this one thing: that we always grow in virtues. And it follows: no one is to be praised or blamed for either virtue or vice of [his] parents. There is no one truly obscure or bright. Instead, as we consider someone let us say even more clearly: I do not know by which hidden design of God and how he does not shine more – because of parents entirely alien to virtues – and still he himself belongs to God by means of marvellous virtue (D.56, c.4).

Likewise Jerome in the letter against Rufinus: to be born of infidels is not the fault of the one who is born. For just so the earth does not sin in the seeds it fosters, nor the seed that lies in the furrow, not humidity, not warmth by whose mildness the grain or bud sprouts. And it follows: do not despise the potter's goodness who created and formed you and made you like he wanted. For he is God's power and God's wisdom that build for himself a house in the virgin Mary's womb.

Jephthah, who is counted among the holy men by the voice of the apostle, was the son of a harlot (Idc 11:1 and Hbr 11:32). Esau [the son] of Rebecca and Isaac, bristly in mind as in body, degraded as though from good wheat to darnel and straw, for not in the seeds, but in the work of the one being born lies the cause for vices and virtues (D.56, c.5 and D.56, c.6). And similarly: the clothes that you are wearing used to be filthy wool. For the crop that is sown by a leprous hand will still be reaped pure (C.1, q.1, c.24).

And also Jerome: our Lord Jesus wanted to be born not only from foreigners but also from adulterous intercourse – namely: from Thamar – to offer us a

deputati de iudiciis ͬ item agustinus inquid vndecumque homines nascantur si parentum vicia non sectantur honesti et salui erint · semen enim hominis ex qualicumque homine dei creatura est ut capite *vndecumque* ·LVI· distincione

ͬ vnde iohannes chrisostomus super matheum omellia ·IIII· numquam de uiciis erubescamus parentum · sed illud vnum queramus semper amplicamur virtutum ͬ et sequitur non est omnino nec de virtute nec de vicio parentum aut laudandus aliquis aut culpandus · nemo inde vere aut obscurus aut clarus est · ymo eciam ut consideramus aliquid dicamus ac expresius nescio qua oculta dei disposicione quomodo ille non magis resplendet racione parentum a virtutibus prorsus alienis ipse tamen fuit dei virtute mirabilis ut capite *numquam* ·LVI· distincione

ͬ item ieronimus in epistula contra rrufinum nasci de infidelibus non est culpa qui nascitur nam sicut in seminibus non pecat terra que confouet nec semen quod in sultis iacitur non humor non calor quibus temperata frumenta uel germen pululant ͬ et sequitur noli despicere bonitatem figuli qui te creauit et plasmauit et fecit ut voluit ͬ ipse est enim dei virtus et dei sapiencia que in vtero virginis marie hedificauit sibi domum ·

inepte inter uiros santos apostoli uoce numeratur meretricis est filius · esau de rebecha et ysac ispidus tam mente quam corpore quasi bonum triticum in lolium auenasque degenerat quia non in seminibus sed in operacione nascentis causa uiciorum est atque virtutum ut capite *nasci* ·LVI· distincione et capite *sponsus* eadem distincione ͬ et iuxta id uestes quas geritis sordida lana fuit · seges enim que leprosa manu seritur munda tamen metitur in capite *quod de xpisto* ·I· quescione ·I·

ͬ ad idem ieronimus dominus noster ihesus uoluit non solum de alieniginis sed eciam de adulterinis conmiscionibus nasci scilicet de thamar nobis magnam fiduciam prestans ut qualicumque modo

---

17 agustinus...**49** distincione A. Díaz de Montalvo, *Tractatus quidam*, 23. **20** vndecumque D.56, c.3. **21** numquam...**28** mirabilis John Chrysostom, *Homilia III in Matthaeum*, 2 and 4. **28** numquam D.56, c.4. **30** nasci... **40** virtutum Jerome, *Contra Ioannem Hierosolymitanum Episcopum ad Pammachium*, 22. **40** nasci D.56, c.5. **41** sponsus D.56, c.6. **43** quod... xpisto C.1, q.1, c.24.

great confidence, that whatever way we are born, we may still follow in his footsteps and not be separated from his body whose members we are made through the faith (D.56, c.8).

The same Jerome: only before God there is freedom not to serve sins. Highest before God is the nobility to be bright by virtues of immortality. For these words are to be obeyed, or attached to him who gains the goods of virtues (D.43, c.2 and D.33, c.6). Hence Ezekiel (Ez 18:20): *the soul that sins itself will die. A son shall not bear the iniquity of the father, and a father shall not bear the iniquity of the son. The justice of a just man shall be upon him, the impiety of an impious man shall be upon him* (C.1, q.4, c.8). For whoever of the seed of Esau and others turns to the Lord and detests the fatherly malice, they will be shown God's mercy, not his wrath (C.1, q.4, c.11).

And Ezekiel (Ez 18:2-4.14.17) cries, saying: *what is it, that you turn this parable among you into a proverb in the land of Israel, saying: Our fathers ate sour grapes, and the teeth of the children are deadened. As I live, says the Lord God, no longer shall this parable be a proverb in Israel! Behold, all souls are mine, as the soul of a father, so the soul of a son is mine. The soul that sins itself will die. A son shall not bear the iniquity of the father nor the other way around.* And it follows: *if he begets a son who sees all of his father's sins that he committed, and is afraid and does not do like him, this one will not die* (X 1.9.10).

It stands according to the theologians, that a father being blessed rejoices in seeing his son in hell. And thus the abbot of Sicily[16] notes it about X 1.5.1. Likewise: a mother's misfortune must not harm the one who is in her womb (Inst. 1,4,1). Because: neither [can] a son [be held liable] for the father nor a father for the son, as Cod. 4,13,1-5 has it, nor a slave for the master (Cod. 4,13,5).

---

[16] Nicolaus de Tudeschis (1386-1445), also called Panormitanus after the Latin name for his Sicilian diocese, was a Benedictine abbot, archbishop of Palermo and famous canonist. The reference is to his *Commentaria super decretalium*. His lifetime just overlapped our author's own by about ten years, so he is one of the most recent scholastic authorities to be cited by name in the *Breue reprehensorium*.

nascamur tamen ut eius uestigia imitemur ab ipsius corporem non separemur cuius per fidem membra efecti sumus in capite *dominus mundi* ·LVI· distincione

ʳ idem ieronimus sola apud deum libertas non seruire pecatis suma apud deum nobilitas clarum esse virtutibus inmortalitatis namque illi verba obedienda sunt siue comictenda qui obtinet bona virtutum capite *in mandatis* ·LXIII· distincione et capite *laici* ·XXIII· distincione ʳ vnde ezechielis ·XVIIIᵒ· capitulo anima que pecauerit ipsa morietur filius non portabit iniquitatem patris et pater non portabit iniquitatem filii iusticia iusti super eum erit impietas impii super eum erit ·I· quescione ·IIII· capite *iam itaque* ʳ quicumque enim de semine esau et ceterorum ad dominum conversi paternam maliciam detestati sunt non odium sed clemenciam dei experti sunt capite *ecclesia* in fine eadem causa et quescione

ʳ et ezechiel ·XIXᵒ· capitulo clamat inquiens quid est quod inter uos vertitis parabolam in proverbium istud in terra israel dicentes patres nostri comederunt vuam acerbam et dentes filiorum obtupescunt viuo ego dicit dominus deus si fuit ultra vobis parabola hec in prouerbium in israel ecce omnes anime mee sunt ut anima patris ita et anima filii mea est anima que pecauerit ipsa morietur filius non portabit iniquitatem patris nec econtra ʳ et sequitur quod si genuerit filium qui uiderit omnia pecata patris sui que fecit et timuerit et non fecerit simile ei hic non morietur facit capitulo *nisi cum pridem de renunciacione*

ʳ hinc est secundum teologos quod pater existens beatus gaudet videndo filium suum in inferno et ergo notat abbas de cicilia in capitulo ·I· *de postulacione prelatorum* ʳ item non debet calamitas matris ei nocere qui in vtero est in § *et ex contrario* institucio *de ingenuis* ʳ quia nec filius pro patre nec pater pro filio ut Codice eodem titulo per totum nec seruus pro domino ut lege fine //·

---

54 anima...57 erit Ez 18:20. 61 quid...69 facit Ez 18:2–4.14.17.

48 dominus...49 mundi D.56, c.8. 53 in mandatis D.43, c.2. | laici D.33, c.6. 57 iam itaque C.1, q.4, c.8. 60 ecclesia C.1, q.4, c.11. 69 nisi... pridem X 1.9.10. 73 capitulo ·I· X 1.5.1. 74 et...contrario Inst. 1,4,0. 75 eodem...76 totum Cod. 4,13,1-5. 76 lege fine Cod. 4,13,5.

Fifth article: that the Saviour came to this world

For our Lord Jesus, the holy Saviour, indeed wanted to do and has done what he was *sent for like crystal* (Ps 147:6) by the Lord in his first coming. For as he says of himself: *everything whatsoever I wanted, I have done* (Ps 113:11; Ps 134:6). And Martha [said]: *I know, whatsoever you ask of the Lord, the Lord will give you* (Io 11:22). Isiah (Is 55:11): *such will be the word that shall go forth from my mouth: it will not return to me empty, but do whatsoever I wanted.*

For first he guided all the saints and friends [of God] since the creation of the world who descended into limbo happily into his glory, and some in body and soul, as is claimed in Catholic faith and is read in the Passion (Mt 27:52-53): *and many bodies of saints who had slept arose and appeared to many. Furthermore, they did not die but are alive with Christ Jesus in glory in body and soul.* Indeed, so he gathered the erring and divided tribes of the nations together and led them back on the path of salvation to heavenly Jerusalem to be one sheepfold.

Ezekiel foretold (Ez 34:15-16): *I will feed my sheep and I will let them lie down, says the Lord. What was lost, I will seek, and what was driven away, I will bring back, and what was broken, I will bandage, and what was weak, I will strengthen, and what is fat and strong, I will protect.* And elsewhere: *listen to me, house of Jacob and all remains of the house of Israel, who are carried by my body, who are born by my womb! Even to old age I am the same, and even to gray hairs I will carry. I have made and I will make [you], and I will carry and save [you]* (Is 46:3-4).

For the ancient fathers cried out from the bosom of Abraham, saying: *that you would already rend the heavens and come!* (Is 64:1). They cried out to the Lord and he raised for them the salvation of Israel and shall save them (Idc 3:15 and D.1, c.69 de poen.). And again: *out of the depths I have cried to you, o Lord* (Ps 129:1 and D.1, c.60 de poen.). And: *if it is delayed, wait for it! For*

quintus articulus quod saluator uenit in hunc mundum

Ad quod enim dominus noster ihesus pius saluator ut xristalum misus domino principaliter in aduentu suo voluit facere ac fecit ͬ quia ut de se ait omnia quecumque uolui feci et marta scio quecumque poposceris a domino dabit tibi dominus ͬ ysaias ·LVᵒ· capitulo sic erit verbum meum quod egredietur de ore meo non revertetur ad me vacuum sed faciet quecumque volui

ͬ primum einm omnes santos et amicos a creacione mundi qui descenderant in limbum ad gloriam suam feliciter perduxit et aliqui in corpore et in anima ut catolice aseritur dum in pasione legitur mathei ·XXVIIᵒ· et multa corpora santorum que dormierant resurrexerunt et aparuerunt multis qui amplius non obierunt sed sunt viui cum xpisto ihesu in gloria in corpore et anima ͬ eciam ut errantes et diuersas nacionum gentes congregaret et ad viam salutis in celestem ierusalem vnum ovile rreduceret

ͬ predixit ezechiel ·XXXIIIIᵒ· Ego pascam oues meos et ego eas acubare faciam dicit dominus quod perierat requiram et quod abiectum fuerat reducam et quod confractum fuerat aligabo et quod infirmum erat consolidabo et quod pingue et forte custodiam ͬ et alibi audite me domus iacob et omne residuum domus israel qui portamini a meo vtero qui gestamini a mea vulua usque ad senectam ego ipse et usque ad canos ego portabo · Ego feci et ego feram et ego portabo et saluabo ysaie ·XLVIᵒ· capitulo

ͬ clamabant enim patres veteres de sinu habrahe dicentes vtinam iam dirumperes celos et venires ysaie ·LXIIIIᵒ· ͬ clamauerunt ad dominum et suscitauit eis salutare israel et saluabit eos iudicum ·IIIᵒ· capitulo *de penitencia* distincione ·I· capite *vide benignum* ͬ et iterum de profundis clamaui ad te domine psalmo ·CXXIX· *de penitencia* distincione ·I· § *denique* ͬ et si moram fecerit expecta illum quia

---

2 ut...misus Ps 147:6. **4** omnia...feci Ps 113:11, Ps 134:6. | scio...5 dominus Io 11:22. **5** sic...7 volui Is 55:11. **11** et...13 anima Mt 27:52–53. **16** Ego...19 custodiam Ez 34:15–16. **20** audite...23 saluabo Is 46:3–4. **24** vtinam...25 venires Is 64:1. **25** clamauerunt...26 eis Idc 3:9.15. **27** de...28 domine Ps 129:1. **29** si...31 uiuet Hab 2:3–4.

---

27 vide benignum D.1, c.69 de poen. **29** denique D.1, c.60 de poen.

what comes will come and will not hesitate. Behold, in him who is unbelieving his soul will not be right. But the just will live in his faith (Hab 2:3-4). And: *he who comes from heaven is above all* (Io 3:31).

I am the living bread that has come down from heaven (Io 6:41; D.2, c.14 de poen.). *He will come like rain on the fleece* (Ps 71:6). *He will rise like a sun of justice* (Mal 4:2). And: *drop down dew, heavens, from above, and let clouds rain the Just One! The earth shall open up and sprout forth the Saviour!* (Is 45:8). *He rejoiced like a giant to run the way. He went out from the highest heaven* (Ps 18:6-7). *He came to his own, [but] his own did not receive him* (Io 1:11). *I came into the world to give testimony for the truth* (Io 18:37). *Blessed is he who has come in the name of the Lord, the king of Israel* (Io 12:13). *He came so that by [his] death he might destroy him who had power over death* (Hbr 2:14). *Therefore the son of man came to save that which had been lost* (Mt 18:11) *and to save his people from their sins* (Mt 1:21) *and to give his life for the redemption of many* (Mt 20:28).

I remembered you, pitying your youth and the love of your betrothal when you followed me in the desert (Ier 2:2). And also: *I will move heaven and earth, sea and dry land, and the one desired by all nations will come* (Hag 2:8.22). And it follows: *great will be the glory of this very last house, greater than of the first one,* says the Lord of hosts (Hag 2:10). And: *at once he will come to his holy temple* (Mal 3:1). Also: *tell the daughter of Zion: your saviour is coming! Behold his reward with him and his work before him!* (Is 62:11). And also Is 35:4-5: *God himself will come and save us. Then the eyes of the blind will be opened* and so

ueniens veniet et non tardabit ecce qui incredulus est non erit recta anima eius in semetipso iustus autem in fide sua uiuet abachuc ·II°· capitulo ͬ et qui de celo venit super omnes est iohannis ·III°· capitulo ͬ ego sum panis viuus qui de celo descendi iohannis ·VI°· capitulo *de penitencia* distincione ·I· *caritas est aqua* ͬ veniet sicut pluuia in uelus psalmo ·LXXI°· ͬ orietur sicut sol iusticie malachie ·II°· capitulo et rorate celi desuper et nubes pluant iustum aperiatur terra et germinet saluatorem ysaie ·XLV· ͬ exultauit ut gigans ad currendam viam a sumo celo egresio cius psalmo ·XVIII°· ͬ in propria uenit sui eum non receperunt iohannis ·I°· ͬ ego veni in mundum peribeam testimonium veritati iohannis ·XVIII°· ͬ beneditus qui uenit in nomine domini rex israel iohannis ·XII°· ͬ venit ut per mortem destrueret eum qui habebat mortis imperium ad ebreos ·II°· capitulo ͬ uenit ideo filius hominis ut saluaret quod perierat mathei ·XVIII°· ͬ et ut saluum faciet populum suum a pecatis eorum mathei ·I°· capitulo ͬ et ut daret animam suam pro redempcione multorum mathei ·XX°· capitulo

ͬ recordatus sum tui miserans adolecenciam tuam et caritatem desponsacionis tue quando secuta es me in deserto ieremie ·II°· capitulo ͬ ad idem ego mouebo celum et terram mare et aridam et ueniet desideratus cuntis gentibus ͬ et sequitur magna erit gloria domus istius nouissime magis quam prime dicit dominus exercituum agei ·II°· capitulo ͬ et statim ueniet ad templum santum suum malachie ·III°· capitulo ͬ item dicite filie sion ecce saluator tuus venit · ecce merces cum eo et opus illius coram illo ysaie ·LXII°· capitulo ͬ ad idem ysaie ·XXXV°· capitulo deus ipse ueniet et saluabit nos tunc

---

32 qui...est Io 3:31.   33 ego...descendi Io 6:41.   34 veniet...uelus Ps 71:6.   35 orietur...iusticie Mal 4:2.   36 rorate...37 saluatorem Is 45:8. 37 exultauit...38 eius Ps 18:6–7.   38 in...39 receperunt Io 1:11. 39 ego...40 veritati Io 18:37.   40 beneditus...41 israel Io 12:13. 41 venit...42 imperium Hbr 2:14.   42 uenit...43 perierat Mt 18:11. 43 ut²...44 eorum Mt 1:21.   44 et...45 multorum Mt 20:28. 46 recordatus...47 deserto Ier 2:2.   48 ego...49 gentibus Hag 2:8.22. 49 magna...50 exercituum Hag 2:10.   51 statim...suum Mal 3:1. 52 dicite...53 illo Is 62:11.   54 deus...55 cecorum Is 35:4–5.

---

34 caritas...aqua D.2, c.14 de poen.

forth. Also: *the scepter shall not be taken away from Judah, nor the rule from his thigh until he comes who is to be sent; he will be the expectation of the nations* (Gn 49:10).

And also Dn 9:24: *seventy weeks are shortened over your people and over your holy city so that transgression be put to an end, iniquity be finished and erased and everlasting justice be brought and vision and prophecy be fulfilled and the most holy be anointed.* Also: *When you will have multiplied and thrived in the land in those days, says the Lord, they will say no longer: the Ark of the covenant of the Lord!, and neither does it come to mind, and they will not remember it, and it will not be visited, and it shall be no more* (Ier 3:16). *A stone* – that is: Christ – *was cut out of the mountain without hands and struck the statue at its feet of iron and clay and crushed them* (Dn 2:34).

For *God sent his Son out of a woman and under the law, to redeem those under the law so that we might receive the adoption as children* (Gal 4:4-5). For *God fulfilled what he had promised* (Ios 23:15). Is 49:8.15: *in a favourable time I heard you, and on the day of salvation I helped you, and even if a mother were to forget her child, I would not forget you*, says the almighty God. *Because the word of God stands in eternity* (Is 40:8).

Return therefore, virgin Israel, return to your cities! For how long will you stray, wandering daughter (Ier 31:21-22)? And: *descend, sit on the earth, virgin daughter of Babylon, sit on the ground! There is no throne for a daughter of Chaldeans. No longer shall you be called tender and delicate. Take a millstone and grind flour! Uncover your veil, bare your legs!* (Is 47:1-2; C. 32, q. 5, c. 11). And so the Saviour has come and has fulfilled what he had foretold by prophets.

aperientur oculi cecorum et cetera ͬ item non aferetur cetrum de iuda nec dux de femore eius donec ueniat qui mictendus est ipse erit expectacio gencium genesis ·XLIX°·

ͬ ad idem daniel ·IX°· septuaginta ebdomade abbreuiate sunt super populum tuum et super vrbem santam tuam ut consumetur preuaricacio et finem accipiat et deleatur iniquitas et abducatur iusticia sempiterna et impleatur visio et prophetia iungatur santus santorum ͬ item cum multiplicati fueritis et credideritis in terra in diebus illis ait dominus non dicent ultra archam testamenti domini nec ascendit super cor nec illius recordabuntur nec visitabitur nec fiet vltra ieremie ·III°· capitulo ͬ excisus est de monte lapis id est xpistus sine manibus et percusit statuam in pedibus eius ferreis et fictilibus et cominuit eos daniel ·II°· capitulo

ͬ misit enim deus filium suum ex muliere factum sub lege ut eos qui sub lege erant redimeret ut adopcionem filiorum reciperemus ad galatas ·IIII°· ͬ adimpleuit enim deus quod promiserat ysaie L° capitulo in tempore placito exaudiui te et in die salutis auxiliatus sum tui et si mulier infantem suum oblita fuerit ego tamen non obliuiscar tui dicit dominus omnipotens ͬ quia verbum dei stabit in eternum ysaia ·XXIX·

ͬ reuertere ergo virgo israel reuertere ad ciuitates tuas usquequo disolueris filia uaga ieremie ·XXXI°· capitulo ͬ et descende sede in terram virgo filia babilonis sede in terra non est filie caldeorum tronus non uocaberis vltra mollis et delicata accipe mollam molle farinam descoperi uellamentum tuum denuda crura tua ysaie ·LII°· XXXII· quescione ·V· capite *si paulus* ͬ et sic saluator venit et quod per prophetas predixit adimpleuit

---

55 non...57 gencium Gn 49:10.   58 septuaginta...62 santorum Dn 9:24.
62 cum...65 vltra Ier 3:16.   65 excisus...67 eos Dn 2:34.   68 misit...69 reciperemus Gal 4:4–5.   70 adimpleuit...promiserat Ios 23:15. | in[1]...73 tui Is 49:8.15   73 quia...eternum Is 40:8.   75 reuertere[1]...76 uaga Ier 31:21–22.   76 descende...79 tua Is 47:1-2.

---

80 si paulus C.32, q.5, c.11.

Sixth article: that men, Jews and Gentiles alike, were divided in errors before the coming of the Saviour

But when the world was in darkness, that same Saviour of ours, Jesus, illuminated every man *by coming into this world* (Io 1:9; D.21, c.1; X 5.7.12). And as Paul says: *the world is dead to me, and I to the world* (Gal 6:14; C.27, q.1, c.43). And: *the world and its desire will pass away* (I Io 2:17; C.1, q.4, c.11). And elsewhere: *let us by no means say uncertainties until the Lord comes, who illuminates what is hidden in darkness and will make visible the intentions of the hearts* (I Cor 4:5; C.2, q.1, c.18; C.30, q.5, c.9).

There was universal darkness before the Saviour's time because the gentile people offered sacrifices to idols and did not know God. According to Ps 95:1.5: *sing to the Lord! All gods of the Gentiles are demons*. And: *pour out your wrath on the nations that did not know you and on the kingdoms that did not call on your name; lest they should say among the Gentiles: where is their God?* (Ps 78:6.10; Ps 113:10; C.23, q.3, c.1). Hence God blames them in the psalm *Listen, you heavens,* saying: *they offered sacrifices to demons and not to God; gods that they did not use to know, newcomers who recently arrived* (Dt 32:17). Also: *they chose new gods [and] war came to their gates* (Idc 5:8). And: *the idols of the Gentiles are silver and gold, the work of human hands* (Ps 113:12; Ps 134:15).

The Jews however misused the knowledge of the law by embracing *the letter that kills* (II Cor 3:6). By leaving the life-giving sense behind, they got entangled in grave sins, as the Lord said to Moses: *go down, because your people has sinned! Let me be, so that my wrath may turn against them and I*

sextus arcticulus quod ante aduentum saluatoris homines tam iudei quam gentiles erant in erroribus diuisi

Set quam mundus in tenebris erat ipse saluator ihesus noster illuminauit omnem hominem uenientem in hunc mundum iohannis ·I°· XXI· distincione capite *cleros de hereticis cum ex iniunto* ʳ et ut paulus ait mundus michi mortus est et ego mundo ad galatas ·VI°· XXVII· quescione ·I· § ultimo ʳ et mundus peribit et concupiscencia eius iohannis ·II°· I· quescione ·I· § *hiis ita* ʳ et alibi incerta nullatenus dicemus donec ueniat dominus qui illuminat abscondita tenebrarum et manifestabit consilia cordium ad corinthios ·XIIII°· II· quescione ·I· capite *multi* ·XXX· quescione ·VIII· capite *incerta*

ʳ vniuerse tenebre erant ante tempus saluatoris ʳ quia gencium populus ydolla inmolabat nec deum nouerat iuxta id psalmo ·XCV· cantate domino omnes dii gencium demonia ʳ et efunde iram tuam in gentes que te non cognouerunt et in regna que nomen tuum non inuocauerunt · ne forte dicant in gentibus ubi est deus eorum psalmo *in exitu* ·CXIII· et psalmo ·LXXVIII°· *deus uenerunt* ·XXIII· quescione ·III· § *hinc* ʳ vnde in psalmo *audite celi* hos reprehendit dominus dicens inmolant demoniis et non deo deos quos non conoscunt nouos qui de circa uenerunt deuteronomii ·XXXII°· ʳ item elegerunt deos nouos uenit guerra ad portas eorum iudicum ·IIII°· capitulo ʳ et simulacra gencium argentum et aurum opera manuum hominum

ʳ iudey vero arci lege abutebantur literam amplectentes que occidit sensum uiuificum relinquentes grauibus pecatis se inmiscebant ʳ dicente domino ad moysem descende quia pecauit populus tuus dimite ut irascatur furor meus contra eos et deleam eos faciamque te

---

4 uenientem...mundum Io 1:9.   6 mundus...mundo Gal 6:14.
7 mundus...8 eius I Io 2:17.   9 ueniat...10 cordium I Cor 4:5.
13 cantate...14 demonia Ps 95:1.5.   14 efunde...16 eorum Ps 78:6.10, Ps 113:10.   19 inmolant...20 uenerunt Dt 32:17.   20 elegerunt...21 eorum Idc 5:8.   22 simulacra...hominum Ps 113:12, Ps 134:15.   23 literam... occidit II Cor 3:6.   25 descende...28 scripsisti Ex 32:10.31–32.

---

5 cleros D.21, c.1. | cum...iniunto X 5.7.12.   7 § ultimo C.27, q.1, c.43.
8 hiis ita C.1, q.4, c.11.   11 multi C.2, q.1, c.18. | incerta C.30, q.5, c.9.
18 hinc C.23, q.3, c.1.

may destroy them; and I will make a great nation out of you. And [Moses] said: *if you forgive sins, forgive them this crime, or if you do not, strike me out of your book that you have written!* (Ex 32:10.31-32; D.45, c.9). And the Lord said also to Moses: *your people, whom you led out of the land of Egypt, out of the power of the Pharaoh, has sinned. They quickly digressed from the way you showed them. I see that this people is stiff-necked* (Ex 32:7-9). And Isaiah like Matthew (Is 29:13, Mt 15:8): *this people honours me with their lips, but their heart is far from me.*

And fearing the people's unfaithfulness, Moses ordered *the book of law to be guarded by the Levites next to the Ark, so that it would be there as a testimony against the people, saying: for I know your obstinacy and your most stiff neck. Even as I am living and going with you, you always act contentiously against the Lord – how much more so as soon as I will be dead? Therefore he let all the ancients and learned ones assemble by tribe and called on heaven and earth against them, shouting: I know that after my death you will act unjustly and quickly turn away from the path that I told you* (Dt 31:25-29).

And the Lord also says through Jeremiah: *this way I will make rot the pride of Judah and the great pride of Israel. This people is very bad, they do not want to hear my words and walked in depravity of heart, they went off after foreign gods to serve them, and they will be like a girdle that is of no use* (Ier 13:9-10). Also: *the princes of my people do not know me. For they are foolish children and not understanding; wise are they in doing evil, but they do not know how to do good* (Ier 4:22; C.16, q.7, c.9).

And elsewhere: *those who depart from me indeed will be wasted, because they have transgressed against me. I, however, redeemed them, and they spoke lies*

in gentem magnam et ait si dimictis pecatum dimicte eis hanc noxiam aut si non facis dele me de libro tuo quem scripsisti exodi ·XXXII°· XLV· distincione *disciplina* ͬ ad idem dominus ad moysem pecauit populus tuus quem eduxisti de terra egypti de potestate pharaonis receserunt cito de via quam hostendisti eis cerno quod popule iste dure ceruicis sit exodi ·XXXII°· ͬ et ysaie ut mathei ·XV°· populus iste labiis me honorat cor autem eorum longe est a me

ͬ et timendo moyses infidelitatem populi iusit leuitis librum legis custodiri in latere archc ut esset ibi in testimonium contra populum dicendo ego enim scio contempcionem tuam et ceruicem tuam durisimam et adhuc uiuente me et ingrediente uobiscum semper contenciosse egistis contra dominum quantomagis cum mortuus fuero ͬ fecit enim congregari omnes maiores natus per tribus et doctos et inuocauit contra eos celum et terram clamando noui enim quod post mortem meam inique agetis et declinabitis cito de via quam precepi uobis deuteronomii ·XXXI°· capitulo

ͬ ad idem dominus per ieremiam ait sic putrescere faciam superbiam iuda et superbiam israel multum populum istum peximum qui nolunt audire uerba mea et ambulabant in prauitate cordis abierunt post deos alienos ut seruirent eis et erunt sicut lumbare quod nullo usui aptum est ieremie ·XIII°· capitulo ͬ item principes populi mei non cognouerunt me filii enim sunt insipientes et non inteligentes sapientes sunt ut faciant mala bene autem facere nescierunt ieremie ·IIII°· XVII· quescione ·VII· *et hoc diximus*

ͬ et alibi qui receserunt a me quoniam uastabuntur quia preuaricati sunt in me · ego autem redemi eos et ipsi locuti sunt contra me

---

52 fol. 1r | fol. 1v | iudit...**9** malicia *marginalia.* | fol. 2r | qui...**36** existam *marginalia.* | est sic: es | qua Vulgate: quo | fol. 2v | vnde...**64** meo *marginalia.* | fol. 3r | actuum...**116** capitulo *interlinear.* | fol. 3v | nos...**156** predestinauit *accidental duplication.* | fol. 4r | fol. 4v | inepte Vulgate: jephte inepte...filius *marginalia.* | quicumque...**60** quescione *marginalia.* | fol. 5r

29 pecauit...**32** sit Ex 32:7–9.   **32** populus...**33** me² Is 29:13, Mt 15:8.
34 leuitis...**42** uobis Dt 31:25–29.   **43** sic...**47** est Ier 13:9–10.
47 principes...**49** nescierunt Ier 4:22.   **51** qui...**57** sue Os 7:13–16.

---

29 disciplina D.45, c.9.   **50** et...diximus C.16, q.7, c.9.

against me. And they have not cried to me with all their heart but howled on their beds, they have thought upon wheat and wine and departed from me. I chastised them and strengthened their arms, and they imagined evil against me. They returned in order to be free from the yoke. They became like a deceitful bow. Their princes will fall under the sword because of the rage of their tongue (Os 7:13-16; D.4, c.20 de poen.). And so these two nations, out of which consisted the entire world, were in various and hostile errors and both guilty of the passion of the Saviour, for although Jews accused him unjustly, Gentiles however, who held the jurisdiction and power, wrongly condemned Jesus to death (D.1, c.23 de poen.). And Jews from the beginning *persecuted the Apostles in order to afflict them with insults and stone them* (Act 3).

Today, however, the arguments that once had been raised between Christians of Gentile and of Jewish origin, are removed, as Jerome says in a preface to the letters of Paul: Paul solves the questions [by determining] that none of them is worthy of salvation by merit of his own justice. He asserts instead that both peoples knowingly and gravely committed offences before baptism: the Jews because they dishonoured God by breaking the law; the Gentiles, on the other hand, because knowing through creation the creator they were obliged to worship God, and yet exchanged his glory for idols made by human hands. He points out with most truthful reason, that both have equally obtained the same pardon, in particular as he shows that Jews and Gentiles are to be called to the faith in Christ in the same law.

Seventh article: that the Saviour brought together his Church out of Jews and Gentiles into one

The eternal God, Jesus Christ, our faithful Saviour and merciful lover of peace, removed those various and hostile errors in his passion and in himself

mendacia et non clamauerunt ad me in toto corde suo · sed ululabant in cubilibus super triticum et vinum et ruminabant et receserunt a me · ego erudiui eos et confortaui brachia eorum et in me cogitauerunt maliciam reuersi sunt ut essent absque iugo facti sunt quasi arcus dolosus cadent in gladio principes eorum a furore lingue sue osee ·VII°· capitulo *de penitencia* distincione ·IV· capite *ve eis* § *porro* et sic isti duo populi quorum totus orbis extabat erant in diuersis et aduersis erroribus et utraque culpabiles in saluatoris pasione ʳ nam licet iudey iniuste eum acusarunt gentes tamen apud quos iurisdiccio erat et imperium ihesum perpere ad mortem condenarunt in capite *periculose de penitencia* distincione ·I· ʳ et iudei cum principibus persecuti sunt apostolos ut contumeliis eos aficerent et lapidarent actuum ·III°·

¶ Toluntur namque hodie argumenta que inter xpistianos ex gentibus et iudeis olim fiebant ut ieronimus in prohemio epistolarum pauli · quod incipit *romani sunt* · paulus dirimit quesciones ut neutrum eorum sua iusticia salutem meruisse afirmet ambos vero populos et scienter et grauiter ante baptismum delinquisse ʳ iudei quia per preuaricacionem legis deum inhonorarunt ʳ gentes vero quia cum cognitum de creatura creatorem ut deum debuerunt uenerari gloriam eius in manu facta mutauerunt simulacra vtrosque simul veniam consecutos equales esse ueracissima racione demonstrat · presertim cum in eadem lege iudeos et gentes ad xpisti fidem vocandos ostendit //·

·VIIᵘˢ· quod saluator ex iudeis et gentibus in vnum congregauit suam ecclesiam

eternus deus ihesus xpistus saluator noster pius et misericors amator pacis istos diuersos et aduersos errores in pasione sua toluit et euulsit

---

et³...23 capitulo *marginalia*. | et...37 ·XLV· *marginalia*. | fol. 5v | item... 55 cetera *marginalia*. | abducatur Vulgate: adducatur | iungatur Vulgate: ungatur | credideritis Vulgate: creueritis | fol. 6r | fol. 6v

63 iudei...64 lapidarent Act 14:5.

58   ve eis D.4, c.20 de poen.   62   periculose D.1, c.23 de poen.
65 Toluntur...74 ostendit A. Díaz de Montalvo, *Tractatus*, 14.

uprooted death for to bring them peace. Hence Is 53:5.8.7: *he was wounded for our sins, he was bruised for our crimes.* And it follows: *for he is cut off from the land of the living, I struck him for the wickedness of my people. And he shall be led like a sheep to the slaughter, and become silent just as a lamb before its shearer.*

As he was in the form of God, he considered it no robbery to be equal to God, yet he emptied himself and took the form of a slave, made in likeness of men and found like a man in habit (Phil 2:6-7). And he prayed for the transgressors saying: *Father, forgive them, because the do not know what they do!* (Lc 23:34; C.1, q.1, c.24; X 1.1.1). He prepared for everyone one holy Church and communion of the faithful, one holy baptism. One Lord, one baptism, one temple, one ministry it shall be (D.95, c.7).

Hence, how beautiful it is written about baptism: *do not fear, my servant Jacob, and most righteous one whom I have chosen! For I will pour out water over the thirsty and I will pour out streams over the drought. I will pour out my spirit over your seed and blessing over your kin, and they will sprout forth among the grass like willows next to waters flowing by. This one will say: I belong to the Lord, and that on will call upon the name of Jacob, and another will write with his hand: for the Lord, and in the name of the Lord he will become like Israel* (Is 44:2-5). According to the gloss, these are the converted from the Gentiles. For the name Israel is applied to them, according to what the apostle [Paul] says (Rm 2).

And again: *I will sprinkle over you pure water, and you will be cleansed of all your impurities, and I will clean you of all your idols, and I will give you my heart, and a new spirit I will put in you* (Ez 36:25-26; D.4, c.127 de cons.).

in se mortem pro illorum pace ferrendo ͬ vnde ysaie ·LIIIᵒ· ipse uulneratus est propter iniquitates nostras actritus est propter scelera nostra et sequitur quia abscisus est de terra uiuencium propter scelus populi mei percusi eum ͬ et tamquam ouis ad occisionem ducetur et quasi agnus coram tondente se obmutescet ysaie ·LIIIᵒ·

ͬ qui cum in forma dei esset non rapinam arbitratus est esse se equalem deo sed semetipsum exinaniuit formam serui accipiens in similitudinem hominum factus et habitu inuentus ut homo ad philipenses ·IIᵒ· ͬ orauitque pro transgresoribus dicens pater ignosce illis quia nesciunt quid faciunt luce ·XXIIIᵒ· I· quescione ·I· § *cum ergo* et in capitulo ·I· *de suma trinitate* ͬ preparauit omnibus vnam santam ecclesiam et comunionem fidelium vnum santum bauptisma ͬ vnus dominus vnum baptisma vnum templum vnum sit ministerium ·XCV· distincione capite *esto*

ͬ vnde quam pulcre scribitur de baptismo ͬ noli timere serue meus iacob et rectisime quem elegi efundam enim aquam super sicientem et efundam fluentam super aridam · efundam spiritum meum super semen tuum et benedicionem super stirpem tuam et germinabunt inter herbas quasi salices iuxta preterfluentes aquas · iste dicet domini ego sum et ille inuocabit in nomine iacob et hic scribit manu domino et in nomine domini israel asimilabitur ysaie ·XLIIIIᵒ· asimilabitur glossa · isti sunt conuersi ex gentibus illis enim aplicatur nomen israel secundum quod dicit apostolus ad romanos ·IIᵒ·

ͬ et iterum aspergam super vos aquam mundam et mundabimini ab omnibus inquinamentis vestris et ab vniuersis ydolis vestris mundabo vos et dabo uobis cor meum et spiritum nouum dabo in uobis ezechiel ·XXXVIᵒ· et *de consecracione* distincione ·IIII· capite *nec*

---

21 fol. 7r

---

5 ipse...**9** obmutescet Is 53:5.7.8.   **10** qui...**12** homo Phil 2:6–7.
13 pater...**14** faciunt Lc 23:34.   **19** noli...**25** asimilabitur¹ Is 44:2–5.
26 illis...israel Rm 2:28–29.   **28** aspergam...**30** uobis² Ez 36:25–26.

14 cum...**15** ergo C.1, q.1, c.24.   **15** capitulo ·I· X 1.1.1.   **18** esto D.95, c.7.   **26** isti...gentibus Nicholas of Lyra, *Postilla super Isaiam*, 44.
31 nec...**32** quemquam D.4, c.127 de cons.

And: *he who touches the corpse of a man and is therefore seven days unclean shall be sprinkled with this water on the third and seventh day, and so will be cleansed* (Nm 19:11-12; D.4, c.127 de cons.).

For through baptism a man is reborn (D.4, c.1 de cons.). And: the flesh is emptied of sin (D.4, c.2 de cons.). Original sin and present sin are rescinded (D.4, c.3 de cons.; D.4, c.6 de cons.; X 3.42.3). And: the baptized receives the grace of heavenly life (D.4, c.4 de cons.). Through the water of baptism an earthly man becomes a heavenly man. He passes from sin to life, from guilt to grace, from wickedness to holiness. And: he who crosses through this water will not die but rise again (D.4, c.9 de cons.). Our Lord Jesus gave through the bath of rebirth the forgiveness of sins to all (Mt 28; C.1, q.1, c.16).

Against this the unlearned try to render the effect of baptism ineffective. They raise scandal among those to whom the one gospel is preached; which is not allowed (X 3.1.11). And although the Saviour ordered: *do not take the path away to the Gentiles and do not enter into the cities of the Samaritans* (Mt 10:5; C.7, q.1, c.9). And: *I am only sent to the sheep that have been lost of the house of Israel* (Mt 15:24; C.17, q.7, c.39). Later he sent the apostles to preach the gospel *to every creature* (Mc 16:15; X 5.7.12-13). And subsequently he said: *I have other sheep that are not of this fold, and I shall restore them to one fold* (Io 10:16; D.4, c.12 de poen.), so that I will have one

quemquam ʳ et qui tetigerit cadauer hominis et propter hoc septem diebus fuerit inmundus aspergatur de hac aqua die tercio et setimo et sic mundabitur numeri ·XIXº· et dicto capite *nec quemquam*

ʳ per baptismum namque renascitur homo ut in capite ·I· *de consecracione* distincione ·IIII· ʳ et caro pecati euacuatur eadem distincione capite ·II· ʳ originale et actuale pecatum aboletur capite *firmisime* et capite *ex quo* eadem distincione et capitulo *maiores de baptismo* ʳ et baptismatus graciam accipit uite celestis ut capite *non potest* eadem distincione ʳ per aquam baptismi de terreno fit homo celestis transit de pecato ad vitam de culpa ad graciam de inquinamento ad santificacionem ʳ et qui per hanc aquam transit non moritur sed resurgit *de consecracione* distincione ·IIII· capite *per aquam* ʳ dominus noster ihesus per lauacrum rregeneracionem omnibus remisionem pecatorum dedit mathei ultimo et capite *cito* ·I· quescio ·I·

ʳ qua ergo fronte indocti efectum baptismi ineficacem facere contendunt suscitant scandalum inter quos vnum predicatur euangelium quod non licet in capitulo *deus qui de vita et honestate clericorum* ʳ Et licet saluator predixerat in viam gencium ne abieritis et in ciuitates samaritanorum ne intraueritis marci ·Xº· XVII· quescione ·I· *denique* ʳ et non sum misus nisi ad oues que perierunt domus israel mathei ·XI· capitulo ·II· quescione ·VII· § *ecce ostensum* ʳ postmodum misit apostolos ad predicandum euangelium omni creature marci ultimo *de hereticis cum ex iniunto* § *quia uero* ʳ et subsequenter dixit alias oues habeo que non sunt de hoc ouili et reducam eas ad vnam ouile iohannis ·Xº·et *de penitencia* distincione ·IIII· § *hanc societatem* ut sit

---

32 qui...**34** mundabitur Nm 19:11–12. **50** in...**51** intraueritis Mt 10:5. **52** non...israel Mt 15:24. **54** ad...creature Mc 16:15. **55** alias...**57** ouile Io 10:16.

---

35 capite ·I· D.4, c.1 de cons. **37** capite ·II· D.4, c.2 de cons. **38** firmisime D.4, c.3 de cons. | ex quo D.4, c.6 de cons. | maiores X 3.42.3. **39** non... **40** potest D.4, c.4 de cons. **43** per...**44** aquam D.4, c.9 de cons. **45** cito C.1, q.1, c.16. **49** deus qui X 3.1.11. **51** denique C.7, q.1, c.9. **53** ecce ostensum C.17, q.7, c.39. **55** quia uero X 5.7.12-13. **57** hanc societatem D.4, c.12 de poen.

fold and I will be the one shepherd for them. That means: one holy Church *whose head is Christ* (Col 1:18).

And also [it is written] in the gospel: *when I will be lifted up from the earth I will draw everything to me* (Io 12:32); therefore of Gentiles as well as of Jews, because, he who says "everything" excludes nothing (Dig. 33,6,16; note to X 1.3.15). For *God did not spare the only son but delivered him for us all* (Rm 8:32; D.2, c.25 de cons.). And: *Jesus died for the people, and not only for the people but also, to gather into one the scattered children of God* (Io 11:51-52; D.4, c.8 de poen.; D.4, c.12 de poen.). In this fashion Moses married an Ethiopian woman,[17] meaning, that the Lord would unite the Church out of the nations (gloss to C.28, q.1, c.15).

And also the Saviour says (Io 21:17): *Peter, do you love me? He answered: You know it, Lord.* Therefore, if you love me, *feed my sheep!* (C.6, q.1, c.10; X 1.33.6). He did not say: feed these sheep and not those, but without difference: *my sheep*. It is evident, however, that he foretold he would have sheep of Israel and also other sheep. Therefore he embraces all, for the indefinite is tantamount to the universal (VI 1.6.4 and Henry[18] on X 5.33.22). Likewise: our Lord Jesus Christ suffered for all to completion (D.2, c.51 de cons.). For *everyone who will call upon the name of the Lord shall be saved* (Ioel 2:32; Rm 10:13). For and in fact *the blood of Christ has cleansed us from every sin* (I Io 1:7). Therefore all who want to be partakers of the effect of [his] Passion will be saved. *For, as God is great, come let us rejoice* (Ps

---

[17] The Vulgate, following the Septuagint, calls the Cushite wife of Moses *Aethiopissa* (Ethiopian) as both terms broadly refer to African or dark skinned people. The Biblical narration is not clear on whether or not this wife is meant to be the same as Zipporah (Ex 2). Gutierre de Palma takes the union of Moses, a Jew, and his wife, a Gentile, to allegorically signify the future unity of Jews and Gentiles in the Christian church.

[18] Henry of Segusio (?–1271), also called Hostiensis after his titular see Ostia, was a leading canonist of the 13th century, an adviser to popes and kings, archbishop and cardinal. The reference is to his comprehensive commentary *Lectura in Decretales Gregorii IX*.

michi vnum ouile et ego illis vnus pastor id est in vna santa ecclesia cuius capud est xpistus iohannis ·IX°· capitulo ad collocenses ·I°·
ʳ ad idem in euangelio cum exaltatus fuero a terra omnia ad me traham ergo tam ex gentibus quam ex iudeis quia qui totum dicit nichil excludit in lege finale digestis *de vino tritico vel oleo legato* et nota in capitulo *sedes de rescriptis* ʳ nam deus pater vnico filio non pepercit sed pro nobis omnibus tradidit illum ad rromanos ·VIII°· *de consecracione* distincione ·II· capite *timorem* ʳ et ihesus mortuus est pro gente et non tantum pro gente sed eciam ut filios dei dispersos congregaret in vnum iohannis ·XI°· *de penitencia* distincione ·IIII· *si uero* et capite *hanc veritatem* ʳ sic moyses duxit ethiopisam significans quod dominus ex gentibus copularet ecclesiam glossa in caput *caue* ·XXVIII· quescione ·I·
ʳ ad idem saluator ait iohannis ·XXI°· petre amas me · qui rrespondit tu scis domine · si ergo diligis me pasce oues meas ·VI· quescione ·I· *inmitare* capitulo *solite de maioritate et obediencia* · non dixit istas oues pasce et illas non · sed indistincte oues meas constat autem quod predixerat se habere oues israel et alias oues ergo omnes comprehendit quia indifinita equipolet vniversali in capite *ut circa de ellecione* libro sexto enrricus in capitulo *quia circa de preuilegiis* ʳ item dominus noster ihesus xpistus pro omnibus pasus est quoad suficienciam ut in capite *quod semel de consecracione* distincione ·II· ʳ nam omnis qui inuocauerit nomen domini saluus erit ioelis ·II°· in fine ad romanos ·X°· ʳ sanguis namque xpisti mundauit nos ab omni pecato iohannis ·I°· capitulo ergo omnes qui uoluerint efectus pasionis esse participes

---

68 fol. 7v

---

59 cuius...xpistus Col 1:18. **60** cum...62 traham Io 12:32. **63** nam...65 illum Rm 8:32. **65** ihesus...68 vnum Io 11:51–52. **68** moyses... ethiopisam Nm 12:1. **71** petre...73 meas Io 21:17. **79** nam...81 erit Ioel 2:32, Rm 10:13. **81** sanguis...pecato I Io 1:7.

---

62 lege finale Dig. 33,6,16. **63** sedes X 1.3.15. **65** timorem D.2, c.25 de cons. **67** si...69 uero D.4, c.8 de poen. **68** hanc veritatem D.4, c.12 de poen. **69** caue C.28, q.1, c.15. **73** inmitare C.6, q.1, c.10. | solite X 1.33.6. **76** ut circa VI 1.6.4. **77** quia circa X 5.33.22. **79** quod semel D.2, c.51 de cons.

94:1.3)! And: *great be his power* (Ps 146:5). Ps 107:2: *my heart is ready.* Therefore the deed and work of salvation will be great, therefore all can be saved by it, because the infinite brings out of itself infinite things.

Hence it is written: *we have an advocate with the Father, Jesus Christ, and he himself is the atonement for our sins. But not only for ours, but for those of the entire world. And this we know since we have come to know God* (I Io 2:1-3; D.2, c.39 de poen.). And: *Christ died for our sins* (Rm 5:9; D.33, c.5). And also those must not be cheated out of the divine silver coin whosoever are working in the vineyard of the Lord (Mt 20; Lc 8; X 5.5.5). And the last one receives as much as the one who had come before him, and equally so, a man being a New Christian is saved as is also an Old Christian who had come before him. And: the holy mother Church keeps no one from her bosom (VI 5.2.4).

Hence the Lord says (Is 65:2): *all day I stretched out my hands to a people that does not believe.* And: *the Lord has compassion since eternity and in eternity on them who fear him. Like a father has mercy for [his] children, the Lord has mercy for those fearing him, because he knows our form* (Ps 102:13-17). Likewise: *the Lord saw they were in tribulation and heard their prayer and was mindful of his covenant and repented according to the multitude of his mercies* (Ps 105:44-45). Likewise the Lord says through the prophet: *I made a covenant with my elect. I have sworn to David, my servant: I will settle your seed forever* (Ps 88:4-5). And it follows: *forever I will keep my mercy for him and the covenant faithful to the name, and I will make his seed to endure for*

salui fient ʳ quia cum sit deus magnus psalmo ·XCIIIIº· uenite
exultemus ʳ et magna sit virtus eius psalmo ·CVII· paratum cor meum
ergo actus et operacio saluacionis erit magna ergo omnes in eo salui   85
esse possunt quia infinitus producit ex se infinita

ʳ vnde scribitur aduocatum habemus apud patrem ihesum xpistum et
ipse propiciacio pro pecatis nostris non pro nostris autem tantum sed
eciam tocius mundi et in hoc scimus quoniam cognouimus deum in
capite *fugerat de penitencia* distincione ·II· ʳ et xpistus pro pecatis   90
nostris mortuus est ad romanos ·Vº· XXXIII· distincione capite *usque
adeo* ʳ ad idem denario diuino fraudari non debent quicumque in
vinea domini laborantes mathei ·XXº· luce ·VIIIº· et capitulo *super
specula de magistris* ʳ et tantum rescipit extremus quantum qui uenerat
ante et sic eque saluatur homo nouus xpistianus sicut et antiqus qui   95
uenerat ante ʳ et pia mater ecclesia nulli claudit gremium in capite
super eo de hereticis libro sexto

ʳ vnde dominus ait ysaie ·LXVº· tota die expandi manus meas ad
populum non credentem ʳ et misericordia domini ab eterno et usque
in eternum super timentes eum quomodo misereretur pater filiorum   100
misertus est dominus timentibus se quoniam ipse cognouit
figmentum nostrum psalmo ·CIIº· ʳ item dominus uidit cum tribu-
larentur et audiuit oracionem eorum et memor fuit testamenti sui et
penituit eum secundum multitudinem misericordie sue psalmo ·CVº·
ʳ item dominus per prophetam ait disposui testamentum electis meis   105
iuraui dauid seruo meo usque in eternum preparabo semen tuum et
sequitur in eternum seruabo illi misericordiam meam et testamentum
fidele nomini et ponam in seculum seculi semen eius et tronum eius

---

108 nomini Vulgate: ipsi

83 uenite...**85** exultemus Ps 94:1.3.   **84**   magna...eius Ps 146:5.
paratum...meum Ps 107:2.   **87**   aduocatum...**88** deum I Io 2:1–3.
90 xpistus...**90** est Rm 5:9.   **92** denario...**94** laborantes Mt 20:1-16, Lc
20:9–16.   **98**   tota...**100** credentem Is 65:2.   **99**   misericordia...**103**
nostrum Ps 102:13–17.   **102**   dominus...**103** sue Ps 105:44-45.
105 disposui...**117** manebit Ps 88:4-5.29–37.

90 fugerat D.2, c.39 de poen.   **91** usque...**93** adeo D.33, c.5.   **93** super...
95 specula X 5.5.5.   **97** super eo VI 5.2.4.

evermore and his throne as the days of heaven. But if his sons forsake my law and walk not in my judgments, if they profane my justice and do not keep my commandments, I will visit their iniquities with a rod and their sins with stripes. But I will not take my mercy away from him, nor will I let my truth fail, nor will I profane my covenant and what proceeds from my lips I will not make void. Once I have sworn by my holiness, I shall not lie to David: his seed will endure forever (Ps 88:29-37).

For and the Lord's heart is open to everyone who repents (C.1, q.7, c.2). And to this the prophet [says]: *As of unicorns he has build his sanctuary on earth which he founded for all times, and he chose David* as king – one may know: our Saviour Jesus Christ – *so that he might feed Jacob his servant and Israel, his inheritance* (Ps 77:69-71).

Hence Eph 2:14-19: *for this same Christ is our peace who made both into one and tore down the separative wall, the enmities, in his flesh. By purging the law of decreed commandments he founded the two in himself as one new man, making peace, reconciling both into one, or rather in one body to God by the cross, killing the hostilities in himself. And by coming he preached also to you* – that is to say: Gentiles – *who were far away the gospel of peace and also peace to those who were near,* the Jews. *Because of this we both have access through him to the Father in one spirit, therefore we are no longer strangers and foreigners but by the bath of baptism we are fellow citizens of the saints and household members of God.*

Therefore, since peace has emerged through our Redeemer, hostility, however, is altogether destroyed, and we have in one spirit access to God, the former disagreement then is thoroughly condemned. Consequently, he who does not keep this indivisible unity and is busy sowing conflict between New and Old Christians shall be punished eternally as a heretic. Because for him who does not keep the unity of the Church, neither baptism nor plentiful alms nor death accepted for the name of Christ will be able to bring

sicut dies celi ʳ si autem derelinquerint filii eius legem meam et in iudiciis meis non ambulauerint · si iusticias meas prophanauerint et mandata mea non custodierint visitabo in virga iniquitates eorum et in verberibus pecata eorum ʳ misericordiam autem meam non dispergam ab eo nec nocebo in veritate me · nec prophanabo testamentum meum et que procedunt de labiis meis non faciam irrita · semel iuraui in santo meo si dauid menciar semen eius in eternum manebit psalmo ·LXXXVIIIº·

ʳ aperta namque sunt vicera domini omni homini penitenti ·I· quescione finale capite *episcopum* ʳ et ad idem propheta edificauit sicut vnicornis sacrificium suum in terra quam fundauit in secula et elegit regem dauid scilicet saluatorem nostrum ihesum xpistum ut pasceret iacob seruum suum et israel hereditatem suam psalmo ·LXXVIIº· //

ʳ vnde paulus ad ephesios ·IIº· ipse enim xpistus est pax nostra qui fecit vtrumque vnum et medium parietem materie soluens inimicicias in carne sua legem mandatorum decretis euacuans et duos condat in semetipsum in vnum nouum hominem faciens pacem reconcilians ambos in vnum aliter in vno corpore deo per crucem interficiens inimicicias in semetipso et ueniens euangelizauit et uobis scilicet gentibus pacem qui longe fuistis et pacem hiis qui prope ut iudeis quoniam per ipsum habemus accesum ambo in vno spiritu ad patrem · ergo iam non sumus hospites et aduene sed per lauacrum baptismum sumus ciues santorum et domestici dey

ʳ cum ergo per redemptorem nostrum pax orta est inimicicia autem totaliter disoluta et in vno spiritu accesum habemus ad deum discordia ergo illa penitus est dampnata ʳ qui igitur hanc indiuisibilem vnitatem non tenet et discordiam inter nouos et ueteres xpistianos satagit facere ut hereticus eternaliter punietur ʳ quia qui ecclesie vnitatem non tenet nec ei baptismus nec elemosina copiosa nec mors pro nomine xpisti suscepta proficere poterit ad salutem in capitulo

---

115 fol. 8r   **124** et Vulgate: ut

118 edificauit…**122** suam Ps 77:69–71.   **122** ipse…**132** dey Eph 2:14-19.

118 episcopum C.1, q.7, c.2.

salvation (X 5.7.3). And elsewhere: *I will awaken a shepherd for you* (Io 10; X 3.42.6), therefore, not two [shepherds], and not two folds, but rather one fold. For one who claims [there to be] two shepherds errs like one who claims [there to be] to folds. Indeed this is proven by the natural order: the cranes follow one [leader, and] among the bees one is master (C.7, q.1, c.41).

Athanasius said: God and man, Christ is one – therefore his Holy Church is one as in the creed of the Church.[19] *The great number of believers was one heart, one soul* (Act 4:32; C.12, q.1, c.2). Also: *one body, one spirit, one hope in our calling,* one prince [sic], *one faith* (Eph 4:4-5; D.95, c.7; C.1, q.1, c.51). Also the Saviour Jesus says: *I and the Father are one* (Io 10:30; C.24, q.3, c.39). And also: we have *one Father who is in heaven* (Mt 23:9; C.29, q.2, c.2).

And for this holy unity the Saviour's human nature prayed to the Father, saying: *holy Father, keep them, whom you have given me, so that they may be one like us.* And: *not only for them do I pray, but also for them who through their word are to believe in me, so that they, too, shall be one in us, in order also for the world to believe, for you have sent me* (Io 17:11.20-21; C.35, q.10, c.1; X 3.41.6). And: *he who hangs on to the Lord is one with him* (I Cor 6:17; X 1.1.2; X 1.21.5). And: *the one who plants and the one who waters are one* (I

---

[19] The reference is to the so-called Athanasian Creed, also known as *Quicumque vult* after its opening words. The somewhat doubtful attribution to the Greek Church Father is nevertheless very old and as such the text was held in high regard especially in the Latin Church.

firmissime de hereticis ͬ et alibi suscitabo uobis vnum pastorem iohannis ·Xº· et capitulo finale *de baptismo* ergo non duos nec duo ouilia   140
sed unum tamen ouile · quia sicut errat qui duos aserit pastores sic qui duo aserit ouilia ͬ probatur enim hoc ordine nature grues vnam secuntur in apibus vnus est dominus in capite *in apibus* ·VII· quescione ·I·

ͬ dixit atanasius deus et homo vnus est xpistus ergo vna santa ecclesia   145
eius ut in simbolo ecclesie ͬ multitudo credencium erat cor vnum anima vna actuum ·4º· capitulo ·XI· quescione ·I· *dilectissimis* ͬ item vnum corpus vnus spiritus vna spes vocacionis nostre vnus dux vna fides ad ephesios ·IIIIº· XCV· distincione *esto iberius* et capite *hi qui* ·I· quescione ·I· ͬ item saluator ihesus ait ego et pater vnum sumus   150
iohannis ·Xº· et capite *quidam* ·XXXIII· quescione ·IIII· ͬ ad idem vnus nobis est pater qui est in celis mathei ·XXIIIIº· XIX· quescione ·II· capite vno

ͬ et pro hac vnione santa orabat vmanitas saluatoris ad patrem inquiens pater sante serua eos quos dedisti michi ut sint vnum sicut et   155
nos et non pro hiis rogo tantum sed pro hiis eciam qui credituri sunt per verbum eorum in me · ut et ipsi in nobis vnum sint ut et mundus credat quia tu me misisti iohannis ·XVIIº· et capite *fraternitatis* ·XXXV· quescione ·X· et capite *cum marthe* § *quesiuisti de celebracione misarum* ͬ et qui adheret deo vnus est cum eo ·Iª· corinthios ·VIº· *de*   160
suma trinitatis capitulo *dampnamus de bigamis* capitulo *debitum* ͬ et qui plantat et qui rrigat unum sunt ·Iª· corinthios ·III· ͬ ad idem

---

157 et² fol. 8v

139 suscitabo…pastorem Ez 34:23, Io 10:11.   **146** multitudo…148 vna Act 4:32.   **148** vnum…150 fides Eph 4:4-5.   **150** ego…sumus Io 10:30.   **152** vnus…celis Mt 23:9.   **155** pater…159 misisti Io 17:11.20–21.   **160** qui…eo I Cor 6:17.   **162** qui¹…sunt I Cor 3:8.

139 firmissime X 5.7.3.   **140** capitulo finale X 3.42.6.   **143** in apibus² C.7, q.1, c.41.   **147** dilectissimis C.12, q.1, c.2.   **149** esto iberius D.95, c.7. | hi qui C.1, q.1, c.51.   **151** quidam C.24, q.3, c.39.   **153** capite vno C.24, q.1, c.19.   **158** fraternitatis C.35, q.10, c.1.   **159** cum marthe X 3.41.6.   **161** dampnamus X 1.1.2. | debitum X 1.21.5.

Cor 3:8). And also the Saviour [says]: *I want them to be one in us, as we are one, so that they may be perfected into one* (Io 17:22-23).

And so, as is universally held to be true, before the end of times all men will be united in Christ Jesus, and all will be Christians, and there will not be any Jews nor Hagarenes because the truth of the Christian faith *prevails and becomes powerful and lives forever and holds fast for all times* (III Esr 4:38; D.8, c.8). Hence Isaiah: *the remnant of Israel will in truth be converted* (Is 10:21; Gloss to C.28, q.1, c.11; John of Imola[20] about Clem 5.2.1). And: all who are wounded in the Saviour's Passion will be saved (C.24, q.1, c.17).

And King Alfonso[21] said in the courts of Alcalá in the law that begins "Por qué se falla", that the Jews according to the prophets are to be converted and saved; therefore they are able to merit the inheritance. And Is 45:17: *Israel is saved in the Lord by an eternal salvation.* And Is 56:8: he *who gathers the scattered of Israel [says]: I will still gather to him all his flock.*

Hence: *it is too little, that you might be my servant to raise up the tribes of Jacob and turn the gates of Israel. I have given you as a light of the Gentiles to be my salvation even to the ends of the earth* (Is 49:6). And also Act 2:39: *to you is the promise and to your children and to all who are far away in whatever way the Lord God will call them near.* [See also] Act 10:47-48. And: *even if you were scattered to the limits of heaven, there the Lord your God would bring you back and accept you and introduce you to the land that your fathers had possessed* (Dt 30:4-5). *They shall know that I am their Lord, for I carried them over to the nations and I gathered them on the land and I have not left any of them behind*

---

[20] John of Imola (c. 1370–1436), also known as Giovanni Nicoletti, was an Italian jurist and supporter of the conciliarist movement. Best known probably for his commentary on the Decretals of Gregory IX, the reference here is to another of his works, *Super Clementinis*.

[21] Alfonso XI (1311–50), also called *el Justiciero* (the Avenger), was king of Castile and Leon. His illegitimate son by Leonor de Guzmán would usurp the throne as Henry II and thus found the Trastámara dynasty that was still in power at the time the *Breue reprehensorium* was written. The legislation cited here was passed at the *cortes* (the representative assembly of the three feudal estates) of Alcalá de Henares (near Madrid) in 1348. Though not as widely famous as the *Siete Partidas* of Alfonso X, the Ordenamiento de Alcalá was in fact a more successful step in the centralisation and unification of the law.

saluator volo ut sint vnum in nobis sicut et nos vnum sumus ut sint consumati in vnum iohannis ·XVII°·

ʳ et sic ut catolice aseritur ante finem seculi omnes homines erunt vni in xpisto ihesu et omnes erunt xpistiani nec erit aliquis iudeorum nec agarenorum ʳ quia veritas xpistiane fidei valet et ualescit et in eternum uiuit et obtinet in secula seculorum ezdre ·IIII°· IX· distincione *consuetudo* ʳ vnde ysaie ·X°· reliquie israel in veritate conuertentur glossa in caput *iudeorum* ·XXVIII· quescione ·I· iohannes de ymola in clementinum *de iudeis* ʳ et omnes qui in pasione saluatoris vulnerati sunt salui fuerunt in capite *petrus* ·XXIIII· quescione ·I·

ʳ et rex alfonsus in curiis de alcala in lege que incipit *por que se falla* ait quod iudei secundum prophetas sunt conuertendi et saluandi ideo posunt emereri hereditatis ʳ et ysaie ·XLV°· israel saluatus est in domino salute eterna ʳ et ·LVI°· idem propheta qui congragat dispersos israel adhuc congregabo ad eum omnes congregatos eius

ʳ vnde parum est ut sis michi seruus ad suscitandas tribus iacob et fores israel conuertendas dedi te in lucem gencium ut sis salus mea usque ad extremum terre ysaie ·XLV°· ʳ ad idem actuum ·II°· uobis est repromisio et filiis vestris et omnibus qui longe sunt quomodocumque aduocauerit dominus deus actuum ·X°· circa finem ʳ et si ad cardines celi fueris disipatus inde rretrahet te dominus deus tuus et asumet atque introducet te in terra quam posederunt patres tui devteronomii ·XXXI°· ʳ Scient quod ego dominus eorum cum transtulerim eos in naciones et congregauerim eos super terram et non reliquerim quemquam ex eis ezechiel ·XXXIX°· in fine ʳ et congregamini omnes

---

179 fores Vulgate: faeces   **184** terra Vulgate: terram

163 volo…**165** vnum Io 17:22–23.   **167** veritas…**169** seculorum III Esr 4:38.   **169** reliquie…conuertentur Is 10:21.   **175** israel…**175** eterna Is 45:17.   **176** qui…**178** eius Is 56:8.   **178** parum…**181** terre Is 49:6. **180** uobis…**183** deus Act 2:39.   **182** si…**185** tui Dt 30:4–5. **185** Scient…**188** eis Ez 39:28.   **187** congregamini…**189** diebus Gn 49:1.

169 consuetudo D.8, c.8.   **170** iudeorum C.28, q.1, c.11.   **171** de iudeis Clem 5.2.1.   **172** petrus C.24, q.1, c.17.   **173** por…falla *Ordenamiento de Alcalá*, title 22, law 2.

(Ez 39:28). And: *gather yourselves all, so that I may tell you what is to come in the last days* (Gn 49:1).

For God shows this congregation and union as an image in the ark of Noah (Gn 5 and 6, C.24, q.3, c.25). Because all who were outside of the ark, while deluge and flood reigned, perished – just so, those who will not go into the holy Church and into Christian unity (C.23, q.4, c.38; gloss to X 5.4.4). They who err in the faith will drown, so to speak, in the water of error, rebellion and disorder. Here the prophet cries: *free me, o Lord, from many waters* (Ps 143:7)! That is: keep me safe in the ark of the Church and in the unity of the faith in Christ that is signified by the image of Noah.

For to do away with the old discord between the peoples, Paul, the *vessel of election*, says (Rm 2:8-11), *that glory, honour, peace be with with those who do good, and hatred, distress, anger with those who do evil, be they from Judea or from Greece. Because before God there is no respect of persons* (Dt 1:17; X 2.1.13). For *God is no respecter of persons, but in every people one is welcome, since the grace of the Holy Spirit is poured out in every nation, for indeed Jews and Gentiles were converted at once by the word of the Lord* (Act 10:35.45; Act 19:10).

For it is not nobility of birth but of virtues and honesty of living that make a pleasing and suitable servant for God to whose rule he has chosen not many nobles according to the flesh and mighty, but some who are of low birth and poor, because there is no exception of persons before him (X 3.5.37). Because before God, there is no finer rank, instead, leading a better life is approved of (C.23, q.4, c.48). And it is not to be regarded who is greater in place or estate, but who is more just (D.40, c.4).

ut anunciem uobis que uentura sunt in nouissimis diebus genesis
·XLIX°· //

¶ hanc enim congregacionem et vnionem figura deus patribus
ostendit per archam noe genesis ·V° · VI° · XXIIII· quescione ·V·
capite *quoniam vetus* ʳ quia omnes qui fuerunt foris extra archam
regnante diluuio et innundacione aquarum perierunt ʳ sic qui non
fuerint intra santam ecclesiam et vnionem xpistianorum de qua in
capite *displicet* ·VIII· quescione ·IIII· glossa in capitulum *querelam ne
prelati vices suas* tamquam crronei in fide demergentur in aqua erroris
sedicionis et confusionis ʳ hinc propheta clamauit libera me domine
ab aquis multis id est conserua me in archa ecclesie et vnitate fidei
xpisti qui figuratus est per noe //

ʳ Tolendo namque antiquam populorum discordiam paulus vas
eleccionis ad rromanos ·II°· ait esse gloriam honorem pacem bene
operanti et odium tribulacionem indignacionem male operanti modo
sit de iudea modo de grecia ʳ quia apud deum non est accepcio
personarum devteronomii ·I°· in capitulo *nouit de iudiciis* ʳ non enim
est personarum acceptor deus sed in omni gente acceptus est illi nam
in omni nacione gracia spiritus santi efusa est iudei namque et gentiles
simul verbo domini conversi sunt actuum ·XIX°·

ʳ quia non generis sed virtutum nobilitas viteque honestas gratum deo
faciunt et ydoneum seruitorem ad cuius regimen non multos
secundum carnem nobiles et potentes elegit sed ignobiles ac pauperes
eo quod non est personarum excepcio apud ipsum in capitulo
uenerabile de prebendis ʳ quia apud deum non est gradus elegancior sed
vite melioris accio comprobatur ·XXIII· quescione ·V· *sicut excelen-
ciam* ʳ nec considerandum quis maior sit in loco uel ordine sed quis
iustior ·XL· distincione *non loca*

---

198 fol. 9r   **211** excepcio Decretals: acceptio

197 libera...**199** multis Ps 143:7.   **200** vas...**202** eleccionis Act 9:15.
201 gloriam...**205** personarum Rm 2:8-11, Dt 1:17.   **204** non...**208** sunt
Act 10:35.45, Act 19:10.

---

192 quoniam vetus C.24, q.3, c.25.   **195** displicet C.23, q.4, c.38.
querelam X 5.4.4.   **204** nouit X 2.1.13.   **212** uenerabile X 3.5.37.
213 sicut excelen-ciam C.23, q.4, c.48.   **215** non loca D.40, c.4.

And Cicero [wrote] to Sallust:[22] I have greater satisfaction in flourishing by my deeds than in rising in the esteem of the elders; an in living in such a way as to be an incentive of nobility to my descendants and an example of virtue. The blessed Bernard says:[23] even though the plain miracles that the Lord worked on this earth were great and divine, yet over everything stood out that he subjugated for himself the whole world and all its highness by the few, the simple and the poor. And: not in the highness of position but in the extend of charity one gains the kingdom of God (X 1.11.5).

Here the psalmist says about this unity: *in order to convert the peoples into one, and kings to serve the Lord* (Ps 101:23). For in the Passion of the Lord peace was made between the different nations. And it was fulfilled what had been prophetically said: *the kings of the earth stand up and the princes gather together against the Lord and against his Christ* (Ps 2:2; Act 4:25; C.23, q.4, c.42). And also it is written: *he will gather to himself all nations and assemble before him all peoples* (Hab 2:5). And: *all nations will worship him, and all kings will serve him* (Ps 71:11; C.23, q.4, c.38).

This holy unity was also proclaimed most delightfully by one of the prophets (Is 60:1.3.5): *rise, Jerusalem, for your light is coming and the glory of the Lord is rising above you!* And shortly after: *nations will walk in your light and kings in the brilliance of your rising. And then you will see and praise and your heart will be amazed and will be raised up when the multitude of the sea will be converted to you and the strength of the nations will come to you.* For what is it to say *multitude of the sea* if not the uncountable multitude of peoples of

---

[22] The invective speeches handed down under the names of M. Tullius Cicero and C. Crispus Sallustius were probably composed by one or more later authors of the Roman Empire. Medieval scholars would have had no reason not to take their attribution to Cicero and Sallust at face value.

[23] The quote is taken from the *Epistola ad fratres de monte Dei*, a work that has been attributed to Bernard of Clairvaux (c. 1091–53), but also, among others, to William of Saint Thierry (c. 1085–1148) and Guigues du Chastel (1083–1137). The eponymous Notre Dame du Mont Dieu is a Carthusian priory in the Ardennes.

ʳ et tulius ad salustium sacius est me meis gestis florere quam mayorum opynione niti et ita viuere ut sim posteris meis nobilitatis inicium et virtutis exemplum ʳ beatus bernardus ait licet magna et diuina fuerint plane miracula que dominus gessit in terris istud tamen super omnia emicuit quod in paucis simplicibus et pauperibus totum mundum et omnem eius altitudinem sibi subiugauit ʳ et non in sublimitate graduum sed in amplitudine caritatis acquiritur regnum dei in capitulo *ad aures de temporibus ordinacionum*

ʳ hinc salmista de hac vnione ait ad convertendos populos in unum reges ut seruiant domino psalmo · quia in pasione domini facta est pax diuersarum gencium ʳ et impletum est quod prophetice dictum fuerat astiterunt reges terre et principes conuenerunt in vnum adversus dominum et aduersum xpistum eius psalmo ·IIº· *quare fremuerunt* et actuum ·IIIIº· capitulo et in capite *si ecclesia* ·XXIII· quescione ·IIII· ʳ ad idem legitur congregabit ad se omnes gentes et aceruabit ad se omnes populos abachuc ·IIº· capitulo ʳ et adorabunt eum omnes gentes et omnes reges seruient ei psalmo ·LXXXIº· *deus iudicium tuum* et ·XXIII· quescione ·IIII· capite *displicet*

℣ hanc eciam vnionem santam prophetarum vnus iocundissime exclamat ysaie ·LXº· capitulo surge iherusalem quia uenit lumen et gloria domini super te orta est et continuo post pauca ambulabunt gentes in lumine tuo et reges in splendore ortus tui et tunc videbis et exaltaberis et mirabitur et eleuabitur cor tuum cum ad te conuersa fuerit multitudo maris et fortitudo gencium uenerit ad te ʳ quid enim est dicere multitudo maris nisi inumerabilis multitudo populorum de

---

224 ad convertendos Vulgate: in conveniendo

224 ad…**226** domino Ps 101:23.   **227** astiterunt…**229** eius Ps 2:2, Act 4:25.   **230** congregabit…**232** populos Hab 2:5.   **231** adorabunt…**233** ei Ps 71:11.   **235** surge…**238** te Is 60:1.3.5.

216 sacius…**217** exemplum Pseudo-Cicero, *In Sallustium declamatio*, 5. **218** licet…**222** subiugauit Bernard of Clairvaux, *Epistola ad fratres de monte Dei*. **223** ad aures X 1.11.5. **229** si ecclesia C.23, q.4, c.42. **233** displicet C.23, q.4, c.38.

which one of the apostles says: a certain *great mass that one cannot count* (Apc 7:9).

Likewise Is 62:2–3 says in order to bring forth all those who had to be converted in the time of the coming of our Saviour Christ: *the nations will see your justice and all the kings of the earth your glory, and you will be given a new name, that the Lord's mouth will designate. You will be a distinguished crown in the hand of the Lord and a diadem of the kingdom in the palm of your God.* And then he confirms: *you will be called priests of the Lord, ministers of God, and for you it will be said: you will consume the strength of the Gentiles and exalt in their glories* (Is 61:6).

Likewise: *we will be glad and rejoice in you,* holy and blessed God (Ct 1:3). And also: *you will be priests for my kingdom and a holy people* (Ex 19:6). And: *for your fathers there are sons born to you. You shall appoint them as princes over all the earth* (Ps 44:17; D.68, c.6). And according to the Apostle [Paul], all those who believe are made into the body of Christ (I Cor 10:17; C.11, q.3, c.58). And: its *head is the Saviour himself* (Col 1:18, Io 4:42; X 5.7.10).

For all Christians are called sheep of Christ (C.23, q.4, c.43). The lost sheep is humankind brought by Christ to the heavenly sheepfold (D.50, c.16; C.26, q.7, c.9). The shepherd, however, is Christ (C.8, q.1, c.9; C.2, q.7, c.39). And: *I will gather them from everywhere to their land* – that is to say: the Christian faith – *and I will make of them a single nation in the land on the mountains of Israel, and one king will rule them all* – one may know: our Saviour Jesus – *and no more shall they be two nations, nor will they be divided further in two kingdoms, nor will they be defiled any more by their idols and*

qua apostolorum vnus inquit quedam turba grandis quam aliquis nummerare non poterat

ʳ Similiter ysaias ·LXIIº· capitulo ortando omnes qui conuerti debebant tempore aduentus saluatoris nostri xpisti ait videbunt gentes iusticiam tuam et omnes reges terre gloriam tuam et erit positum tibi nomen nouum quod os domini signabit erisque tu corona excelens in manu domini et diadema rregni in palma dei vestri ʳ Et continuo ait vos eritis sacerdotes domini vocati ministri dei et pro uobis dicetur comedetis virtutem gencium et in gloriis suis exaltabimini

ʳ item exultabimus et letabimur in te deo santo et benedicto cantico ·Iº· capitulo ʳ ad idem uos eritis regno meo sacerdotes et populus santus exodi ·XIXº· capitulo ʳ et pro patribus tuis nati sunt tibi filii constitues eos principes super omnem terram psalmo ·XLIIIIº· ·LXVIII· distincione capite *quorum merces* ʳ et secundum apostolum omnes credentes xpisti corpus eficiuntur ·Iª· corinthios ·XIº· et capite *si quis hominem* ·XII· quescione ·III· ʳ et capud eius est idem saluator ad colossenses ·Iº· et iohannis ·IVº· et in capitulo *vergentis de hereticis*

ʳ oues enim xpisti dicuntur omnes xpistiani ·XXIII· quescione ·IIII· capite *quis enim potest* ʳ ouis perdita est genus humanum per xpistum ad ouile celeste reperata ·L· distincione *quia tua* ·XXVI· quescione ·VII· *penitentem* ʳ pastor autem est xpistus ·VIII· quescione ·I· *in scripturis* ·II· quescione ·VII· *testes* ʳ et congregabo eos vndique ad humum suam scilicet fidem xpistianam et faciam eos in gentem vnam in terra in montibus israel et rex vnus omnibus imperans scilicet saluator noster ihesus et non erunt ultra due gentes · nec diuidentur

---

241 fol. 9v

---

241 quedam...**243** poterat Apc 7:9.   **244** videbunt...**248** vestri Is 62:2-3.
248 vos...**250** exaltabimini Is 61:6.   **250** exultabimus...te Ct 1:3.
251 uos...**253** santus Ex 19:6.   **252** pro...**254** terram Ps 44:17.
255 omnes...eficiuntur I Cor 10:17.   **256** capud...saluator Col 1:18, Io 4:42.   **262** congregabo...**268** suis Ez 37:21–23.

---

254 quorum merces D.68, c.6.   **256** si...hominem C.11, q.3, c.58.
257 vergentis X 5.7.10.   **259** quis...potest C.23, q.4, c.43.   **260** quia tua D.50, c.16.   **261** penitentem C.26, q.7, c.9. | in...**263** scripturis C.8, q.1, c.9.   **262** testes C.2, q.7, c.39.

their abominations (Ez 37:21-23). And also: *I will gather the lameness* – that is to say: the law of Moses that was believed in figuratively – *and I will pick up her whom I had cast out* – one may know: the Gentile people – *and whom I had afflicted I will console* (Mi 4:6, So 3:19).

For Christ saved with the one Passion the entire world (D.2, c.71 de cons.). Hence I find a threefold "truly" in this: first, Isaiah (Is 45:15): *truly, you are a hidden God*. Second, also Isaiah (Is 53:4): *truly, he bore our infirmities, and carried our pains himself* (X 3.41.6). Third, the centurion said in the Saviour's Passion as he hung on the cross and he beheld an earthquake: *truly, this one was a son of God* (Mt 27:54, Mc 15:39, Lc 23:47).

I conclude therefore truly, that our Saviour Jesus joined together his one holy Church out of Jews and Gentiles, for every old discord to be taken away.

Eighth article: that in the present age the sinners must not be separated from the righteous

For this reason, no one in this age is to be separated or judged; accept therefore what is found written in the gospel of the cockle: *allow both to grow, otherwise by wanting to root out the cockle, you might root out with it also the wheat* (Mt 13:29-30).[24] Hear therefore the scripture saying that the children of Judah could not destroy the Jebusites, instead *they lived with them in Jerusalem until today* (Idc 1:21). Therefore, *do not give what is holy to the dogs* (Mt 7:6; C.11, q.3, c.22)!

---

[24] The parable of the weeds between the crops was the most important biblical argument against religiously motivated violence in the whole middle ages. The maxim "Suffer both to grow!" thus became the basis for what tolerance premodern Christianity could muster. Against it stood frequently the parable of the great supper (Lc 14:16–24) where the command "Compell them to come in!" *(compelle intrare)* served as a reason to believe that even forced conversions could be legitimate.

amplius in duo regna · nec poluentur ultra in ydolis suis et
abominacionibus suis ezechiel ·XXXVIIº· ʳ ad idem congregabo
clauditatem scilicet legem moysi que sub figura credebat et eam quam
eieceram colligam scilicet gentilem gentem et quam aflixeram
consolabo micheas ·IIIIº· sophonias capitulo ultimo

ʳ nam xpistus vna pasione totum mundum saluauit *de consecracione*
distincione ·II· capite *iteratur* ʳ vnde triplex vere in hoc reperio ʳ
primum ysaie ·XLVº· vere tu es deus absconditus · ʳ secundum idem
ysaias vere languores nostros ipse tulit et dolores nostros ipse portauit
in capite *cum marthe de celebracione misarum* ʳ tercium dixit centurio
in pasione saluatoris cum penderet in cruce viso terremotu · vere filius
dei erat ille mathei ·XXVIIº· marci ·XVº· luce ·XXIIIº·

ʳ concludo ergo vere quod saluator ihesus ex iudeis et gentilibus
copulauit suam unam santam ecclesiam omnem discordiam antiquam
tolendo ·

·VIIIᵘˢ· articulus quod in presenti seculo pecatoris non debent separari a iustis

Ideo nemo est in hoc seculo separandus nec iudicandus sumite ergo
quod scriptum legi in euangelio de zizaniis sinite utraque crescere ne
forte uolentes erradicare zizaniam erradicetis cum ipsis et triticum
mathei ·XVIIº· et marci ·XIIIº· ʳ audite ergo scrituram dicentem quod
non potuerunt filii iuda disperdere iebuseos sed habitauerunt cum
ipsis in iherusalem usque in odiernum die · nolite ergo mictere
santum canibus in capite *nolite* ·XI· quescione ·III·

---

4 fol. 10r   7 iuda Vulgate: benjamin

267 congregabo...271 consolabo Mi 4:6, So 3:19.   273 vere...absconditus
Is 45:15.   274 vere...portauit Is 53:4.   276 vere...278 ille Mt 27:54, Mc
15:39, Lc 23:47.   4 sinite...5 triticum Mt 13:29–30.   7 habitauerunt...8
die Idc 1:21.   8 nolite...9 canibus Mt 7:6.

---

272 iteratur D.2, c.71 de cons.   275 cum marthe X 3.41.6.   9 nolite C.11,
q.3, c.22.

And: you as the good one, tolerate the evil one, for our Saviour, knowing Judas as a thief and a traitor, tolerated him and sent him with the other apostles to preach (Mt 10:4-7). And beforehand he gave him the [Eucharistic] host (Lc 22; Io 6; C.23, q.4, c.2; C.23, q.4, c.2; X 1.31.2; X 5.38.12). And: he who does not tolerate the evil ones, is by his intolerance a witness against himself, that he is not good (C.23, q.4, c.15).

And elsewhere: we tolerate a few whom we cannot correct. Neither do we leave the Lord's field because of the chaff, nor do we rip the Lord's net because of the bad fishes, nor do we abandon the Lord's fold because of the goats that are to be separated in the end, nor do we move out of the Lord's house because of *the vessels made unto dishonour* [Rm 9:21] (C.23, q.7, c.1). And: *the learning of a man is known by his patience* (Prv 19:11). *Be holy therefore, for I am holy, says the Lord* (Lv 19:2; D.81, c.23).

All are Christians, therefore the Church receives all. For if Abraham and Lot had not received all who were coming to the city, perhaps they would not have hosted the angels of God (Gn 16; Gn 19; D.42, c. 1-2). And if blessed Martin had not given every alms, perhaps he would not have covered the naked Christ with half of his cloak. Without difference alms must be extended to all (C.16, q.1, c.5). And alms must not sweat in the hand. *Because every creature of God is good, and nothing is to be rejected that is*

ʳ et tu bonus tolera malum quia saluator licet sciuit iudam furem et traditurum tolerauit et cum aliis apostolis ad predicandum misit mathei ·Xº· et prius hostiam dedit luce ·XXIIº· iohannis ·VIº· in capite *tu bonus* ·XXIII· quescione ·IIII· et capite *quid ergo* et in capitulo *sacerdos de officio iudicis ordinarii* et capitulo *omnis de penitenciis et remisionibus* ʳ et qui malos non tolerat sibi ipsi per intolerancia conscius est quod bonus non sit capite *hec autem* ·XXIII· quescione ·IIII·

ʳ et alibi nonnullos toleramus quos corrigere non posumus ʳ nec propter paleam relinquimus aream domini · nec propter pices malos rumpimus rectia domini · nec propter edos in fine segregandos deserimus gregem domini · nec propter uasa facta in contumeliam migramus de domo domini in capite *quicumque* ·XXIII· quescione ·VII· ʳ et doctrina viri per pascienciam noscitur prouerbiorum ·XIXº· ʳ santi ergo stote quia santus sum ego dicit dominus leuitici ·XIXº· et capite *oportet* ·LXXXI· distincione

ʳ omnes sunt xpistiani ergo omnes ecclesia recipit quia si habraham et loth · omnes ad ciuitatem uenientes non admiserant forte dei angelos non hospitauerant genesis ·XVIº· et ·XIXº· capitulo et capite *quiescamus* et capite *ospitalem* ·XLII· distincione ʳ et si beatus martinus cuntis elemosinam non dederat forte xpistum nudum cum mediatete palii sui non coperuerat ʳ indistinte omnibus debet patere elemosina in capite *si cupis* ·XVI· quescione ·I· nec debet sudare elemosina in manu ʳ omnis namque creatura dei bona et nichil reiciendum quod

---

32 nec Didache: et

11 traditurum...**11** misit Mt 10:4–7.   **12** hostiam dedit Io 13:26.
23 doctrina...noscitur Prv 19:11. | santi...dominus Lv 19:2.   **26** si...**27** hospitauerant Gn 18-19, Hbr 13:2.   **33** omnis...**33** percipitur I Tim 4:4.

13 tu bonus C.23, q.4, c.2. | quid ergo C.23, q.4, c.3.   **14** sacerdos X 1.31.2. | omnis X 5.38.12.   **16** hec autem C.23, q.4, c.15.   **22** quicumque C.23, q.7, c.1.   **25** oportet D.81, c.23.   **28** quies-camus D. 42, c.1.   **29** ospitalem D. 42, c.2.   **32** si cupis C.16, q.1, c.5. | nec...**32** manu *Didache*, I,6.

received with thanksgiving (I Tim 4:4). And: *like the green herbs I have given you all things* (Gn 9:3).

Let us therefore do everyone good, most to those of the household of the faith (Gal 6:10; X 1.15.1). And there is an example in the Gospel (Lc 10:25-37) that the one who showed mercy to the beaten, half-living, forsaken man was nearer to him even though he was of another nation. Likewise the Saviour says: *love your enemies and do good to those who hate you* (Mt 5:44; Lc 6:27; C.23, q.4, c.16). And: *if your enemy is hungry, feed him, if he is thirsty, give him to drink!* (Rm 12:20; Prv 25:21; C.23, q.4, c.15). For *God guides the meek in judgment and teaches the gentle his ways* (Ps 24:9; C.16, q.1, c.30).

For in one simple peasant may perchance the entire city be sustained. This means that where good people are, there is the Roman Curia (gloss to D.21, c.3). For *no one knows, whether he is worthy of hate or love* (Ecl 9:1). And: *God's foundation stands firm, having this seal: the Lord does know indeed who belongs to him* (II Tim 2:19; D.2, c.25 de poen.).

And Peter plainly denied the Saviour during the Passion (Mt 26:70-74). In vain therefore did he foretell: *Peter, I have prayed for you that your faith might not fail.* And it follows: *Simon, behold, he said, Satan demands to sift you like wheat. But I have prayed for you, that you faith might not fail* (Lc 22:31-32; D.2, c.40 de poen.). Not even in the virgin mother of Christ was the entire faith sustained according to the Abbot of Sicily[25] on X 1.6.4.

---

[25] Nicolaus de Tudeschis, see note 16.

cum graciarum accione percipitur ad timotheum ·4º· et quasi olera virencia dedi uobis omnia genesis ·IXº·

ʳ operemur igitur bonum ad omnes maxime ad domesticos fidei ad gallatas ·IIIIº· *de sacra vncione* capitulo vno § *hoc vnguento* ʳ et exemplum in euangelio luce ·Xº· quod qui misericordiam fecit cum percuso semiuiuo rrelicto fuit illi proximior licet alterius nacionis esset ʳ similiter saluator ait diligite inimicos vestros et beneficite hiis qui oderunt uos mathei ·Vº· luce ·VIº· XXIII· quescione ·IIII· capite *cum in lege* ʳ et si exurierit inimicus tuus ciba illum · si sitit potum da illi ad rromanos ·XIIº· XXIII· quescione ·I· § *ex hiis omnibus* ʳ nam deus dirigit mictes in iudicio et docet mansuetos vias suas psalmo ·XXIIIIº· *ad te domine* ·XI· quescione ·I· *nos autem*

ʳ quia forte in vno simplici rustico tota ciuitas substinetur ʳ hinc est quod ubi sunt boni ibi est curia romana glossa in caput *quamvis* ·XXI· distincione ʳ quia nemo scit an sit dignus odio uel amore ecclesiastici ·IXº· capitulo ʳ et firmum fundamentum dei stat habens signaculum hoc enim scit dominus qui sunt eius Iª ad timotheum ·IIº· capitulo *de penitencia* distincione ·II· *firmum*

ʳ et manifeste petrus in pasione negauit saluatorem mathei ·XXVIº· frustra ergo predixisset petre oraui pro te ne deficeret fides tua ʳ et sequitur simon ecce inquid satanas postulat vos ut cribaret quasi triticum ego autem oraui pro te ne deficeret fides tua in capite *fugerat de penitencia* distincione ·II· nisi quia in virgine matre xpisti tota fides ecclesie substinebatur secundum abbatem de cicilia in capitulo *significasti de ellecione*

---

46 fol. 10v

---

34 quasi...34 omnia Gn 9:3.   36 operemur...fidei Gal 6:10.   38 qui...38 esset Lc 10:25-37.   40 diligite...40 uos Mt 5:44, Lc 6:27.   42 si¹...illi Rm 12:20, Prv 25:21.   44 dirigit...suas Ps 24:9.   48 nemo...amore Ecl 9:1.   49 firmum...49 eius II Tim 2:19.   52 petrus...saluatorem Mt 26:69-75.   53 petre...54 tua Lc 22:31-32.

---

37 capitulo vno X 1.15.1.   41 cum...41 lege C.23, q.4, c.16.   43 ex... omnibus C.23, q.4, c.15.   45 nos autem C.16, q.1, c.30.   47 quamvis D.21, c.3.   51 firmum D.2, c.25 de poen.   55 fugerat D.2, c.40 de poen. 58 significasti X 1.6.4.

And neither do we accept sinners for their being sinners, but rather do we treat them with human consideration because they, too, are human beings (C.23, q.4, c.35). And: sins deserve hatred, not men (D.86, c.2; C.23, q.4, c.35). And: *that you may be children of your Father, who is in heaven, who lets it rain and makes his sun rise over the sinners and the righteous* and casts no one out (Mt 5:45; C.23, q.4, c.15).

Therefore, no one in the present age is to be slighted nor separated.

Ninth article: that frivolous words, from which scandal may arise, are to be cut short

And said words are not out of themselves as hurtful as out of the intention in which "confesos" are usually called so; as in the aforementioned depicted words (Dig. 47,2,54; Dig. 47,10,3; Cod. 9,35,5). For the intention is inferred through the appearance (Cod. 2,20,6; Dig. 49,16,5; Salicetus[26] in great part about Dig. 48,8,4).

And: the speech must be understood according to the condition of the person at whom it is directed (Dig. 29,1,11 and there Bartolus[27] notes: Dinus[28] on VI 5.12.26). And it cannot have been spoken in the heat of passion and thus be without punishment as the gloss says on X 4.19.5 and D.1, c.22 de poen. and Dig. 50,17,48. For, since it has been written and depicted on an altarpiece, it cannot have been said in the heat of passion but deliberately (D.1, c.22 de poen.). *For corrupt is the heart of man and*

---

[26] Bartolomeo de Saliceto (c. 1330–1412) was an important Italian jurist and commentator of Roman law. Born in Bologna into a family of scholars that originally hailed from Saliceto he also worked in Padua and Ferrara. The reference is to his *Lectura super secunda parte Digesti*.

[27] Bartolus de Saxoferrato (1313–1357) was one of the most famous Italian jurists and a prolific author of commentaries on the Roman law. The reference is to his *Lectura super secunda parte Digesti*.

[28] Dinus de Rossonis (c. 1253–1303), also called Mugellanus after his home town Mugello near Florence composed legal commentaries on both civil and canon law. The reference is to his commentary on the last title in Pope Boniface VIII's Liber Sextus, a collection of short legal maxims titled *De regulis iuris*.

ʳ nec enim suscipiamus pecatores propter hoc quod sunt pecatores sed tamen eos ipsos quia et homines sunt humana consideracione tractemus in capite *duo* ·XXIII· quescione ·IIII· ʳ et hodio habeantur pecata non homines ·LXXXVI· distincione *odit* et dicto capite *duo* ʳ et ut sitis filii patris vestri qui in celis est qui pluit et solem suum oriri facit super pecatores et iustos et neminem euictat mathei ·Vº· et in § *ex hiis* ·XXIII· quescione ·IIII·

ʳ ergo nemo in presenti seculo est nictandus nec segregandus

·IXᵘˢ· articulus quod leuia uerba ex quibus nascitur scandalum sunt resecanda

Nec dicta verba sunt ex se tan iniuriossa quam ex animo quo dici solent confessos ut in predictis depictis articulo lege *iniurie* digestis *de furtis* et lege ·III· digestis *de iniuriis* et lege *si non conuicii* Codice eodem titulo ʳ animus enim per exteriora colligitur ut Codice *de dolo* lege *dolum* et digestis *de re militari* lege *non omnes* § *a barbaris* salicetus plere in lege cornellia *de sicaris*

ʳ et sermo debet inteligi secundum condicionem persone ad quam dirigitur ut lege *ex militari* digestis *de testamento millitis* et ibi bartolus notat dynus in regula *ea que* libro sexto ʳ nec potest dici calore iracundie dictum et sic pena carere ut dicit glossa in capitulum *ex literis de diuortiis* et capite *si quis iratus de penitencia* distincione ·I· et lege *quidquid calore* digestis *de regulis iuris* ʳ quia ex quo fuit scriptum et depictum in retabulo altaris iracundie calorem non potest dici sed deliberate ut nota in dicto capite *si quis iratus* ʳ prauum enim est cor hominis et inscrutabile quis conoscet illud ego dominus scrutans cor et renes ieremie ·XVIIº· capitulo

---

63 ut...63 euictat Mt 5:45.   16 prauum...18 renes Ier 17:9–10.

61 duo C.23, q.4, c.35.   62 odit D.86, c.2.   65 ex hiis C.23, q.4, c.15.
4 iniurie Dig. 47,2,54.   5 lege ·III· Dig. 47,10,3. | si...conuicii Cod. 9,35,5.
7 dolum Cod. 2,20,6. | non omnes Dig. 49,16,5.   8 de sicaris Dig. 48,8,4.
10 ex militari Dig. 29,1,11.   11 ea...11 que VI 5.12.26.   12 ex literis X 4.19.5.   13 si...iratus D.1, c.22 de poen.   14 quidquid calore Dig. 50,17,48.

unsearchable. Who knows it? I, the Lord, am searching heart and kidneys (Ier 17:9-10).
I read an example in IV Rg 1:9-10; C.23, q.4, c.29, that the king of Israel commanded the prophet Elijah to be called by his captains [and] soldiers who said: *Man of God, the king calls you.* The prophet answered: *if I am a man of God, may fire from heaven burn you up!* And so it happened, for with evil intention was he called a man of God; as is commonly said as a byword "son of a good woman", that is: of a whore. Therefore Elijah rightly replied, *if I am a man of God*; like you bear one thing in mind to say it and something else in mind and in spirit, against X 2.24.26, for as it goes forth from the mouth so it shall come from the heart.

Who was therefore that drunk fool thinking in bad faith who dared to put such words in public next to the Lord's altar where his true body is sacrificed? And the divine and prophetic and also the evangelic law and the holy canons teach how much this is detestable to God and hostile to the saints, and it is obvious to almost all right believers (C.1, q.3, c.9).

And so, *may the almighty God rise up* and scatter such wicked plans by *judging his cause* (Ps 73:22; D.21, c.7). *For a fool says foolish things* (Is 32:6; D.93, c.24). And: *the words of the wicked lay traps, the blood of the just has liberated them* (Prv 12:6). *The just shall detest a deceitful word; the wicked brings disorder and shall be dismayed* (Prv 13:5; C.5, q.5, c.5). And: *he who guards his mouth guards his soul; but he who speaks unadvisedly will experience [evil]* (Prv 13:3).

A very severe sentence is passed on him by Jesus our Saviour in the scriptures. Mt 18:6 and Mc 9:41: *he who scandalizes one of these little ones who believe in me, it were better for him that a millstone be hanged around his*

ʳ exemplum legi ·4°· regum capite *si illic* ·XXIII· quescione ·IIII· quod rex israel fecit uocari eliam prophetam per quinquagenarios milites suos qui dicebant homo dei rex uocat te · respondit propheta si vir dei sum ignis de celo vos comburat et sic factum est · quia malo animo vocabatur homo dei · ut comuniter dicitur vade pro filio bone mulieris id est meretricis ʳ ideo elias recte rrespondit si vir dei sum sicut uos mente geritis vnum ore dicendo et aliud mente et animo contra capitulum *etsi xpistus de iureiurando* quia sicut procedit ex ore ita procedat ex corde

ʳ quis ergo fuit ille ebrius fatuus de fide male senciens qui iuxta altare domini ubi verum eius corpus inmolatur ausus fuit talia verba in publico proferre ʳ et quantum hoc sit detestabile deo santisque sit contrarium diuina et prophetica nec non euangelica lex et sacri canones docent et fere omnibus recte credentibus manifestum existit ·I· quescione ·III· capite *ex multis*

ʳ Exsurgat itaque deus omnipotens et tam nephanda consilia disipet iudicans causam suam psalmo ·LXXIII°· capite *nunc autem* ·XXI· distincione ʳ fatuus enim fatua loquitur ysaie ·XXXII°· in capite *legimus* ·XCIII· distincione ʳ et verba impiorum insidiantur sanguis iustorum liberauit eos proverbiorum ·XII°· ʳ verbum mendax iustus detestabitur impius confundit et confundetur idem sapiens et in § *sed illud* ·V· quescione ·V· ʳ et qui custodit os suum custodit animam suam · qui autem inconsiderate loquitur senciet proverbiorum ·XIII°·

ʳ Sentencia crudelisima contra eum per ihesum saluatorem nostrum lata est in scriptis mathei ·XVIII°· et marci ·IX°· capitulo qui scandalizauerit vnum de pusilis istis qui in me credunt expedit ei ut suspendatur mola asinaria in colo eius et demergatur in profundum

---

25 fol. 11r **41** senciet Vulgate: sentiet mala

---

20 rex...**22** comburat IV Rg 1:9–10.   **34** Exsurgat...**34** suam Ps 73:22. **36** fatuus...loquitur Is 32:6.   **37** verba...**37** eos Prv 12:6.   **38** verbum... **38** confundetur Prv 13:5.   **40** qui...**40** senciet Prv 13:3.   **43** qui...**45** maris Mt 18:6, Mc 9:41.

---

19 si illic C.23, q.4, c.29.   **26** etsi xpistus X 2.24.26.   **33** ex multis C.1, q.3, c.9.   **35** nunc autem D.21, c.7.   **37** legimus D.93, c.24.   **39** sed...**39** illud C.5, q.5, c.5.

neck and he be drowned in the depth of the sea (X 1.9.10). For the newly converted are and are held to be little and pitiable people according to [Pope] Innocent [III] in X 5.6.13.

From this follows, that attackers of their goods can be summoned before an ecclesiastic judge, as the abbot of Sicily[29] notes on X 1.29.38 and Anthony[30] on X 2.2.11. This the townsfolk of Toledo should have enjoyed, because we must work to gain them so that provoked by gentleness and reason they may be willing to follow us, not flee us (D.45, c.3; C.2, q.1, c.18). Hence property is permitted to be given so that someone converts to the faith (C.23, q.4. c.53 and C.23, q.7, c.3; gloss to X 5.3.28 and X 5.9.5 and C.23, q.6, c.4).

For Paul said he did not expect any reward from God, but to have gained those who were under the law (I Cor 9:18-20). And: we have to flatter the infidels for them to be converted (C.1, q.2, c.2). And that is a good deceit.[31] Therefore no one must raise scandal over this. Hence Ps 49:20: *you spoke against your brother and laid scandal against the son of your mother* (C.6, q.1, c.13). And also: *if my victual should scandalize my brother, I will not eat meat ever again* (I Cor 8:13; C.23, q.3 and X 1.9.10). And: *if your eyes or foot or right hand scandalizes, it shall be removed from the compound of the body, for it*

---

[29] Nicolaus de Tudeschis, see note 16.

[30] Antonius de Butrio (1338–1408) was a well known teacher of canon law at Bologna and confidant of Pope Gregory XII. The reference is to his commentary *Super secundo libro decretalium*.

[31] The term *bonus dolus* (good deceit) in the Latin legal tradition orinially marked a degree of sagacity in business transactions that was deemed to be competitive but fair as opposed to the criminal and punishable *malus dolus* (bad deceit). Our author now applies this maxim to the question of alleged *converso* opportunism and favouritism. In a quite remarkable spin he does not even deny the well known Old Christian grievance that certain New Christians had supposedly gained undue advantages from their conversion, but rather argues, in essence, that the end justifies the means.

maris in capitulo *cum pridem de renunciacione* in § *pro graui* ͬ quia nouiter conuersi sunt et censentur pusiles et miserabiles persone dictum est innocencius in capitulo *iudei de iudeis et sarracenis* ͬ ex quo sequitur quod suorum bonorum inuasores posunt coram ecclesiastico iudice conuenire ut notat abbas de cicilia in capitulo *significantibus de officio et potestate iudicis delegati* antonius in capitulo *ex tenore de foro competente* de quo gauderent vicani toletani ͬ cum laborare debeamus eos lucrifacere ut mansuetudine et racione prouocati sequi nos uelint non fugere in capite *qui sincera* ·XLV· distincione et capite *multi in vnum* ·II· quescione ·VII· ͬ vnde licite datur pecunia ut quis conuertatur ad fidem ·XXIII· quescione ·IIII· capite penultime et quescione ·VII· capite *quod autem* glossa in capitulum *dilectus de symonia* et in capitulum *a nobis de apostatis* et capite *iam vero* ·XXIII· quescione ·VI·

ͬ paulus enim nullam mercedem a deo dicebat sperare nisi cum lucrifaciebat eos qui sub lege erant ad rromanos ·Xº· ͬ et debemus infidelibus blandiri ut conuertantur glossa in caput *quam pio* ·I· quescione ·II· et iste est bonus dolus ͬ igitur nemo debet super hiis scandalum suscitare ͬ vnde propheta psalmo ·XLIXº· aduersus fratrem tuum loquebaris et aduersus filium matris tue ponebas scandalum ·VI· quescione ·I· capite *ex merito* ͬ ad idem si sca mea scandalizauerit fratrem meum non manducabo carnem in eternum ad corinthios ·VIIIº· XXIII· quescione ·III· in principio et dicto capitulo *cum pridem* § *pro graui* ͬ et si uos oculus aut pes aut destera scandalizauerit manus a compage corporis auferatur quia melius est hiis in seculo

---

69 fol. 11v

---

60 nullam...**60** erant I Cor 9:18–20. **64** aduersus...**64** scandalum Ps 49:20. **66** si...**66** eternum I Cor 8:13. **69** si...**70** deputari Mt 18:8-9, Mc 9:43–47.

---

46 cum pridem X 1.9.10. **48** iudei X 5.6.13. **51** significantibus X 1.29.38. **52** ex tenore X 2.2.11. **54** qui sincera D.45, c.3. **55** multi...vnum C.2, q.1, c.18. **57** capite penultime C.23, q.4. c.53. | quod autem C.23, q.7, c.3. **58** dilectus X 5.3.28. | a nobis X 5.9.5. **59** iam vero C.23, q.6, c.4. **62** quam pio C.1, q.2, c.2. **66** ex merito C.6, q.1, c.13. **68** in principio C.23, q.3. | cum...**68** pridem X 1.9.10.

is better to be without these members forever than be assigned to eternal sufferings with them (Mt 18:8-9, Mc 9:43-47; C.24, q.3, c.34). Similarly the Saviour [says]: *woe to him through whom scandal will come* (Mt 18:7, Lc 17:1).

And if something horrible or serious is feared by a good man, he would be careful not to raise so much scandal through its repetition by good people (X 5.12.10; X 5.32.2 and X 5.39.3). Neither did Pilate sin by desisting in that case, where he probably considered that by delaying, he would save the accused (C.23, q.8, c. 21; C.11, q.3, c.23). Hence I have read there to be written against those insurgents: *behold, my witness is in heaven* (Iob 16:20). And it follows: let us set the fools free to speak what they want! For what else are the slanderers doing but to blow in the dust and to stir up dirt in their eyes? The more slander they are blowing around, the more they shall see nothing of the truth (C.11, q.3, c.55). For and those insurgents fall by law under capital punishment, because it is a crime against the royal majesty[32] (Cod. 9,30,1-2). Therefore said words are to be avoided altogether. Hence [King] David in Ps 119:2: *Lord, deliver my soul from hostile lips and a deceitful tongue!* (Ps 119:2).

Tenth article: that in this age the good suffer and the reprobate pride themselves

However, it was not wrong of the Israelites to rob the Egyptians (Ex 3 and 12). For that was ordered by God who knew what everyone was due to suffer. Nor did the Israelites commit theft, but they rendered a service to God who commanded them (C.14, q.5, c.12). And as luck would have it, the just consumed the work of the wicked (C.23, q.7, c.1; X 3.50.7). And

---

[32] Laws against the *laesae maiestatis crimen* are as old as the Roman republic and targeted various offences that were considered treason against the state. In Roman imperial and in medieval times this was most often understood as a crime that injured the dignity of the ruling monarch.

carere membris quam cum ipsis supliciis eternis deputari mathei ·V°· actuum ·XVIII°· marci ·IX°· XXIIII· quescione ·III· capite *illud sane* ʳ similiter saluator ve illi per quem scandalum veniet mathei ·XVIII°· luce ·XVII°·

ʳ et si quid orridum uel graue timetur bono viro non consuleret ut pro repeticione bonorum tantum suscitaret scandalum in capitulo *suscepimus de homicidio* et capitulo ·II· *de noui operis nunciacione* et innocencius in capitulo *si uero de sentencia excomunicacionis* ʳ nec hoc casu pecat pilatus supersedendo ubi verisimiliter arbitratur quod diferendo tempus reparabit rem suam ·XXIIII· quescione ·VII· capite *conuenior* et capite *quando* ·XI· quescione ·III· ʳ vnde contra istos sediciosos scriptum legi ecce in celo testis meus et sequitur dimitamus stultos foris loqui quod uolunt quid enim aliud detrahentes faciunt nisi in puluuerem suflant et in oculos suos terram excitant vnde plus detraccionis perflant vnde magis nichil veritatis videant in capite *inter verba* ·XI· quescione ·III· ʳ isti namque sediciosi de iure capitaliter puniuntur cum sit lese iulie magestatis crimen in lege ·I· et ·II· Codice *de sediciosis* · ergo dicta verba sunt omnino cauenda ʳ vnde dauid in psalmo ·CXIX°· domine libera animam meam a labiis iniquis et a lingua dolosa ·

·Xᵘˢ· articulus quod in hoc seculo boni paciuntur et reprobi gloriantur

Non tamen fuit erroneum israelitarum spoliandi egipcios exodi ·III°· et ·XII°· illud enim deus iussit qui nouerat quid quemque pacti oportuerat ʳ nec israelite furtum fecerunt · sed deo iubenti ministerium prebuerunt in capite *dixit dominus* ·XIIII· quescione ·IIII· ʳ et forte ut labores impiorum iusti ederent capite *quicumque*

---

73   ve...veniet Mt 18:7, Lc 17:1.   82   ecce...meus Iob 16:20.
89   domine...89 dolosa Ps 119:2.   3   spoliandi egipcios Ex 3:21-22, Ex 12:35–36.

---

72   illud sane C.24, q.3, c.34.   77   suscepimus X 5.12.10. | capitulo ·II· X 5.32.2.   78   si uero X 5.39.3.   81   conuenior C.23, q.8, c.21. | quando C.11, q.3, c.23.   85   inter...85 verba C.11, q.3, c.55.   87   lege....II· Cod. 9,30,1-2.   6   dixit dominus C.14, q.5, c.12.   7   quicumque C.23, q.7, c.1.

often what is stowed away by wolves becomes the plunder of foxes (Prv 11) [sic].³³ And the voice of the Lord [says]: *the kingdom of God will be taken away from you and will be given to a people doing justice* [Mt 21:43] (C.23, q.7, c.1-2). And also the Saviour says: *I have sent you to reap what you did not sow. Others have worked and you entered into their work* (Io 4:38).

They in turn who rob the greedy rich in order to give to the poor – their thinking is prompted by the devil's cunning. For [even] if they divided all of what they carried off, they would rather add [to their] sin than reduce it (C.14, q.5, c.3). For *he who offers a sacrifice out of the livelihood of a poor man is the same as one who would sacrifice a son in the sight of his father. The bread of the needy is the life of the poor, and who defrauds him is a man of blood. The one who spills blood and the one who commits fraud against a dependent are brothers* (Sir 34:24-25.27; C.1, q.1, c.27; C.14, q.5, c.2). And about these pillagers I have read: *I have seen the likeness of adulterers and the way of lying. And they strengthened the hands of the worst people so that not a single one turned away from their wickedness* (Ier 23:14). Not even to redeem the life of a captive is the crime of usury allowed to be involved (X 5.19.4).

Vices should not secretly enter under the guise of virtues (X 5.7.14; D.41, c.6). For there must be no wickedness committed under the pretext of piety (C.30, q.1, c.3). And: there must be no evil done under the pretext of good (C.1, q.1, c.27; the admirable gloss to X 3.50.3). And: pretended righteousness is twofold wickedness. And: often vices introduce themselves and falsely claim to be virtues, like avarice wants to be seen as parsimony,

---

33) The quote seems to be taken from the legal commentary by Giovanni d'Andrea (or Johannes Andreae, c. 1270–1348) on X 3.50.5. His *Novella Commentaria in quinque libros decretalium* actually attribute this aphorism to the Roman playwright Titus Maccius Plautus (ca. 254–184 BC) but cross-reference it with Prv 11. Giovanni was a celebrated doctor of law at the universities of Padua, Pisa and Bologna. A great number of (ahistorical) quaint anecdotes surrounding his life bears witness to his enormous fame, both contemporary and posthumous.

·XXIII· quescione ·VII· et capitulo *relatum ne clerici uel monachi* ʳ et sepe recondita luporum sunt rapine vulpium sapiencie ·XI°· ʳ et illa vox domini auferetur regnum dei a uobis et dabitur genti facienti iusticiam in capite *si de rebus* et capite *quicumque* ·XXIII· quescione ·VII· ʳ ad idem saluator ait misi uos metere quod non seminastis · alii laborauerunt et vos in labores eorum introistis iohannis ·V°· capitulo

ʳ sed qui rapiunt diuitibus auaris ut dent pauperibus huius cogitacio diaboli caliditate sugeritur · nam si totum tribuerunt quod abstulerunt adunt pocius pecatum quam minuant in capite *forte* ·XIIII· quescione ·IIII· ʳ qui enim ofert sacrificium de substancia pauperis idem est acsi victimet filium in conspectu patris · panis egencium vita pauperis est et qui defraudat illum homo sanguis est qui efundit et qui sanguinem fraudem fecit necessario fratres sunt ecclesiastici ·XXIIII°· ·I· quescione ·I· *non est putanda* ·XIIII· quescione ·I· *inmolans* ʳ et de hiis depredatoribus legi · vidi similitudinem adulterii et iter mendacii confortauerunt manus peximorum ut non conuerteretur a malicia sua vnusquisque ieremie ·XXIII°· ʳ nec pro redimenda vita captiui usurarum crimen debet inuolui in capitulo *super eo de usuris*

ʳ ne vicia sub specie virtutum subintrent in capitulo *sicut de hereticis* ·XLI· distincione capite *seppe* ʳ quia pretestu pietatis non est inpietas comictenda ·XXX· quescione ·I· capite *nosse* ʳ et pretestu boni malum non est faciendum ·I· quescione ·I· *non est putanda* glossa mirabilis in capitulum *non magno ne clerici uel monachi* ʳ et simulata equitas est duplex iniquitas ʳ et seppe vicia se ingerunt et se virtutes esse menciuntur ut tenecia parsimonia efusio largitas crudelitas zelus iusticie

---

25 fol. 12r

---

10 auferetur...**11** iusticiam Mt 21:43.   **12** misi...**13** introistis Io 4:38.
17 qui...**20** sunt Sir 34:24–25.27.   **22** vidi...**24** vnusquisque Ier 23:14.

8   relatum X 3.50.7. | et²...**9** vulpium Giovanni d'Andrea: *Novella Commentaria in quinque libros decretalium* on X 3.50.5.   **11** si...rebus C.23, q.7, c.2. | quicumque C.23, q.7, c.1.   **16** forte C.14, q.5, c.3.   **21** non... putanda C.1, q.1, c.27.   **22** inmolans C.14, q.5, c.2.   **25** super eo X 5.19.4.
27   sicut X 5.7.14.   **28**   seppe D.41, c.6.   **29**   nosse C.30, q.1, c.3.
30 non²...putanda C.1, q.1, c.27.   **31** non magno X 3.50.3.

lavishness as liberality, cruelty as fervour for justice, negligence as forgiveness (D.41, c.6). By this the gloss to X 4.20.7 is rejected that demands that if a ward has nothing from which to eat but his estate, the guardian is obliged to lend some of it (gloss to D.46, c.10).

And in this age those who are robbed say with Job: *the Lord has given, the Lord has taken, his name be praised! And as it pleased him, so it is done* (Iob 1:21). And in the holy scriptures it is written not only to chastise an unruly son, but to beat his flanks, so that he be compelled to good discipline and guided by the Lord. Hence the wise affirms: *you beat him with a rod! But you will liberate his soul from death* (Prv 23:14; C.23, q.4, c.38). And: *a father chastises a son whom he loves* [Prv 3:12] (X 5.34.12; C.5, q.5, c.2).

And also Paul: *my son, do not neglect the discipline of the Lord, and do not get weary when you are rebuked by him. For the Lord punishes whom he loves. He flogs every son whom he receives. Hold out in discipline, God behaves towards you as to children. For who is a son whom the father does not chastise? And if you are without the discipline of which all are made partakers, then you are illegitimate and not children* (Hbr 12:5-8). And elsewhere: *behold, I will surround your ways with thorns and fortify them with square stones*, that is: I shall take away the ability of sinning (Os 2:6; C.23, q.4, c.22).

And: it was more wholesome to lose goods than bodies, and [more wholesome to lose] bodies than souls. For *a man will give everything for his life* (Iob 2:4). And: *what good is it for a man if he gains the whole world but*

remisio pietas vellit videri in capite *sepe* ·XLI· distincione ʳ per hec reprobatur glossa capitulum *per vestras de dote post diuorcium restituenda* que uult quod si pupillus non habet nisi pecuniam vnde alatur tutor cogitur ex illa fenerari glossa in caput *sicut non suo* ·XLVI· distincione

ʳ Et isto tempore derrobati dicent cum iob ·I°· capitulo dominus dedit dominus abstulit sit nomen eius beneditum ʳ et sic ei placuit sic factum est ʳ et in sacris scripturis scribitur filium durum non solum corripere sed latera eius tundere ut ad bonam disciplinam cohatus et domino dirigatur · vnde sapiens ait tu percute eum virga animam autem eius liberas a morte in capite *displicet* ·XXIII· quescione ·IIII· ʳ et pater filium quem diligit corripit in capitulo *cum in iuuentute de purgacione vulgari* et capite *non omnis* ·V· quescione ·V·

ʳ ad idem paulus filii mi nolli negligere disciplinam domini nec fatigeris dum ab eo argueris quem enim deligit dominus castigat flagelat autem omnem filium quem rescipit in disciplina perseuerate tanquam filiis ofert se deus uobis · quis enim filius quem non corripit pater et si extra disciplinam estis cuius participes facti sunt omnes ergo adulteri et non filii estis ad ebreos ·XII°· capitulo ʳ et alibi ecce ego sepiam vias tuas spinis et muniam eas lapidibus quadratis id est tolam facultatem pecandi osee ·II°· capitulo ·XXIII· quescione ·IIII· capite *nabuchodonosor*

ʳ Et salubrius fuit perdere bona quam corpora et corpora quam animas · quia cunta dabit homo pro anima sua iob ·II°· capitulo ʳ et quid prodest homini si vniuersum mundum lucretur anime vero sue detrimentum paciatur mathei ·XVI°· marci ·VIII°· et capitulo *matheus*

---

47 filii Vulgate: fili

---

39 dominus…**41** est Iob 1:21. **43** tu…**44** morte Prv 23:14. **45** pater… corripit Prv 3:12. **47** filii…**52** estis Hbr 12:5–8. **52** ecce…**53** quadratis Os 2:6. **57** cunta…sua Iob 2:4. **58** quid…**59** paciatur Mt 16:26, Mc 8:36.

34 sepe D.41, c.6. **35** per vestras X 4.20.7. **37** sicut…suo D.46, c.10. **44** displicet C.23, q.4, c.38. **45** cum…iuuentute X 5.34.12. **46** non omnis C.5, q.5, c.2. **55** nabuchodonosor C.23, q.4, c.22. **59** matheus X 5.3.23.

suffers the loss of his soul (Mt 16:26, Mc 8:36; X 5.3.23)? Hence: *do not fear those who kill the body, but cannot kill the soul, but rather fear him who can destroy soul and body in hell* (Mt 10:28, Lc 12:5; C.11, q.3, c.86).

And how greatly does the Saviour console those who are persecuted and robbed by saying: *blessed are those who suffer persecution for the sake of justice and hunger for it. Blessed are the sorrowful. Blessed are they who mourn* (Mt 5:5.10; Lc 6:21). And it follows: *blessed shall you be when people curse you and do every evil against you for my sake* – that is: because you are Christians and have faith – *rejoice on that day, for your reward is plentiful in heaven* (Mt 5:11-12, Lc 6:22-23; D.2, c.92 de cons.; C.23, q.4, c.42). An so the Saviour promises eternal glory to them who are persecuted in this age. And elsewhere: often the evil persecute the good (Gn 21; C.23, q.4, c.37).

These plunderers are lamented by the prophet in Is 5:20, where he says: *woe to those who put bitter for sweet, for honey poison. Woe to those who grant favours to have the widows and orphans of my people plundered* (Is 10:1-2). *Who does such things shall not have the kingdom of God* (I Cor 6:10; D.3, c.18 de poen.). For they go directly against what is said in Is 1:16-17: *remove your evil intention from my eyes! Learn to do good! Cease to act perversely! Help the oppressed! Judge for the orphan, defend the widow!* These persecuted people are something pitiful. But one must not wonder if God allows this to happen, for he had foretold in the gospel that near the end of time *false messiahs [and] false prophets arise and seduce many,* (Mt 24:24-25, Mc 13:22-23) and

de simonia ʳ unde nolite timere eos qui occidunt corpus animam autem non posunt occidere sed pocius timete eum qui potest animam et corpus perdere in gehenam mathei ·X°· luce ·XII°· XI· quescione ·III· *nolite timere*

ʳ et saluator quam valde consolatur persecutos et derrobatos inquiens · beati qui persecucionem paciuntur propter iusticiam et eam exuriunt · beati tristes · beati qui lugent et sequitur · beati eritis cum maledixerint vos gentes et fecerint omne malum aduersus vos propter me id est quia xpistiani estis et fidem habetis gaudete in illa die quoniam merces vestra copiosa est in celis mathei ·VI°· luce ·VI°· *de consecracione* distincione ·II· capite *acceserunt de penitencia* distincione ·I· *fleat* et capite *si ecclesia* ·XXIII· quescione ·IIII· ʳ et sic saluator policitus est gloriam eternam in hoc seculo persecutis ʳ et alibi seppe mali persecuti sunt bonos genesis ·XXI°· et capite *nimium* ·XXIII· quescione ·IIII·

ʳ hos depredatores lamentat propheta ysaie ·V°· capitulo dicens ue illis qui ponunt pro dulci amarum pro mele uenenum · ve illis qui prestant fauorem ut depredentur uiduas et orfanos populi mei ʳ qui talia agunt regnum dei non posidebunt ad corinthios ·VI°· *de penitencia* distincione ·III· capite *sane* ʳ isti enim directo veniunt contra dictum ysaie primo capitulo auferte malum cogitacionum vestrarum ab oculis meis discite benefacere quiescite agere peruerse · subuenite opreso · iudicate pupillo defendite viduam ʳ isti persecuti sunt mendicum ʳ Sed ne mirandum si hec permictat deus fieri cum predixerat in euangelio circa finem seculi pseudo xpistos pseudo prophetas surgere et multos seducere et fideles suos in mundo multas

---

69 fol. 12v

---

60 nolite...**62** gehenam Mt 10:28, Lc 12:5.   **65** beati...**69** celis Mt 5:5.10–12, Lc 6:21–23.   **74** ue...**77** mei Is 5:20, Is 10:1–2.   **76** qui...**78** posidebunt I Cor 6:10.   **79** auferte...**82** viduam Is 1:16–17. **83** pseudo[1]...**85** seducere Mt 24:24–25, Mc 13:22–23.

---

63 nolite timere C.11, q.3, c.86.   **70** acceserunt D.2, c.92 de cons. | fleat D.1, c.79 de poen.   **71** si ecclesia C.23, q.4, c.42.   **73** nimium C.23, q.4, c.37.   **78** sane D.3, c.18 de poen.

his faithful are to suffer many hardships, but still *the gates of hell are not to prevail* [Mt 16:18].

So then, as the apostle affirms, *it is proper that there are heresies, so that they who are tested become evident*. It is necessary for us with the prophet [Ezekiel] to *rise against odds and put up a wall for he house of Israel* and with the apostle [Paul] to *enter through many tribulations into the kingdom of God, for the fellow sufferings of this time are not worth as much as the future glory that will be revealed in us* (Ez 13:5; Rm 8:18; C.1, q.3, c.8). And: they shall be mindful – as is written in Idt 8:21-25 – for *our fathers were tempted to be proven if they truly worshipped their God. And Abraham was tempted [and] being proven by many tribulations he was made a friend of God. So Isaac, so Jacob, so Moses and all who pleased God passed as faithful through many tribulations. But those who did not accept the temptations with fear of the Lord and brought forth their impatience and murmured reproach against the Lord were destroyed by the destroyer and perished by serpents*, as follows there.

It is therefore expedient with the apostle Paul (Rm 12:18) to *maintain charity towards the hateful; and if they would not have peace with us, still we would no doubt have [peace] with them* (C.11, q.3, c.55). For *a furnace tries a potter's vessels, but temptation [tries] just men* (Sir 27:6; D.2, c.40 de poen.). And *if they are tested, they will receive the crown that God promised to those who love him* (Iac 1:12). And elsewhere: if the church is the true one, it is she herself that suffers persecution (C.23, q.4, c.42). And Io 12:4: *if a grain –* that is: a man – *does [not] fall into the earth*; one may know: were not killed

habituros presuras · sed tamen portas inferi non preualituras marci ·XIII°· mathei ·XXIIII°·

ʳ proinde ut ait apostolus oportet esse hereses ut qui probati sunt magnifesti fiant · oportet nos cum propheta ex aduerso consurgere et murum oponere pro domo israel et cum apostolo per multas tribulaciones intrare in regno dei quoniam non sunt condigne compasiones huius temporis ad futuram gloriam que reuelabitur in nobis in capite *saluator* ·I· quescione ·III· ʳ et sint memores illorum que scribuntur iudit ·V°· capitulo quia temptati sunt patres nostri ut probarentur si uere colerent deum suum et abraham temptatus est per multas tribulaciones probatus amicus dei efectus est sic ysac · sic iacob sic moises et omnes qui placuerunt deo per multas tribulaciones transierunt fideles ʳ illi autem qui temptaciones non susceperunt cum timore domini et inpacienciam suam et properium murmuracionis sue contra dominum protulerunt exterminati sunt ab exterminatore et a serpentibus perierunt ut ibi sequitur

ʳ expedit ergo cum apostolo paulo caritatem erga obedientes seruare et si illi nobiscum pacem non habeant nos tamen cum illis sine dubio habeamus in capite *inter uerba* ·XI· quescione ·III· ʳ vasa enim figuli probat fornax homines autem iustos temptacio ecclesiatici ·VI°· *de penitencia* distincione ·II· *si enim* ʳ et cum probati fuerint recipient coronam quam repromisit deus diligentibus se iacobi ·I· *de renunciacione* capitulo *nisi cum pridem* verso *verum* ʳ et alibi si ecclesia vera est ipsa est que persecucionem patitur in capite *si ecclesia* ·XXXIII· quescione ·IIII· ʳ et in euangelio iohannis ·XII°· si granum id

---

90   regno Vulgate: regnum   98   properium Vulgate: improperium
101 obedientes Vulgate: odientes   109 si Vulgate: nisi

---

85 portas...preualituras Mt 16:18.   87 oportet...89 fiant I Cor 11:19.
89 murum...israel Ez 13:5. | per...91 nobis Rm 8:18.   92 sint...101 sequitur Idt 8:21–25.   101 caritatem...104 habeamus Rm 12:18.
103 vasa...105 temptacio Sir 27:6.   105 cum...107 se Iac 1:12.   109 si...112 manet Io 12:24.

---

92 saluator C.1, q.3, c.8.   103 inter uerba C.11, q.3, c.55.   105 si enim D.2, c.40 de poen.   107 nisi...pridem X 1.9.10.   108 si ecclesia C.23, q.4, c.42.

in this time – that is: if there were no persecutions and difficulties – *it remains alone.* That is: *woe to the lonely, for if he should fall, he will have no one to lift him up* (Ecl 4:10; X 3.35.2). However, if it is killed it will bear fruit in virtue and holiness. Here [says] the apostle [Paul]: *when I am weak, then I am stronger* (II Cor 12:10). For sometimes the weakness of the body brings strength to the will, and ardour of the spirit raises one to higher things (X 1.9.10).

On that account, no one shall be troubled by seeing mean people enjoy prosperity. For here there is no retribution of malice nor of virtue. And if it sometimes happens that there be some retribution of either malice or virtue, it is still not according to what is befitting, but simply like a certain taste of justice or judgment, so that by such things be taught those who do not believe in resurrection. Thus when we see someone evil grow rich, we should not be worried; when we see someone good suffer bad things, we should not be disturbed – there a crown, there torments. There is also another reason, for an evil man cannot be evil in everything but has some good, nor [can] a good man be good in everything but has some sin. When therefore the evil man has prosperity, it is unfortunate for his life, for if he receives the recompense for that little good here, he will be punished even harder then (D.3, c.48 de poen.). And: *every friend of this world is an enemy of God* (Iac 4:4; C.23, q.4, c.15).

Hence the apostle greatly commended the faith of Moses and proclaimed it to be worthy of praises, when *he denied himself to be a pharaoh's son and preferred to be afflicted with [his] brethren rather than enjoy the pleasure* of an elder's palace; when he out of compassion for a brother buried a [slain] Egyptian in the sand; *when he, [not] fearing the king's wrath, left Egypt* (Hbr 11:24-27; Ex 2; D.2, c.39 de poen.).

est homo in terra cadens scilicet in hoc seculo non mortificatum fuerit   110
id est non habuerit persecuciones et angustias ipsum solum manet id
est ve soli quia si ceciderit non habebit subleuantem in capitulo
monachi de statu monachorum ʳ si autem illud mortificatum fuerit
frutificabit in virtute et santitate ʳ hinc apostolus cum infirmor forcior
sum quia nonnumquam infirmitas corporis fortitudinem inducit   115
animi et feruor spiritus ad superiora ascendit in capite *nisi cum pridem
de renunciacione*

ʳ idcirco nemo videns malignos prospcritate gaudere turbetur non
enim est hic retribucio malignitatis nec virtutis ac si aliquando contin-
geret ut aliqua sit retribucio uel malicie et virtutis non tamen secun-   120
dum quod dignum est sed simplice ueluti quidam gustus uel iusticie
uel iudicii ut qui resureccionem non credunt talibus doceantur ·
quando itaque uidemus malignum ditescere non subrruamur quando
videmus bonum mala pati non turbemur illic corona illic suplicia ʳ est
et alia racio quia non potest malus in omnibus malus esse sed aliqua   125
bona habet nec bonus in omnibus bonus esse sed habet aliqua pecata ·
quando ergo prosperitatem habet malus malo capitis sui cum enim
pro illis paucis bonis retribucionem hic accipit illic iam plenius
punietur in capite *quid ergo de penitencia* distincione ·III· ʳ et omnis
amicus huius seculi inimicus dei est iacobi ·IIIIº· XXIII· quescione   130
·IIII· § *ex hiis omnibus*

ʳ vnde apostolus valde comendauit fidem moisi dignisque preconiis
eius merita predicauit dum se negauit esse filium pharaonis malens
afligi cum fratribus quam perflui iocunditate presbiteralis palacii dum
fratri compaciens egypcii fabulo obrruit dum ueritus animositate regis   135
egyptum reliquit exodi ·IIº· *de penitencia* distincione ·II· § *oponitur*

---

114 fol. 13r   **134** perflui Vulgate: perfrui   **135** fabulo Vulgate: sabulo
animositate Vulgate: animositatem

112 ve...subleuantem Ecl 4:10.   **114** cum...**116** sum II Cor 12:10.
129 omnis...est Iac 4:4.   **132** fidem...**137** reliquit Hbr 11:24–27, Ex 2.

113 monachi X 3.35.2.   **116** nisi...pridem X 1.9.10.   **129** quid ergo D.3,
c.48 de poen.   **131** ex...omnibus C.23, q.4, c.15.   **136** oponitur D.2, c.39
de poen.

Because of this the impious Saracens grow strong in this age, but it is unfortunate for their lives. Against them it is allowed to fight, for they occupy the Holy Land consecrated by the blood of Jesus Christ, which belongs to us, as [Pope] Innocent [III] notes in X 3.34.8. Hence the prophet [says] in Ps 17:38: *I will pursue my enemies and seize them and not turn back until they pass away* (C.23, q.4, c.42). And: *he will perish, for he told a lie* (Ps 5:7). And about his lie the gloss to Clem 5.2.1 notes: and because those Hagarenes are children of a slave girl, they must not inherit the Holy Land. As Gn 21:10 [has it]: *cast out Hagar the slave girl*, from whom, we read, the Hagarenes descend, *and her son* Ismael, from whom they also descend, *for that same son of a slave girl shall not be an heir together with my son Isaac*, from whom we Christians descend (C.32, q.2, c.12; C.32, q.4, c.2; C.32, q.4, c.9); most of all if the Hagarenes were at first Christians, as the gloss to the word "Mohammed" in said Clem 5.2.1 notes. And: they sinned against Christ. Like erring heretics their children who follow the parents' errors must lose goods and possessions and the Holy Land (X 5.7.10 and there the gloss at the end). For their goods are confiscated (VI 5.2.19 and the note in X 5.40.26).

From this follows that the Hagarenes will perish in short time and leave the Holy Land to us. So it was prophesied by Is 21:16-17, where *the children of Cedar*, the children of Ismael *will be destroyed and their strongmen will be devastated*. And so, with God as leader, their perdition will not be delayed,

ʳ hinc est quod improbi sarraceni in hoc seculo ualde prosperantur sed malo suorum capitorum ʳ contra quos licitum est punare quia detinent terram santam consecratam sanguine ihesu xpisti que ad nos pertinet ut notat innocencius in capitulo *quod super de uoto et uoti rredempcione* ʳ vnde propheta in psalmo ·XVIIº: persequar inimicos meos et comprehendam illos et non conuertar donec deficiant in capite *si ecclesia* ·XXIII· quescione ·IIII· ʳ et perdetur quia locutus est mendacium psalmo ·V· *verba mea* et de mendacio eius notat glossa in clementinum unicum *de iudeis et sarracenis* ʳ et cum isti agareni sint filii ancile non debent hereditare terram santam iuxta id genesis ·XXIº· eice agar ancila a qua agarenos descendise legimus et filium eius ismael a quo eciam descendunt quia non erit heres ipse filius ancile cum filio meo ysac a quo xpistiani descendimus in capite *non omnis* ·XXXII· quescione ·II· et quescione ·IIII· capite *recurrat* et capite *dicat* ʳ maxime cum prius agareni fuerunt xpistiani ut notat glossa in verbo *machometi* in dictum clementinum unicum *de iudeis et sarracenis* · et prevaricati sunt in xpistum ut erronei heretici debent eorum filii qui errorem parentum sunt secuti perdere bona et posesiones et terram santam in capitulo *uergentis de hereticis* et ibi bona glossa fine ʳ quia sunt eorum bona confiscata in capitulo *cum secundum de hereticis* libro sexto et nota in capitulo *super quibusdam de verborum significacione*

ʳ ex quo sequitur quod agareni in breui tempore peribunt et relinquent nobis terram santam sic prophetauit ysaias ·XXIº· capitulo ubi filii cedar filii ismael destruentur et fortes eorum uastabuntur ʳ et sic deo duce non morabitur eorum perdicio secundum quod legi in

---

162 fol. 13v

---

141 persequar...**143** deficiant Ps 17:38. **143** perdetur...**145** mendacium Ps 5:7. **147** eice...**150** ysac Gn 21:10. **161** filii[1]...uastabuntur Is 21:16–17.

---

140 quod super X 3.34.8. **143** si ecclesia C.23, q.4, c.42. **145** de... sarracenis Clem 5.2.1. **149** non...**151** omnis C.32, q.2, c.12. **150** recurrat C.32, q.4, c.2. **151** dicat C.32, q.4, c.9. **155** uergentis X 5.7.10. **156** cum...**158** secundum VI 5.2.19. **157** super quibusdam X 5.40.26.

according to what I have read in a consolatory work that someone highly skilled in this city composed about the destruction of Constantinople.[34]

And I am not to be refuted if I tried to prove something well-known, for Augustine proved something well-known, that is, that the Church does not fail to exist (C.24, q.1, c.33). And: for we blush with shame to speak without right (Nov. 18,5).

Eleventh article: that for many reasons misdeeds must be set right

I admonish you therefore, brothers, friends in Christ Jesus our Lord, that you have these aforementioned insulting letters removed and erased, so that by no means offences arise from where justice is begotten. And to correct this error should not make you ashamed who are ready to correct the error of others (X 5.1.24). And: he who must defend me, must not attack me.[35] And: where the pardon of sinners is to be demanded, there the opportunity to sin must not be granted, or else sins being committed must be arrested in the act (VI 3.23.2). Is it not because of you that the prophet says: *the Lord disdained the tabernacle and the tent in which he dwelt among men* (Ps 77:60)? And: he who provokes me to anger sins more gravely than I (gloss to D.55, c.13). From this is concluded, that if I move against you because of a word or deed of yours, for you I am not to be judged (Dig. 9,1,1). For out of just pain I committed the deed (Dig. 9,2,52).

And you are not allowed to conceal said words, because they verge on an offence to God. For we must not hide a disgrace of him who took away our disgrace (X 5.6.14). At least on Judgment Day the Saviour will bring forth

---

[34] The Ottoman conquest of Constantinople was not only a traumatic event for Greek Orthodox Christianity but resounded throughout the Latin west as well. Numerous authors struggled to come to terms with the fact that Muslims now ruled over one of Christianity's oldest and most famous strongholds. Cf. Agostino Pertusi, *La caduta di Costantinopoli*, vol. II: *L'eco nel mondo* (Milan, 1976). The work here referenced can not be attributed with certainty and may well be lost today.

[35] This maxim is derived from the gloss to X 1.2.13, though its origins are much older going back at least to Dig. 8,5,15. Apparently the author meant to insert a citation but ultimately failed to do so.

consolatoria quam fecit quidam prudentisimus super destrucionem constantinopole in hac vrbe ·

ͬ nec sum redarguendus si notoria probare conaui quia agustinus probat notorium scilicet ecclesiam non esse nullam ·XXIIII· quescione ·I· capite *pudenda* ͬ et quia erubescimur cum sine lege loquimur in auctentica *de triente et semisse* § *consideremus*

·XI^{us}· articulus quod multis ex causis maleficia sunt corrigenda

Moneo ergo vos fratres amici in xpisto ihesu domino nostro ut predictas literas iniuriosas abolere ac delere faciatis ne forte inde nascantur iniurie vnde iura nascuntur ͬ et ne pudeat vos errorem illum corrigere qui positi estis ut aliorum corrigatis errorem in capitulo *qualiter et quando* ·II⁰· *de accusacionibus* ͬ et qui me debet defendere non me debet impunare ͬ et ne ubi pecatorum est venia postulanda ibi pecandi detur ocasio · aut deprehendantur pecata commicti in capitulo *decet de inmunitate ecclesiarum* libro sexto ͬ ne forte propter vos dicat propheta psalmo ·LXVIII⁰· dedignauit dominus tabernaculum et tentorium in quo habitabat inter homines ͬ et grauius pecat qui me ad iracundiam prouocat quam ego glossa in caput *si euangelica* ·LV· distincione ͬ ex quo elicitur quod si ego dicto uel facto tuo intuli tibi ex hoc non sum tibi condempnandus articulum lege ·I· § *cum arietes* digestis *si quadrupes pauperiem fecisse* ͬ quia iusto dolore motus feci articulo lege *si ex plagis* § *tabernarius* digestis *ad legem aquilam*

ͬ nec licet vobis · dicta verba disimulare cum vergant in iniuriam dei quia non debemus illius dissimulare obprobrium qui probra nostra deleuit in capitulo *postulasti de iudeis et sarracenis* ͬ saltem in die iudicii saluator contra vos dictas literas ducat in testes iuxta id lapis de pariete clamabit et lignum quod inter iuncturas est respondebit

---

10 dedignauit...**11** homines Ps 77:60.   **21** lapis...**22** respondebit Hab 2:11.

167 pudenda C.24, q.1, c.33.   **168** consideremus Nov. 18,5.   **6** qualiter... quando X 5.1.24. | qui...**7** impunare X 1.2.13, Dig. 8,5,15   **9** decet VI 3.23.2.   **13** si euangelica D.55, c.13.   **15** cum arietes Dig. 9,1,1.   **16** si... plagis Dig. 9,2,52.   **20** postulasti X 5.6.14.

said letters as witnesses against you; similarly: *a stone in the wall will call out, and a beam that is between the joints will answer* (Hab 2:11). And to that the Lord [says]: *I am the judge and the witness* (Ier 29:23). And since said letters are written publicly you will not be able to pretend ignorance of them (X 1.5.1). And since they are depicted on the altar of yours of your convent where you live, I presume all the more that you are aware of and know [them] (X 2.23.7).

Hence the Lord says: *if someone sins before me, I will strike him out of the book of life* (Ex 32:33, Apc 3:5; D.4, c.7 de poen.). And it is no excuse for you, as it is not for a shepherd, when a wolf eats the sheep and he says: I do not know it (X 5.41.10). Be wary, therefore, of what is written! Ez 3:26: *I will make your tongue stick to the roof of your mouth* (X 1.9.10). He who does not set right such things, is to be called a lewd dog[36] rather than a prelate (D.83, c.2). And since said letters are *not of the faith, therefore they are a sin* (Rm 14:23; C.1, q.1, c.50; X 2.23.14).

They should therefore refrain themselves from a show of so much crime, for if Dina, the daughter of Jacob, had held herself back and had remained among her own, she would not have been defiled by the foreign Sichem (Gen 34:1-2; D.5, c.1 de poen.). And: I am not telling you to come out in public (D.1, c.87 de poen.). *The wicked shall therefore leave his way, and the sinful man his thoughts* (Is 55:7; D.1, c.87 de poen.)!

And unless you were laymen and common people it is about you and against you that the prophet [Sophonias] says in the person of the Lord: *my*

---

[36] An allusion to the play on words *dominicani* (Dominicans) – *domini canes* (the Lord's dogs) may be intended here.

abachuc ·II°· capitulo ʳ et ad idem dominus ego ero iudex et testis geremia ·XIX°· ʳ et quia dicte litere publice sunt scripte earum ignoranciam non poteritis pretendere in capitulo ·I· *de postulacione* *prelatorum* ʳ et cum in vestro altari vestri cenobii ubi degitis sint depicte tanto melius presumitur quod scistis et cognouistis in capitulo *quosdam de presumpcionibus*

ʳ vnde dominus ait si quis pecauerit ante me delebo eum de libro vite exodi ·XXXII°· *de penitencia* distincione ·IIII· *si quis pecata* ʳ nec est vestra excusacio cum nec sit pastoris si lupus comedat oues et ipse dicat nescio in capitulo *quamuis de regulis iuris* ʳ cauete ergo eorum que scribuntur ezechiel ·IIII°· linguam tuam adherere faciam palato tuo et in capitulo *nisi cum pridem de renunciacione* ʳ qui talia non corrigit magis dicendus est canis inpudicus quam prelatus in capite *nemo* ·LXXXIII· distincione ʳ et cum dicte litere ex fide non sunt ergo pecatum sunt ad rromanos ·XIIII°· capite *non sanat* ·I· quescione ·I· et capitulo *literas de presumpcionibus*

ʳ cohibeant ergo se a manifestacione tanti facinoris nam si dina filia iacob se cohibuisset et inter suos remansiset ab extraneo sichem corrupta non esset in capite *consideret de penitencia* distincione ·V· ʳ et non tibi dico quod te prodeas in publicum in capite *lacrime de penitencia* distincione ·I· ʳ derelinquat igitur impius viam suam et vir iniqus cogitacionem suam ysaie ·LV· *de penitencia* distincione ·I· § *hiis auctoritatibus*

ʳ et ne forte layci et plebei de uobis et contra uos cum propheta in persona domini dicat · sacerdotes mei contaminant santa et

---

39 fol. 14r

---

23 ego...testis Ier 29:23. **29** si...vite Ex 32:33, Apc 3:5. **33** linguam... **34** tuo Ez 3:26. **36** ex...**37** sunt Rm 14:23. **39** si...**41** esset Gen 34:1-2. **43** derelinquat...**44** suam Is 55:7. **47** sacerdotes...**48** legem So 3:4.

25 capitulo ·I· X 1.5.1. **28** quosdam X 2.23.7. **30** si...pecata D.4, c.7 de poen. **32** quamuis X 5.41.10. **34** nisi...pridem X 1.9.10. **36** nemo D.83, c.2. **37** non sanat C.1, q.1, c.50. **38** literas X 2.23.14. **41** consideret D.5, c.1 de poen. **42** lacrime D.1, c.87 de poen. **44** hiis... **45** auctoritatibus D.1, c.87 de poen.

priests pollute the sanctuaries and reject the law (So 3:4). And again: *o you priests who deceive my name and have said: wherein do we deceive your name? To which the answer is: by offering unclean breads at my altar, there is no good will for me in you, says the Lord* (Mal 1:6-7.10). And: *I will not accept sacrifices from your hands*, for you are unclean (Mal 2:13; D.81, c.23). For they who call by the name of *confesos* those who are called Christians after Christ deceive the name of our Saviour Jesus Christ and dishonour and reproach by such deception their own name of Christians. And also: is it not against you said with reason what I read written in C.24, q.3, c.33: all evils proceed from priests.

And this from the psalmist: *let their ways be dark and slippery, and the Lord's angel pursue them* (Ps 34:6; C.23, q.4, c.33). And also this: *their sacrifices are like breads of sorrow. All who eat [them] are defiled* (Os 9:4; C.1, q.1, c.70).

But that year of rebellion and uproar, when pillage sprang up in this city of distinguished men, shall be remembered no more. As Cato says: it is of evil to recall hostilities after friendly relations.[37] The aforementioned letters must be scratched out from before the eyes of the faithful, for what is written always speaks and does not cease to speak until it is deleted (Cod. 1,5,5).

Anyhow, in order not to betray the most famous King John II of glorious memory, our lord King Henry[38] must assume filial vengeance, for it is a most vile crime that taints an entire genealogy and passes to the descendants (X 5.7.9) and it is treason and a crime against the royal majesty.

And in cursing that year a short time before in order to mourn the misfortune over this city, the sun over the earth near noon went into a great

---

[37] The quote is taken from the *Disticha Catonis* (2:15), a collection of proverbs and aphorisms attributed to the ancient Roman statesman Cato the Elder (234–149 BC). Despite having more likely been composed under that pseudonym half a millennium later, the work was widely popular and generally believed to be authentic until modern times.

[38] As opposed to a later instance (cf. note 51), the appeal to King Henry IV is here not altered by a later amendment in favor of his half-brother and pretender to the throne Alfonso.

rreprobant legem ʳ et iterum O vos sacerdotes qui falitis nomen
meum et dixistis in qua rre fallimus nomen tuum · quibus
rresponsum est · offerentes ad altare meum panes polutos non est   50
michi uoluntas in uobis dicit dominus ʳ et sacrificium non accipiam
de manibus vestris quia poluti estis in capite *opportet* ·LXXXI·
distincione ʳ nomen enim saluatoris nostri ihesu xpisti falunt qui
xpistianos a xpisto vocatos uocant confessos et proprium nomen
xpistianorum falacia quadam dehonestant et vituperant ʳ et ad idem   55
ne contra vos cum racione dicatur quod scriptum legi in capite
transferuntur ·XXIIII· quescione ·III· omnia mala a sacerdotibus
proceserunt

ʳ et illud psalmiste fiant vie illorum tenebre et lubricum et angelus
domini persequens eos in capite *nabuchodonosor vires itaque* ·XXIII·   60
quescione ·IIII· ʳ et eciam illud sacrificia eorum tanquam panes luctus
omnes qui manducant contaminantur osee ·IXº· I· quescione ·I· *si
quis inquid*

¶ Sed annus ille sedicionis et tumultus quo in hac vrbe celeratorum
hominum preda inualuit non memoretur amplius ʳ cum dicat cato est   65
malorum post amicicias inimicicias meminisse ʳ rradantur predicte
litere ab oculis fidelium ʳ quia scriptatur semper loquitur et nec cesat
loqui donec resecatur articulo lege *ariani* Codice *de hereticis*

ʳ saltim ne prodicionis comisse contra illustrissimum regem gloriose
memorie iohannem secundum dominus noster rrex enrricus sumat   70
ulcionem filiorum cum sit uilissimum crimen totam genolosiam
corrumpens et transeat in posteros ut dictum capitulum *vergentis de
hereticis* et sit perdulionis et lese magistatis

ʳ et in detestacionem anni illius modico tempore ante lugendo mala
ventura super ciuitatem hanc sol circa meridiem per orbem terrarum   75
magnam fuit pasus eclipsim et ego illo tunc cum essem paruulus in

---

48 O...51 dominus Mal 1:6–7.10.   51 sacrificium...52 estis Mal 2:13.
59 fiant...60 eos Ps 34:6.   61 sacrificia...62 contaminantur Os 9:4.

---

52   opportet D.81, c.23.   57   transferuntur C.24, q.3, c.33.
60 nabuchodonosor C.23, q.4, c.23.   62 si...63 inquid C.1, q.1, c.70.
65 est...66 meminisse *Disticha Catonis* 2,15.   68 ariani Cod. 1,5,5.
72 vergentis X 5.7.9.

eclipse. And I myself saw it then when I was young, spending my time studying in Salamanca.[39] In that abominable year a warlike heresy grew strong, straining to produce sedition and a separation between faithful Christians. The divine and prophetic and also the evangelical law and the holy canons teach, how much this is abominable to God and against his saints, and it is obvious to almost all right believers (C.1, q.3, c.9). Therefore the almighty *God shall rise* and scatter such impious plans by *judging his cause* (Ps 73:22; D. 21, c. 7).

And if said letters are not deleted out of charitable love, they must at least be deleted out of fear of punishment. Hence the Lord says: *mine is vengeance. I will repay them in time so that their foot may slide.* And it follows: *praise his people, you nations, for he will avenge the blood of his saints* (Dt 32:35.43). For *whosoever belittles his brother is a murderer, and a murderer has no part of the kingdom of God* (I Io 3:15; C.6, q.1, c.16). And also the Lord [says]: *he who curses you shall be cursed, and he who blesses you shall be filled with blessings* (Gn 27:29; C.24, q.3, c.11). Also: *I will curse your maledictions* (Mal 2:2; D.81, c.15; C.1, q.1, c.76; C.1, q.1, c.84).

For according to a law of the Siete Partidas (7,25,3), calling a Christian *tornadizo* or *confeso* or something similar is to be severely punished as the judge seems fit. And because the law says *as the judge seems fit,* I say that considering place and time, persons and offensiveness, one can impose the death penalty (Dig. 48,11,7; most beautiful and singular the gloss to Inst. 4,4,10). And further: those who say words of the like pay 300 maravedi for

---

[39] Ramón Gonzálvez Ruiz links this mention to a documented eclipse in 1448 and thereby estimates the author's year of birth to be between 1430 and 1435 (see introduction).

studio salamantice degens vidi ʳ isto tan detestabili anno marcialis inualuit heresis que sedicionem et seccionem xpistianorum fidelium satagebat facere · quantum hoc sit detestabile deo santisque suis contrarum diuina et prophetica nec non euangelica lex et sacri canones docent et fere omnibus recte credentibus minifestum existit ·I· quescione ·III· capite *ex multis* ʳ exsurgat itaque deus omnipotens et tam nephanda consilia disipet iudicans causam suam psalmo ·LXXIIIº· capite *non autem* ·XXI· distincione

ʳ Et si non delentur dicte litere caritatis amore deleantur saltim formidine pene ʳ vnde dominus ait mea est ulcio ego retribuam eis in tempore ut labatur pes eorum ʳ et sequitur laudate gentes populum eius quia sanguinem santorum suorum ulciscetur deuteronomii ·XXXIIIº· ʳ omnis namque qui detrahit fratri sui homicida est et homicida non habet partem in regno dei iohannis ·IIIº· VI· quescione ·I· in *suma* ʳ et ad idem dominus qui maledixerit tibi sit maledictus qui benedixerit tibi benedicionibus repleatur genesis ·XXVIIº· XXIIII· quescione ·III· capite *sed qui* ʳ item maledicam maledictionibus vestris malachie ·IIº· capitulo ·LXXXI· distincione *si qui presbyteri* ·I· quescione ·I· *maledicam* et capite *multi*

ʳ nam de lege partite vocans xpistianum tornadiso o confesso uel quid simile crudeliter punietur ut iudici uisum fuerit ut ·VIIª· partita titulo ·XXVº· lege ·III· ʳ et quia lex dicit ut iudici uisum fuerit dico quod consideratis loco et tempore personis et scandalo poterit penam mortis infligere articulo lege *hodie* digestis *de penis* glossa est pulcherrima et singularis in § *in suma* institucionibus *de iniuriis* in verbo *extraordinaria* ʳ et ultra hec similia verba dicentes pro qualibet

---

80 fol. 14v

82 exsurgat…83 suam Ps 73:22. 86 mea…88 ulciscetur Dt 32:35.43.
89 omnis…90 dei I Io 3:15. 91 quiˡ…92 repleatur Gn 27:29.
93 maledicam…vestris Mal 2:2.

79 quantum…84 distincione A. Díaz de Montalvo, *Tractatus*, 5. 82 ex multis C.1, q.3, c.9. 84 non autem D.21, c.7 91 suma C.6, q.1, c.16.
93 sed qui C.24, q.3, c.11. 94 si…presbyteri D.81, c.15. 95 maledicam C.1, q.1, c.76. | multi C.1, q.1, c.84. 98 lege ·III· *Las Siete Partidas*, 7,25,3.
100 hodie Dig. 48,11,7. 101 in suma Inst. 4,4,10.

every instant, and if they do not have any wealth they shall be jailed for 15 days (ordinances of John II, 21st petition). The authors of those words therefore committed [the crime of] a defamatory publication,[40] and are to be severely punished (Cod. 9,36,2).

You, however, brothers – remove said words and do what the Lord orders when he tells you: *bestow my name upon the children of Israel* – that is: call them by the name of Christians after Christ Jesus – *I the Lord shall bless them* (Nm 6:27; C.1, q.1, c.96).

Twelfth article: that one who tolerates seditious evil is severely punished.

I am rising and leaving you, dearest brothers, so that you set right that error and the enraged God may not strike [your] souls (X 3.13.6). As an example, Eli who was a high priest, although he himself was good, nevertheless because he did not effectively censure the digressions of his sons drew equally on himself and on them the vengeance of deserved reproach. While his sons were slain in battle, he himself *falling from a stool died with his neck broken* (I Re 2; X 5.3.31).

Hence Ez 3:17-19: *son of man! I gave you to the house of Israel as a watchman, and you will hear the word from my mouth, and you shall announce it to them from me. And if I am telling the impious: you will die! And you do not announce it to him and you do not speak out so that he turns away from his impious path, this same impious man will die in his sin. I will, however, demand his blood from your hand.* And it follows: *if you do announce [a warning] to an impious man and he will not convert, he will die in his sin but you have delivered your soul.*

For they who act and they who consent are to be punished according to the testimony of scripture with equal sentence for the consent of a gross

---

[40] The legal term *libellus famosus* (slanderous pamphlet) dates back to ancient Roman times and denotes for juridical purposes any kind of punishable written insult or public denigration.

vice soluent ·CCC⁰ˢ· morapetinos et si non habent bona incarcerabuntur per ·XV· dies in ordinariis forie domini rregis iohannis secundi in ·XXI· peticione ʳ illa ergo verba depingentes comiserunt famosum libellum et grauiter essent puniendi lege ·I· Codice *de famosis libellis*

ʳ vos tamen fratres tolite dicta verba et facite quod precipit dominus dicens vos ponite nomen meum super filios israel id est vocate nomine xpistianos a xpisto ihesu ego dominus benedicam eos numeri ·VIº· I· quescione ·I· capite *dictum*

·XIIᵘˢ· articulus quod ualde punitur qui tolerat malum sediciosum

Ortor et secedo vos fratres amicissimi ut corrigatis errorem illum ne ob id iratus deus animas percuciat in capitulo *si quis presbyterorum de rebus ecclesie non alienandis* ʳ exemplo hely qui sumus sacerdos licet in se bonus existeret quia tamen filiorum excessus eficaciter non corripuit in se pariter et in ipsis animaduersionis digne vindictam excepit dum filiis suis in bello peremtis ipse de sella corruens fractis ceruicibus expirauit ·Iº· regum ·IIº· capitulo et capitulo *licet heli de symonia*

ʳ vnde ezechielis ·IIIº· filli hominis speculatorem dedi te domui israel et audies de ore meo verbum et anunciabis eis ex me et si dicente me ad impium morte morieris non anunciaueris ei nec locutus fueris ut auertatur a uia sua impia et uiuat ipse inpius in iniquitate sua morietur · sanguinem autem eius de manu tua requiram ʳ et sequitur si anunciaueris impio et non fuerit conuersus ipse in iniquitate sua morietur tu autem animam tuam liberasti ·

ʳ cum agentes et consencientes pari pena scripture testimonio puniuntur in consensu negligencie crase que est in prelatis in capitulo

---

12 fol. 15r

109 ponite...**110** eos Nm 6:27.   **8** dum...**8** expirauit I Sm 4:11.18.
10 filli...**16** liberasti Ez 3:17–19.

105 ·XXI· peticione *Ordenanzas reales de Castilla* 8,9,4.   **106** lege ·I· Cod. 9,36,2.   **111** dictum C.1, q.1, c.96.   **4** si...presbyterorum X 3.13.6.
9 licet heli X 5.3.31.   **18** capitulo...**19** ·I· X 1.29.1.

negligence (X 1.29.1). And: Catholic authority judges those to be punished with equal sentence, understanding them to support the wrongdoers, who desist from confronting an obvious crime, although they could [do so] (X 5.39.47). Also: an error not opposed is approved of; and truth when least defended is oppressed. To neglect where one could disturb the wicked is of course nothing else but to foster [them]. And: what good does it do not to be tainted by his own error to him who gives his consent to the erring? And: seen to consent with the erring is he who does not oppose that which is to be restricted and must be corrected. However, if it is not allowed to flatter the vices of others, than also not to delight the evil with praises (D. 83, c.3-5). For they who raise up with praises the evil deeds of men promote what must be rebuked (D.46, c.2).

Here Ez 13:18 [says]: *woe to them who sew cushions for every elbow and hand and make pillows for heads of all ages.* And it follows: *they themselves built a wall, but those plastered it* (Ez 13:10). And also, just as Job does not value the good of bad people, so he refuses to judge the good of bad people when he says: *far be it from me to judge you just. Until I die I will not part from my innocence* (Iob 27:5). On that account you will have to tear down the aforementioned wickedly depicted letters, most of all, as I believe you already know from the bull of the Holy Father, Lord Nicolas V,[41] vicar of Jesus Christ whose soul my rest in peace, that said seditious opinion is condemned which strains to make a division between Christians and without purpose tears apart little by little the *tunic of Christ, which is woven seamlessly from the top* [Io 19:23]. And: foxes destroy the vineyard of Christ among exhausted cisterns that have no water – that is to say: wisdom – that can hardly be understood there with the fount sealed and that garden closed (C. 24, q.1, c.25).
To those who denied the mandate of the Saviour's Passion he replied: I am coming to Rome to be crucified again (X 4.17.13) – an opinion that a

---

[41] Pope Nicolas V held office at the time of the 1449 insurrection of Toledo and condemned the actions taken there against the New Christians in several bulls. His ban of any discrimination against the *conversos* on pain of excommunication was generally held to be in effect at least until Alexander VI practically overturned it by granting a statute of blood purity to the Order of Saint Jerome in 1495.

·I· *de officio delegati* ʳ et pari pena plectendos catolica condempnat auctoritas eos delinquentibus fauere interpretans qui cum posint magnifesto facinori designunt obuiare in capitulo *quante de sentencia excomunicacionis* ʳ item error cui non resistitur aprobatur et veritas cum minime defensatur opprimitur ʳ negligere quippe est cum possit perturbare peruersos nichil est aliud quam fouere ʳ et quid prodest illi suo errore non polui qui consensum prestat erranti ʳ et consentire videtur erranti qui ad resecanda que corrigi debent non occurrit · si autem aliorum uicia palpare non debet ita nec malorum laudibus delectari in capite *error* et capite *quid prodest* et capite *consentire* ·LXXXIII· distincione ʳ augent enim quod increpare debuerunt qui dum malefacta hominum laudibus eferunt in capite *sunt nonnulli* ·XLVI· distincione

ʳ hinc ezechiel ·XXXIIIº· ve qui confluunt puluilos sub omni cubitu et manus et faciunt ceruicalia sub capite vniuerse etatis et sequitur ipsi enim edificabant parietem illi autem liniebant eum ʳ ad idem iob ·XXVIº· sicut mala de bonis non extimat ita iudicare bona de malis recusat dicens absit a me ut iustos vos iudicem donec deficiam non recedam ab inocencia mea · ʳ idcirco predictas literas nequiter depictas laniare debetis ʳ premaxime cum iam credo nostis per bullam santisimi patris domini nicholai quinti vicarii ihesu xpisti cuius anima in pace quiescat dictam sediciosam oppynionem esse dampnatam que diuisionem xpistianorum satagebat facere et indecisam domini tunicam desuper contextam minutatim per frustra discerpit ʳ et xpisti vineam exterminant vulpes inter lacos contrictos qui non habent aquam scilicet sapienciam dificile est ut ibi fons signatus et ortus ille conclusus posit inteligi ut capite *quoniam uetus* ·XXIIII· quescione ·I·

ʳ quibus saluatoris pasionis ministerium negantibus rrespondet venio rromam iterum crucifigi in capitulo *per venerabilem qui filii sint*

---

32 confluunt Vulgate: consuunt | cubitu…33 manus Vulagte: cubito manus

---

32 ve…33 etatis Ez 13:18.   33 ipsi…34 eum Ez 13:10.   36 absit…37 mea Iob 27:5.   42 tunicam…contextam Io 19:23.

---

21 quante X 5.39.47.   28 error D. 83, c.3. | quid prodest D. 83, c.4. consentire D. 83, c.5.   30 sunt nonnulli D. 46, c.2.   45 quoniam uetus C.24, q.1, c.25. 47 per venerabilem X 4.17.13.

foolish fig tree – namely: Pero Sarmiento[42] – produced in this imperial city in that year. And in order to cut down barren, pestilential and harmful branches Pope Boniface VIII of happy memory stood up against you (VI 5.3.1). And in memory and exaltation of our orthodox faith the same Roman pontiffs of the same most holy Church that is fertile with new offspring (X 3.1.11) consecrate white lambs.[43] And they are of great virtue in that they signify the new faithful of Christ and they are handed to us like relics that are allowed to be worn around the neck, as Henry[44] concludes in a comparison he makes about X 5.21.1; D.20, c.3 at the end. And there he notes: he who therefore raises division among Christians will not have the Holy Spirit who only comes to those assembled as one in the name of Jesus Christ (Mt 18:19-20; X 2.12.3).

Hence the Saviour as he was about to ascend to heaven said to the holy apostles and their followers: *behold, I am with you for all days until the end of time* (Mt 28:20; Clem 3.16.1). To give testimony for this he also said: *I give you my peace, I leave you peace* (Io 14:27; C. 23, q.1, c.1). For Christ came to teach peace (Mc 9:49, Mt 10:12-13, Io 14:27). And among other things he had given it first and to those among the children who are truly his own (Dig. 28,2,11; enough what is noted in the rest of the title about X 3.26.16 and VI 3.11.1). And: *if it is possible, for your part, have peace with all men*

---

[42] The abbreviation "pe. pal." does not spell out the name as such but very likely points to Pero Sarmiento, the leader of the 1449 anti-*converso* uprising in Toledo. The literal meaning (vine branch) of *sarmiento* in Spanish and *palmes* in Latin is here used as a play on words: Jesus calls his disciples branches of himself, the vine, meant to bear fruit (Io 15:1–8), whereas he curses a fig tree for not doing so (Mc 11:12–21).

[43] This remark possibly refers to a custom associated with the feast of Saint Agnes in Rome. Two lambs are traditionally blessed by the Pope and their wool later used for new pallia, the liturgical insignia worn around the neck by archbishops.

[44] Henry of Segusio, see note 18.

legitimi ʳ quam opynionem ficus fatua scilicet pe · pal · in hanc imperialem vrbem anno illo produxit ʳ et ad suscidendos infructuosos palmites pestiferos et nociuos bonifacius papa ·VIII^{us}· felicis memorie vos ortatur ut in capitulo *ad suscidendos de scismaticis* libro sexto ʳ Et in memoriam et exaltacionem nostre orthodoxe fidei idem rromani pontifices eiusdem sacrosante ecclesie que noua prole est fecunda ut in capitulo *deus qui de vita et honestate clericorum* agnos cereos consecrant ʳ et sunt magne uirtutis per illos designantes nouos xpistifideles et ut rreliquie nobis traduntur ʳ quos suspendere licet ad colum ut in simili determinat enrricus in capitulo *in tabulis de sortilegiis* facit capite *de quibus* ·XX· distincione in fine et ibi notatur ʳ qui igitur suscitat diuisionem inter xpistianos non habebit spiritum santum qui non uenit nisi in congregatos in vnum in nomine ihesu xpisti mathei ·XVIII⁰· et in capitulo *cum ecclesia subtrina de causa posessionis et proprietatis*

ʳ vnde saluator accensurus in celum dixit santis apostolis et eorum secacibus · Ecce ego uobiscum sum omnibus diebus usque ad consumacionem seculi in clementinis *si dominem* § *in hac de reliquiis et veneracione santorum* ʳ quibus eciam testando dixit pacem meam do uobis pacem relinquo uobis iohannis ·XIIII⁰· et capite *nisi bella* ·XXIII· quescione ·V· ʳ xpistus enim venit docere pacem marci ·X⁰· mathei ·IX⁰· iohannis ·XIIII⁰· ʳ et cum alia prius donauerat et inter filios qui sunt vere sui ut in lege *in suis* digestis *de liberis et postumis* · suficit quoquo relicto titulo nota in capitulo *raynucius* in verbo *relinquens de testamentis* et in capitulo *si pater* eodem titulo libro sexto ʳ et si fieri potest quod ex uobis est pacem cum omnibus hominibus

---

51 fol. 15v

60 in¹...**61** xpisti Mt 18:19–20.   **64** Ecce...**65** seculi Mt 28:20.
66 pacem...**67** uobis² Io 14:27.   **68** venit...pacem Mc 9:49, Mt 10:12-13, Io 14:27.   **73** si...**74** habentes Rm 12:18.

51 ad suscidendos VI 5.3.1.   **54** deus qui X 3.1.11.   **57** in tabulis X 5.21.1.
58 de quibus D.20, c.3.   **61** cum...subtrina X 2.12.3.   **65** si dominem Clem 3.16.1.   **67** nisi bella C.23, q.1, c.1.   **70** in suis Dig. 28,2,11.
71 raynucius X 3.26.16.   **72** si pater VI 3.11.1.

(Rm 12:18; C.11, q.3, c.55). And: for *the Romans signed a peace treaty with the Jews* (I Mcc 8:29; C.22, q.1, c.16).

However, he who does not want unity does not want peace, for the Lord says: *he who does not gather with me scatters* (Lc 11:23; Mt 12:30; C. 24, q.1, c.25). And he will not be an heir of his bequest without the Saviour's inheritance – that is to say: peace. And he will not enter into the holy *Jerusalem which is above, the free one*, city of God, a sight of peace (Gal 4:26; C.23, q.4, c.42). And he will not be fed on the abounding mountains of Israel, nor at the rivers or in any other habitation of the earth. Rather they will be *scattered on the day of gloom and darkness*, for they did not want to be in the unity and congregation of the sheepfold – one may see: the Church under Christ the shepherd (Ez 34:12). And he will not be able to say with the elect: *the Lord is part of my inheritance and I will stay in the inheritance of peace* (Sir 24:11.16).

And those do not believe in Christ who do not have charity and do not perform the faith through [works of] love (D.2, c.14 de poen.). To them it is to be said furiously: o you enemies of God and madmen, who have dishonoured the only bride of Christ – that is to say: the Catholic faith – who is so very worthy of the only bridegroom; as you have finally destroyed the seamless robe of Christ (C.16, q.7, c.19). Against you says the Lord God through the prophet [Jeremiah]: *you have scattered my flock and driven them away and have not visited them. I will visit upon you the malice of your workings, says the Lord. And I will gather together the rest of my flock from all the lands to which they expelled them, and I will bring them back to their tents. And they shall grow and multiply, and I will appoint [pastors] over them, and they will feed them, and they will no longer fear and be frightened, and none*

habentes ad romanos ·XII°· XI· quescione ·III· capite *inter uerba* ͬ et quia rromani pacem firmarunt cum iudeis mathei ·VIII°· XXII· quescione ·I· § *sic eciam*
ͬ qui tamen non vult vnionem non vult pacem dicente domino qui mecum non coligit dispergit mathei ·XII°· luce ·VI°· XXIIII· quescione ·I· *quoniam uetus* ͬ nec erit heres illius relicti sine hereditatis saluatoris scilicet pacis ͬ nec intrabit in santam iherusalem que sursum est libera ciuitas dei visio pacis ad gallatas ·IIII°· et capite *si ecclesia* ·XXIII· quescione ·IIII· ͬ nec pascetur in montibus uberrimis israel nec in riuis et in cuntis sedibus terre · sed dispergentur in die nubis et caliginis quia noluerunt esse in vnione et congregacione ouilis videlicet ecclesie sub xpisto pastore ut ezechielis ·34°· capitulo ͬ nec poterit cum electis dicere dominus pars hereditatis mee et in pacis hereditate morabor ecclesiastici ·XXIII°·

ͬ nec isti credunt in xpistum qui non habent caritatem nec operantur fidem per dileccionem in capite *amen dico de penitencia* distincione ·II· ͬ quibus furibunde dicendum est ͬ O deo infesti insanique qui maculastis vnicam xpisti sponsam scilicet catolicam fidem vnico tantum sponso condignam tunc inconsutilem xpisti tunicam demum lacerastis ut capite *sunt domini* ·XVI· quescione ·VII· ͬ contra uos dicit dominus deus per prophetam uos dispergistis gregem meum et eiecistis eos et non uisitastis eos · Ego uisitabo super uos maliciam studiorum vestrorum ait dominus ͬ et congregabo reliquias gregis mei de omnibus terris ad quas eiecerant eos illud et conuertam ad thentra sua et crescent et multiplicabuntur et suscitabo super eos et pascent eos et non formidabunt ultra et non pauebunt et nullus queretur ex

---

93 fol. 16r   97 thentra Vulgate: tentoria

75 quia…iudeis I Mcc 8:29.   77 qui²…78 dispergit Lc 11:23, Mt 12:30. 80 iherusalem…81 libera Gal 4:26.   82 pascetur…84 caliginis Ez 34:12-14.   86 dominus…87 morabor Sir 24:11.16.   94 uos…103 mei Ier 23:2–4.19–20.27.

74 inter uerba C.11, q.3, c.55.   76 sic eciam C.22, q.1, c.16.   79 quoniam uetus C.24, q.1, c.25.   81 si ecclesia C.23, q.4, c.42.   89 amen dico D.2, c.14 de poen.   90 O…104 ieremia A. Díaz de Montalvo, *Tractatus*, 54. 93 sunt domini C.16, q.7, c.19.

shall be missed out of [their] number, says the Lord. And it follows: *behold, a whirlwind of the Lord's anger will go forth, and a shattering storm will come over the head of the wicked. The Lord's wrath will not turn back until he fulfils his heart's plan, for they want to make my people forget my name* (Ier 23:2-4.19-20.27).

Just so the spiteful scribes of said words, against whom God is angered, want to forget the name of Christians derived from Christ our God in calling [them] "confesos".

Thirteenth article: that the power of the pope and the Church is great.

But *woe to me, for I have become like one who collects straw during harvest and like a bunch in the grape-gathering, when there are no early grapes to eat. Woe to my soul, for the God-fearing has perished from the earth and there is no one among all men who would set right* (Mi 7:1-2). And this from the gospel: *when Jesus saw Jerusalem he wept over her* (Lc 19:41). With even more reason will he weep over a Church *built out of living stones* (I Pt 2:5) for her *to be a house of prayer* (Is 56:7), but made by disgraceful words of criminals *into a den of robbers* (Ier 7:11, Mt 21:13, Mc 11:17, Lc 19:46; C.16, q.7, c.9). But since the religious of the same monastery imitate the insensibility of the pharaoh and stop up their ears after the habit of the asp, they despise his warnings with proud stubbornness (VI 2.14.2).

I have resolved to appeal to the pious, sweet, distinguished watchman of souls, the pastor of this most holy church of Toledo,[45] which the depth of the unknowable divine universal providence by an unchangeable order preferred to [all other] churches and wanted to hold the office of primate of all Spain.[46] She is worried by constant cares and urged by incessant

---

[45] Alonso Carrillo, see note 4.

[46] In the fifteenth century the primacy of Toledo was indeed well established, but not altogether undisputed. Burgos, Braga and Santiago de Compostela had their own traditions of primacy or at least of being independent from Toledo. The repetition of Toledo's claim in this treatise is therefore more a pledge of allegiance than a statement of the self-evident. On the other hand, what exactly constitutes "all of Spain" in this epoch is a rather vague concept and could or could not encompass Portugal, Aragon, Granada and even parts of North Africa. Cf. Jorge Díaz Ibáñez, 'Alonso de Cartagena y la defensa de la exención del

numero dicit dominus ʳ et sequitur Ecce turbo dominice indignacionis egredietur et tempestas dirumpens super capud impiorum ueniet · non reuertetur furor domini usque dum impleat cogitacionem cordis sui quia volunt facere ut obliuiscatur populus meus nominis mei ieremia ·XXIIIº·

ʳ sic maligni depingentes dicta uerba uolunt obliuisci nomen xpistianorum a xpisto deo nostro dicti uocando confessos contra quos furor est dei

·XIIIᵘˢ· articulus quod magna est potestas pape et ecclesie

Set ve michi quia factus sum sicut qui coligit stipulam in mese et sicut rracemum in uendemia cum non sint botri ad manducandum primogeniti ʳ ve anime mee quia periit timoratus a terra et qui corrigat in omnibus hominibus non est michee ·VIIIº· capitulo ʳ et illud euangelii cum uidisset ihesus ierosolimam fleuit super eam racionabilius flebit super ecclesiam lapidibus uiuis edificatam ut esset domus oracionis · factam autem propter turpia verba celeratorum derrobancium speluncam latronum in capite *et hec dicimus* ·XVI· quescione ·VII· ʳ quia tamen eiusdem monasterii religiosi pharaonis imitati duriciam et obturantes more aspidis aures suas huius monita elata obstinacione despiciunt ut in capitulo *ad apostolice de re iudicata libro sexto*

¶ Cogitaui recurrendum ad pium dulcem egregium vigilem animarum pastorem huius sacrosante toletane ecclesie ʳ quam inperscrutabilis diuine prouidencie altitudo vniuersis ordinacione incomutabili pretulit ecclesiis ʳ et tocius ispanie primatum obtinere uoluit magistratum ʳ curis solicitatur continuis et asidua meditacione urgetur ʳ et in subditorum comodis prosperatur ʳ cuius mores et vita apud deum et homines merito comendatur

---

20 fol. 16v

---

2 Set…**5** est Mi 7:1-2. **6** cum…eam Lc 19:41. **7** lapidibus…edificatam I Pt 2:5. **8** domus oracionis Is 56:7. | celeratorum…**9** latronum Ier 7:11, Mt 21:13, Mc 11:17, Lc 19:46.

---

9 et…dicimus C.16, q.7, c.9. **12** ad apostolice VI 2.14.2.

contemplation; and she whose manners and life before God and men is deservedly commended prospers to the benefit of [her] subordinates.

Besides, her name is glorious on account of the etymology of her own name.[47] Hence Sir 41:15: *take care of a good name! For this will prevail more than thousand treasures.*

Don Ildefonsus[48] speaks as a deep fountain out of which sweeter waters flow over the thirsting people of Spain (Ex 12; D.2, c.69 de cons.). Of this deep fountain I read in Ioel 3:18: a *fountain will spring forth from the house of the Lord and water the torrent of thorns*. About the same fountain prophesied Za 13:1: *on that day there will be a fountain open to the house of David and to the inhabitants of Jerusalem for the washing of sinners*. From its living water will the leprosy found on said wall be cleansed, as did Elisha (IV Rg 2:19-22). And he shall cast his shepherd's staff into the bitter water of those in error, *and the water's nature will lose its bitterness* (Ex 15:25). For he shall strike the rock with the rod of his power and it will pour out waters (D.2, c.83 de cons.). And on account of the massiveness of his deep fountain many peoples will arise (Apc 12; X 3.41.6). And: *blessed shall be those who will have sown by the waters* of this fountain (Is 32:20).

obispado burgalés frente al primado toledano', *En la España medieval*, 34 (2011), 325–42.

[47] Although the author does not elaborate this point, he most likely alludes to the folk etymology from the Latin *tollere* (to lift, to raise) making Toledo "the elevated one". It is worthy to note that a Hebrew folk etymology also exisited interpreting Toledo as the city of "generations" *(toledot)*. Historically though the latinised name of *Toletum* is probably derived from an ancient Celtic name possibly designating a "settlement on the hill".

[48] Ildefonsus (c. 607–67) was a famous archbishop of Toledo under Visigothic rule. He played an important part in the 8th and 9th council of Toledo and continued the historiographic work of Isidor of Seville. At the time of the *Reprehensorium* he was already one of the city's most revered patron saints. Legends surrounding his life include him receiving a chasuble by the virgin Mary herself and the brief resurrection of Saint Leocadia related in this treatise. The historic background of these miraculous episodes is probably Ildefonsus's ardent devotion to Mary and his propagation of her worship. Our author introduces him with a play on words, *altus fons* (deep fountain) being phonetically close to Ildefonsus.

⁋ tum ex sui proprii nominis ethimologia gloriosum est nomen eius ʳ vnde ecclesiastici ·XLI· curam habe de bono nomine hoc enim magis preualebit quam mille tasauri ·
dominus yllefonsus altus fons sonat ex quo dulciores aque dilabuntur super sicientem populum yspanie ut exodi ·XIIº· et capite *revera de consecracione* distincione ·II· ʳ de quo alto fonte legi ioelis in capitulo finale ʳ fons de domo domini egredietur et irrigabit torrentem spinarum ʳ de eodem fonte prophetauit zaccharias ·XIIIº· capitulo in die illa erit fons patens domui dauid et habitantibus in iherusalem in ablucionem pecatorum ʳ ex cuius aqua viua mundabitur lepra in dicto pariete reperta ut fecit eliseus ·IIIIº· regum ·IIº· ʳ mictetque bachulum sue pastoritatis in aquam amaram errancium et amaritudinem suam aquarum natura disponet exodi ·XVº· ʳ percuciet enim petram cum virga sue dominacionis et efundet aquas capite *in calice de consecracione* distincione ·II· ʳ et propter multitudinem eiusque alti fontis fient populi multi apocalypsis ·XIIº· et capitulo *cum marthe de celebracione misarum* ʳ et beati erunt qui seminauerint apud huius fontis aquas ysaie ·XXXIIº·

---

22 curam...23 tasauri Sir 41:15.   24 aque...25 populum Ex 17:6.
27 fons...28 spinarum Ioel 3:18.   28 in...30 pecatorum Za 13:1.
31 ut...eliseus IV Rg 2:19–22. | mictetque...33 disponet Ex 15:25.
35 propter...36 multi Hbr 11:12.   37 beati...38 aquas Is 32:20.

---

25 revera D.2, c.69 de cons.   34 in calice D.2, c.83 de cons.   36 cum marthe X 3.41.6.

Due to the merits of life then – I speak the truth and I do not lie – that what I take time to praise is what justly deserves to be praised; for with silent tongues her praises spring forth by divine power:

O virgin, most precious martyr by the name of Leocadia,[49] remember your miraculous resurrection, when on that feast day of yours, on which our bishop Saint Ildefonsus celebrated a solemn mass in your church before the glorious King Recceswinth,[50] the tomb was opened, the slab turned from above – you approached the altar! Embracing the same Saint Ildefonsus before the entire Christian people you commended [him] and said with a clear voice: "On account of Ildefonsus's life my lady [the virgin Mary] lives in the heavens", and you returned to the place of your rest. At the request of the same king who wished for your relics, Saint Ildefonsus seized with a sword one half of your most sacred head scarf, and the other half you held back as though with force and kept it until now. And for what did you keep it, blessed lady, crowned by God? To which she the benign seems to give me a response: "For another Ildefonsus I have kept the other half of my head scarf, so that I be joined to both in the glory of God that he has prepared for those who love him and that one be at my right and the other at the left."

Therefore, *the grace given from heaven is not to be neglected* (I Tim 4:14; D.93, c.24; D.95, c.6). And: *the grace of God makes just through him, Jesus Christ, our Lord* (Rm 7:25; Tit 3:6-7;D.4, c.154 de cons.). God has [indeed] bestowed grace on us and his mother, the immaculate virgin Mary, for they awakened for us another Ildefonsus worthy of finding the body of the most blessed Leocadia and like the first one united with a most illustrious king, our Lord Henry.

He who once had reigned with him seemed to harden. God's voice is heard through a prophet as in I Sm 16:1: *how long will you mourn [for Saul] while*

---

[49] Leocadia of Toledo was according to local tradition a Christian martyr in the times of Emperor Diocletian and as such died around the year 304. Her veneration dates back at least to the sixth century and three synods were held in the church dedicated to her in Toledo.

[50] Recceswinth ruled over the Visigothic kingdom 649–72. His reign was mostly remembered as a peaceful one, associated also by other fifteenth century authors with the contemporary Saint Ildefonsus, cf. e.g. Alonso de Cartagena, *Liber genealogie regum Hyspanie*, ed. Bonifacio Palacios Martín (Valencia, 1995), p. 246–47.

¶ tum ex vite meritis · veritatem dico non mencior · vt quid moror laudare quod iuste laudari meretur ʳ nam tacentibus linguis excelssa sua diuina potencia pulularunt

¶ O virgo martir preciossima nomine <u>leocadia</u> estis memor vestre miraculose resureccionis ʳ dum die quadam vestre festiuitatis santo illefonso pontifice nostro intra ecclesiam vestram coram glorioso rege recisuindo misarum solempnia celebrante aperto sepulcro reuoluto desuper lapide ad altare accesistis ʳ eumdem santum illefonsum amplexum coram omni xpistiano populo comendastis et lucida voce dixistis propter vitam illefonsi uiuit domina mea in cellis et reuertens in locum vestre stacionis ʳ ad preces eiusdem regis reliquias vestras optantis cum gladio santus illefonsus dimidiam partem velli vestri sacratissimi capitis arripuit et aliam dimidiam quasi violenter retinuistis et hactenus conseruastis ʳ et ad quid conseruastis domina beata et a deo coronata · ʳ que michi visa est benignam prestare responsum pro altero <u>yllefonso</u> conseruaui alteram dimidiam velli capitis mei ut sim sociata hiis duobus in gloria dei quam preparauit diligentibus se · et sit michi unus a destris alter vero ad sinistris

ʳ non est igitur negligenda gracia celitus data ·I· ad timotheum ·IIII· XXIII· distincione *legimus* ·XCV· distincione *ecce ergo* ʳ et gracia dei iustificat per ipsum ihesum xpistum dominum nostrum ad romanos ·VII· et ad titum ·III· *de consecracione* distincione ·IIII· *placuit* ʳ graciam contulit deus nobis eius intemerata virgo mater maria quia suscitarunt nobis alterum illefonsum dignum reperire corpus beatissime leocadie ʳ qui asociatus ut alter cum illustrissimo rrege domino nostro <u>enrrico</u>

qui cum illo tunc regnasset putabatur durare ʳ audiata est vox dei per prophetam ut habetur in ·Iº· regum ·XVIº· usquequo tu luges ʳ cum ego proiecerim eum ne regnet super israel imple cornu tuum oleo ut

---

57 fol. 17r **65** qui...**70** exodi *marginalia*.

39 veritatem...mencior I Tim 2:7; Rm 9:1. **57** non...data I Tim 4:14.
58 gracia...**59** nostrum Rm 7:25, Tit 3:6–7. **66** usquequo...**68** noster I Sm 16:1.

---

58 legimus D.93, c.24. | ecce ergo D.95, c.6. **60** placuit D.4, c.154 de cons.

I have rejected him to reign over Israel? Fill your horn with oil, so that I may send you to the great men in order for the lord our king to be anointed, Ildefonsus! For *although he is the younger brother he shall be greater then him. His seed will grow into nations and peoples and will multiply* (Gn 48:19).[51]
He will receive the other half of the veil which the same saint, miraculously discovered, will give voluntarily, for she has guarded it until then for him. Rightly she will then say to him: "On account of the life of our bishop Ildefonsus my Lady lives in heaven and on earth", defending the unity of the church militant and seeking to carry whichever erring Christian away from sin (X 2.1.13; X 4.17.13). Not unmerited have I therefore come forward in revocation of the error of said words, as much out of the excellence of his name as of his life; but rather so that I might speak of his successive power:

To know that God in the beginning created heaven and earth and everything that is in them, angelic and human nature, spiritual and worldly things that he rules by himself. Just like a maker is in the habit of directing his product, he also gave orders to the man he made and by himself imposed a punishment for transgression, namely: on Adam and Eve (Gn 3:16-19). The same way he also punished Cain by himself and Lamech and certain others (Gn 4:10-12; Gn 5:29). This way God ruled the world by himself until Noah.

From the time of Noah onward God began to rule his creations through servants, the first of whom was Noah. That he was a ruler is obvious from the fact that the Lord entrusted to him the steering of the ark by which the Church is signified, as I said above; also, that the Lord gave Noah and [his] sons the leadership (Gn 9:1-3). There he also – despite not being invested as a priest – executed the office nevertheless at once after leaving the ark, before he gave the law to the people (Gn 9:4-7). *And Noah built [an altar for God]* and so forth (Gn 8:20). For Abel and Cain had likewise executed the ministry of a priest. And in this vicarage there followed patriarchs, judges of the law, priests and others who for a time took the lead in ruling the Jews.

---

[51] This paragraph (an addition on the page margin) must have been made as a last minute redaction before presenting the work to the author's patron: Archbishop Alonso Carrillo (cf. note 4). The latter openly withdrew his allegiance from Henry IV in the summer of 1465 and supported his younger half-brother's claim to the throne. The author of the *Breue reprehensorium* probably completed his work around this time and inserted the remark to better accommodate the archbishop's political stance.

mictam te ad magnates ut vngatur rex noster dominus illefonsus ͬ licet frater enim iunior maior illo erit semen eius crescet in gentes et in populos et multiplicabitur ut habetur exodi ·XLVIIIº·
recipiet alteram dimidiam velli ͬ quam sponte eadem beata miraculose rreperta tradet quia hactenus pro eo custodiuit ͬ recte tunc ei dicet propter vitam <u>illefonsi</u> pontificis nostri uiuit domina mea in celis et in terris ͬ cum defensat vnionem militantis ecclesie ͬ et quemquam errantem xpistianum spectat de pecato corripere ut in capitulo *nouit de iudiciis* et capitulo *per uenerabilem qui filii sint legitimi* ͬ igitur ne inmerito pro dictarum literarum errore rreuocando tam ex eccelencia nominis sui quam uite prosilii ͬ Sed ut de eius succesiua potestate dicam

ͬ Sciendum quod deus a principio creauit celum et terram et omnia que in eis sunt angelicam et humanam naturam spiritualia et temporalia ͬ que per se ipsum regit sicut factor rem suam gubernare solet ͬ et homini quem fecit precepta dedit et transgrediendi penam inposuit per se ipsum scilicet adde et eve genesis ·IIIº· ͬ qualiter eciam cahim per se ipsum puniuit et lamech et quosdam alios in eodem libro genesis ·IIIIº· et ·Vº· capitulo sic deus regit mundum usque ad noe per se ipsum

ͬ Ex tempore noe cepit deus creaturas suas regere per ministros ͬ quorum primus fuit noe de quo quod fuit rector populi ex eo patet quod dominus sibi gubernacionem arche per quam ecclesia significatur comisit ut supra dixi · ͬ item quod dominus noe et filiis rectoriam dedit genesis ·IXº· ubi eciam licet non legatur · sacerdos fuisse · officium tamen sacerdotis exercuit statim post egresum arche antequam legem populo daret genesis ·IXº· edificauit autem noe et cetera ͬ quia officium sacerdotis simul abel et cahim perfecerant ͬ in hac autem vicaria succeserunt patriarche iudices legis sacerdotes et alii qui pro tempore prefuerunt in regimine iudeorum

---

68 licet…70 multiplicabitur Gn 48:19.   83 transgrediendi…84 eve Gn 3:16–19.   84 qualiter…85 alios Gn 4:10-12, Gn 5:29.   91 noe…92 dedit Gn 9:1–3   94 antequam…daret Gn 9:4-7. | edificauit…noe Gn 8:20.

---

75 nouit X 2.1.13.   76 per uenerabilem X 4.17.13.

And so it continued until our Lord Jesus Christ who was born our lord and king, of whom the psalmist said: *God, give your judgment to the king* (Ps 71:2). And Is 33:22: *the Lord is our judge and the Lord is our lawgiver*. And: *out of the number of your brothers you will appoint a king over yourself* (Dt 17:14-15). And: *how glorious is the king of Israel today* (II Sm 6:20)! And: *he himself is king of kings, Lord of lords* (Apc 19:16, I Tim 6:15). And: *the king of Israel changed [his] dress and went into battle* (III Rg 22:30). And: *the Lord of hosts, he is the king of glory* (Ps 23:10). And: *I am the Lord, your Holy One, king of Israel who created the heavens* (Is 43:15).

Our Lord, our king Jesus Christ appointed as his vicar Peter and [his] successors when he gave him the key to the heavens (Mt 16:19; X 4.17.13; C.24, q.1, c.6; X 1.33.6). About this power of the keys Is 22:22 prophesied: *on that day the Lord will put the key of the house of David on his shoulder. He will open and no one will close; and he will close and no one will open*. He did as described in Ex 26 where the Lord orders Moses to make an ark and put in it the tablets of the spiritual commandments and turn it over to the sons of Aaron. And its key was committed to the priests and Levites (Nm 10:8, Nm 18:6). And also: *if there is anything doubtful and uncertain, go to the priests* of Levite descent who have said keys (Dt 17:8). And: *you are a priest forever according to the order of Melchizedek*, who only offered bread and

ʳ et sic durauit usque ad dominum nostrum ihesum xpistum qui fuit naturalis dominus et rex noster ʳ de quo dixit psalmista deus iudicium tuum regi da ʳ et ysaie ·XXXVIIIº· dominus iudex noster ʳ et dominus legisfer ʳ et de numero fratrum tuorum pones super te regem deuteronomii ·XVIIº· ʳ et quam gloriosus hodie rex israel ·IIº· regum ·VIº· capitulo ʳ et ipse est rex regum dominus dominancium apocalypsis ·XIXº· ʳ et rex israel mutauit habitum et ingresus est bellum ·IIIº· regum ·XXIIº· ʳ et dominus virtutum ipse est rex glorie psalmo ·XXIIIº· ʳ et ego dominus santus vester rex israel creans cellos ysaie ·XLIIIº· capitulo

ʳ dominus noster · rex noster ihesus xpistus vicarium suum constituit petrum et succesores quando ei dedit claues regni celorum in capitulo *pro humani de homicidio* libro sexto et dicto capitulo *per uenerabilem* et capite *quodcumque* ·XXIIII· quescione ·I· et capitulo *solite de maioritate et obediencia* ʳ de hac potestate clauium prophetauit ysaias ·XXIIº· capitulo in die illa dominus ponet clauem domus dauid cum humero suo ipse aperiet et nemo claudet et claudet et nemo aperiet ʳ facit quod habetur exodi ·XXVIº· capitulo vbi precepit dominus moisi facere archam et in ea poni tabulas preceptorum spiritualium et tradi filiis aaron et clauis eius fuit tradita sacerdotibus et leuitis ut numeri ·Xº· capitulo ʳ ad idem cum aliquid fuerit dubium et ambiguum ite ad sacerdotes leuitici generis qui dictas claues habent numeri ·XVIIº· capitulo ʳ et tu es sacerdos in eternum secundum ordinem melchise-dec qui solum panem et vinum oferebat in templo psalmo ·CIXº·

---

104 fol. 17v

---

99 deus...100 da Ps 71:2. 100 dominus[1]...101 legisfer Is 33:22. 101 de...regem Dt 17:14–15. 102 quam...israel II Sm 6:20. 103 ipse... dominancium Apc 19:16, I Tim 6:15. 104 rex...105 bellum III Rg 22:30. 105 dominus...glorie Ps 23:10. 106 ego...cellos Is 43:15. 109 ei... celorum Mt 16:19. 113 in...114 aperiet[2] Is 22:22. 117 clauis...leuitis Nm 10:8, Nm 18:6. 118 cum...119 generis Dt 17:8–9. 120 tu... melchise-dec Ps 109:4. 121 qui...templo Gn 14:18.

---

110 pro humani VI 5.4.1. | per uenerabilem X 4.17.13. 111 quodcumque C.24, q.1, c.6. | solite X 1.33.6.

wine in the temple (Ps 109:4, Gn 14:18; D.2, c.83 de cons.; D.2, c.88 de cons.).

And the priesthood was handed over from Noah and Moses to Peter and his successors (X 1.2.3).[52] And: a sentence is nullified if vetoed by the one who mandated the judgment or one who has greater authority (Dig. 5,1,58).

For I have heard what during the transfiguration of mount Tabor was heard, a clamour from heaven over the Saviour saying: *I have glorified and I will again glorify [my name]* (Io 12:28; D.3, c.30 de cons.). The same Saviour forbade Moses to further use the priesthood and the power of the keys and transferred his representation to Peter to whom he said before the Passion: *to you I will give the keys to the kingdom of the heavens* (Mt 16:19; C.2, q.7, c.41; D.20, preface). And he said to him: *whatsoever you will bind on earth shall be bound in the heavens* (Mt 16:19; C.24, q.1, c.6). And also: *if you forgive someone's sins, they shall be forgiven.* That is: the Holy Spirit forgives them, not you (C.1, q.1, c.82; D.4, c.141 de cons.). And: amen, I tell you, *seeing that you will judge angels, how much more then earthly matters* [I Cor 6:3] (X 4.17.13; X 5.39.28)?

Therefore, no one should disregard the bonds of the Church! For it is God who binds, not a man who wanted to give priests so much power (C.11, q.3, c.31; C.11, q.3, c.31). For priests are called by merit of God. And elsewhere:

---

[52] This passage is exemplary for the kind of supersessionism proposed also by other pro-*converso* authors of the time: on one side it emphasises the continuity between Biblical Judaism and Christianity as a means to advocate the full integration of Jewish converts. On the other side it leaves no doubt about the so-called Old Covenant being allegedly null and void after the foundation of a New Covenant by Jesus Christ.

dixit dominus et genesis ·V°· capitulo et *de consecracione* distincione ·II· capitulo *in calice* et capitulo *accipite*

ʳ et translatum fuit sacerdocium de noe et moisi in petrum et eius succesores ut in capitulo *translato de constitucionibus* ʳ et iudicium   125
soluitur uetante eo qui iudicare iusit uel eo qui maius imperium habet in lege *iudicium* digestis *de iudiciis*

ʳ quia ut audiui quod in transfiguracione montis tabor audito clamore de celo super saluatorem dicente clarificaui et iterum clarificabo iohannis ·XII°· capitulo *de consecracione* distincione ·II· capite *omnes*   130
quos · idem saluator uetuit moisi ne amplius uteretur sacerdocio et potestate clauium et transtulit in petrum eius vicarium ʳ cui ante pasionem dixerat tibi dabo claues regni celorum mathei ·XVI°· XXIIII· quescione ·I· § *sed notandum* et in capite *decretales* ·XX· distincione ʳ et eidem dixit quodcumque ligaueris super terram erit   135
ligatum in celis ut dicto capite *quodcumque* ʳ ad idem si cui dimiseritis pecata dimituntur ei hoc est spiritus santus dimictit non uos ut in capite *euidenter* ·I· quescione ·I· et capite *nemo tollit de consecracione* distincione ·II· ʳ et amen dico uobis quoniam angelos iudicabitis quanto magis temporalia dicto capitulo *per uenerabilem* et capitulo *a*   140
nobis elemento ·2°· *de sentencia excomunicacionis*

ʳ Ideo · nemo contempnat uincula eclesiastica deus enim est qui ligat non homo qui uoluit dare tantam potestatem sacerdotibus in capite *nemo* et capite *per principalem* ·XI· quescione ·III· ʳ quia sacerdotes per excelenciam dii uocantur exodi ·XXII°· et iohannis ·X°· capitulo ʳ et   145

---

142 fol. 18r

---

128   transfiguracione…tabor Mt 17:1–5, Mc 9:2–7, Lc 9:28–35.
129   clarificaui…clarificabo Io 12:28.   **133**   tibi…celorum Mt 16:19.
135   quodcumque…**136** celis Mt 16:19.   **139**   quoniam…**140** temporalia I Cor 6:3   **144**   sacerdotes…**145** uocantur Ex 19:22, Io 10:39.

---

123 in calice D.2, c.83 de cons. | accipite D.2, c.88 de cons.   **125** translato X 1,2,3.   **127** iudicium Dig. 5,1,58.   **130** omnes…**131** quos D.3, c.30 de cons.   **134** sed notandum C.2, q.7, c.41. | decretales D.20, preface.
136 quodcumque C.24, q.1, c.6.   **138** euidenter C.1, q.1, c.82. | nemo tollit D.4, c.141 de cons.   **140** per uenerabilem X 4.17.13. | a…**141** nobis X 5.39.28.   **144** nemo C.11, q.3, c.31. | per principalem C.9, q.3, c.21.

you shall not speak ill of God (Ex 22:28), that is: the priests (X 5.7.12). And the same power was given to Peter and his successors. Otherwise the Church would have remained without a shepherd after Peter (gloss to VI 5.4.1). Indeed, the pope is greater than Paul in the administration. For he is in the place of Peter who was greater than Paul in the administration (C.2, q.7, c.35; D.21, c.2).

What then shall I say about the power of the Church and of the vicar of Christ? For as the Ostian[53] says about X 2.1.12: he can turn squares into circles and arrange everything as much as the Lord, unless it were a violation of the faith. Giovanni d'Andrea[54] says it even stronger about X 2.13.13: speaking of the power of the pope is *to set one's mouth against heaven* [Ps 72:9]. With this power therefore the most noble prelate is charged to defend said unity of the faithful. For Christ did not only choose apostles but bishops and priests (Mt 4:17-25, Act 6:1-7).

Fourteenth article: that those who err in faith are to be corrected first by the Church and her pastors and finally by the secular princes.

And since the Dominican Order is in a way particular in the Church of God, you who are members of said order are obliged by duty of office to defend said holy unity. For it is not right for the members to withdraw from the head (D.12, c.1; X 2.26.12). And said errors [must be] erased. Hence, *if your brother should sin*, according to evangelical advice, *go and rebuke him* (Mt 18:15; X 2.1.13)! And: *if your brother and your friend who sleeps on your*

---

[53] Herny of Segusio, see note 18. Henry was a die-hard defender of the papal *plenitudo potestatis* (fullness of power).

[54] Giovanni d'Andrea, see above, at note 33.

alibi non detrahes diis id est sacerdotibus in capitulo *cum ex iniunto de hereticis* ⌐ et eadem potestas fuit data petro et eius successoribus alias post petrum sine pastore remansisset ecclesia ut dicit glossa in capitulum *pro humani de homicidio* libro sexto ⌐ ymo papa maior est paulo in administracione ·XXI· distincione § ·I· ⌐ est enim loquo petri · qui fuit maior paulo in administracione ut ·II· quescione ·VII· *puto* ·XXI· distincione capite *in nouo*

⌐ quid enim dicam de potestate ecclesie et vicarii ihesu xpisti quia ut dicit hostiensis in capitulo *cum uenissent de iudiciis* potest mutare quadrata rotundis et omnia disponere tanquam dominus salua violacione fidei ⌐ magis dicit iohannes andree in capitulo *literas de restitucione spoliatorum* quod loqui de potestate pape est ponere os in celum ⌐ hac igitur potestate dictam fidelium vnionem preclarissimus antistes defendere tenetur ⌐ quia xpistus elegit non solum apostolos sed episcopos et presbyteros mathei ·IIII°· actuum ·VI°· //·

150

155

160

·XIIII^us· articulus quod errantes in fide sunt corrigendi prius per ecclesiam et eius pastores finaliter per principes seculares ·

Cumque predicatorum ordo sit quasi precipuus in ecclesia dei · vos qui dicti ordinis membra estis ex debito oficii tenemini dictam vnionem santam defensare ⌐ quia non decet a capite membra recedere in capite *cum non decet* ·XII· distincione et capitulo *cum non liceat de prescripcionibus* ⌐ et dictos errores tollere vnde si frater tuus pecauerit secundum euangelicam monicionem uade et corripe eum in capitulo *nouit de iudiciis* ⌐ et si frater tuus et amicus tuus qui in sinu tuo dor-

5

---

146 non...diis Ex 22:28. **157** ponere...**158** celum Ps 72:9. **159** xpistus...**160** presbyteros Mt 4:18-22, Act 6:2–7. **7** si...**8** eum Mt 18:15. **9** si...**11** eorum Dt 13:6–9.

---

146 cum...iniunto X 5.7.12. **149** pro humani VI 5.4.1. **150** § ·I· D. 21, preface. **151** puto C.2, q.7, c.35. **152** in nouo D.21, c.2. **154** cum uenissent X 2.1.12. | potest...**156** fidei Henry of Segusio, *Lectura in Decretales Gregorii IX*. **156** literas X 2.13.13. **157** loqui...**158** celum Giovanni d'Andrea, *Novella sive commentarius in decretales epistolas Gregorii IX*. **6** cum¹...decet D.12, c.1. | cum²...liceat X 2.26.12. **9** nouit X 2.1.13.

bosom should want to distort the truth, *your hand shall be upon them and you shall spill their blood!* (Dt 13:6–9; C.23, q.8, c.13).

Ah, but alas! For *his watchmen are all blind, they do not know anything, dumb dogs that are unable to bark, seeing vain things, sleeping and loving dreams; and most impudent dogs that are never satisfied. The shepherds themselves do not know understanding, they all strayed on their way, everyone to his own greed* (Is 56:10-11). Accept therefore what is written in the parables of Prv 30:17: *the eye that mocks the father and despises the birth by his mother – may the ravens of the brooks pick it out and may the young of the eagle eat it*. These words of the wise man can of course be understood according to a Catholic mind:

The eye is a treacherous man who is stubborn in faith. Hence the prophet says: *save me! Let their eyes be darkened, so that they do not see, and their back [always] be crooked* (Ps 68:2.24; D.37, c.15)! Also: *while they have eyes wounded by a great beam, they notice a mote in the eyes of others* (Mt 7:3; Lc 6:41; C.1, q.1, c.84). And: the vice of ambition blinds the eyes of certain people (VI 1.6.24). Hence it is the eye of the mind that has to be pure (C.2, q.1, c.18). It is the eye of the heart that has to be chaste (C.32, q.5, c.13). It is the eye of the administration that has to be foresightful (C.6, q.1, c.9). Hence someone is not a heretic and does not sin in a manner that his obstinacy ceases and he does not defend his error and believes the same as the Church believes, believing so, and places his opinion under the faith of the Church. For even though he supposes wrongly, still that is not his faith, but rather his faith is the faith of the Church (X 1.1.2; Pope Innocent in X 1.1.1).

mit deprauare uoluerit veritatem sit manus tua super eos et efundes
sanguinem eorum deuteronomii ·XIIIº· ·XXII· quescione ·III· *legitur*
ͬ Sed heu heu quia speculatores eius ceci omnes nescierunt vniuersi
canes muti non ualentes latrare uidentes uana dormientes et amantes
sompnia et canes inpudentissimi nescientes saturitatem ipsi pastores
nescierunt inteligenciam omnes in uiam suam declinauerunt
vnusquisque ad auariciam suam ysaie ·LVI· ͬ Sumite ergo illud quod
scribitur in parabolis proverbiorum ·XXXº· capitulo <u>oculum qui
subsanat patrem et qui despicit partum matris sue sufodiant eum
corui de torrentibus et comedant eum filii aquile</u> ͬ que verba sapientis
sane secundum catolicam mentem posunt inteligi

ͬ // <u>oculus</u> iste est infidelis homo errans pertinaciter in fide ͬ vnde
saluum me fac psalmo ·LXVIIIº· ait propheta · obscurentur occuli
eorum ne videant et dorsum eorum super incurua ·XXVII·
distincione § *ut itaque* ͬ item magna trabe uulneratos oculos habentes
festucam conspiciunt in aliorum occulis mathei ·VIIº· luce ·VIº· I·
quescione ·I· capite *multi* ͬ et oculos quorundam uicium ambicionis
excecat in capitulo *quorundam de elleccione* libro sexto ͬ vnde est
oculus mentis qui purus esse debet ·II· quescione ·I· capite *multi* ͬ est
oculus cordis qui debet esse pudicus ·XXXII· quescione ·V· *qui viderit*
ͬ est oculus administracionis qui debet esse prouidus ·VI· quescione ·I·
oues ͬ vnde non est hereticus nec pecat dum modo ceset pertinacia et
errorem suum non defendat et hoc ipsum credat quod credit ecclesia
sic credere et suam opynionem · fidei ecclesie supponit ͬ quia licet sic
male opinetur tamen non est illa fides sua · ymo fides sua fides est
ecclesie in capitulo *dampnamus de suma trinitate* circa finem
innocencius in capitulo *firmiter* eodem titulo in fine //

---

19 fol. 18v   **23** super Vulgate: semper

---

12 speculatores...**18** suam Is 56:10–11.   **17** oculum...**21** aquile Prv 30:17.
22 saluum...fac Ps 68:2. | obscurentur...**25** incurua Ps 68:24.
24 magna...**27** occulis Mt 7:3, Lc 6:41.

---

11 legitur C.23, q.8, c.13.   **24** ut itaque D.37, c.15.   **26** multi C.1, q.1,
c.84.   **27** quorundam VI 1.6.24.   **28** multi C.2, q.1, c.18.   **29** qui viderit
C.32, q.5, c.13.   **31** oues C.6, q.1, c.9.   **35** dampnamus X 1.1.2.
36 firmiter X 1.1.1.

He mocks the father, that is to say: God. Hence Ier 3:19: *you will call me father*. For he mocks the father by claiming a difference in the Christian people, just as if it had not one Father, God, and our Saviour, Jesus. This erring eye reveals the shameful parts of his father, therefore it is cursed as Cham was to be his brothers' slave (Gn 9:25-27; C.2, q.7, c.27). And this erring eye deserves indeed to be called a wolf, not a Christian. For they lie about being Christians if they depart from Christ and do not do his works (C.23, q.5, c.20) and make an effort to divide the Christian unity (C.23, q.5, c.35).

For they are heretics who understand the scripture in a different way than demands the sense of the Holy Spirit, by whom it was written (C.24, q.3, c.27), and who teach a perverted doctrine against the faith (C.24, q.3, c.26) and follow new and false opinions, and those who believe them are fooled by a certain fancy of truth (C.24, q.3, c.28). For and they are heretics because they hold sick and deformed things to be true [and] insist on defending pestilential doctrine (C.24, q.3, c.31). They attempt to defend their false and perverse opinions with their obstinate boldness and recklessness of their presumption (C.24, q.3, c.29). For *God hates them who sow discord among brethren* (Prv 6:19). Brethren indeed are all Christians (C.11, q.3, c.24). By necessity therefore, the prelates must root those errors out of the Church (Clem 5.3.3).

Who despises the birth by his mother, that is to say: them who are born again by holy baptism in which the Church is fertile with offspring and is said to beget her children (VI 3.4.33), them he despises by calling them *confesos*,

subsanat patrem scilicet deum ʳ vnde ieremia ·IIIº· patrem uocabis me subsanat enim patrem aserendo diferenciam inter xpistianum populum quasi si non esset eis vnus pater deus et saluator noster ihesus ʳ iste erroneus oculus pudenda patris sui demonstrat ideo maleditus est ut cham seruus fratrum suorum erit genesis ·IXº· I· quescione ·IIII· § *ex hiis* ʳ iste namque oculus erroneus non xpistianus sed lupus nominari meretur ʳ nam xpistianos se esse menciuntur cum a xpisto deuiant et opera eius non faciunt in capite *cauete* ·XXIII· quescione ·V· ʳ et xpistianam vnitatem separare contendunt ut capite *si uos* ·XXIII· quescione ·V·

ʳ heretici enim sunt qui aliter scripturam intelligunt quam sensus spiritus santi flagitat a quo scripta est ut capite *heresis* ·XXIIII· quescione ·IIII· ʳ et peruersum dogma contra fidem docent ut capite *inter scisma* eadem causa et quescione ʳ et nouas et falsas oppyniones secuntur et qui hii credunt ymaginacione quadam veritatis sunt illusi ut capite *hereticus* eadem causa et quescione ʳ heritici namque sunt quia morbum prauumque sapiunt pestifera dogmata defendere persistunt capite *qui in ecclesia* ·XXIIII· quescione ·III·ʳ suas falsas ac peruersas sentencias sua pertinaci animositate et sue presumpcionis audacia defendere conantur ut in capite *dixit apostolus* eadem causa et quescione ʳ odit enim deus inter fratres seminantes discordias prouerbiorum ·VIº· ʳ fratres enim sunt omnes xpistiani ·XI· quescione ·III· *ad mensam* ʳ hos ergo errores neccessario prelati ab ecclesia extirpare tenentur ut clementinis fine *de hereticis*

ʳ qui despicit partum matris sue scilicet eos qui renascuntur per sacrum baptisma in quo ecclesia est prole fecunda et dicitur generare filios suos in capitulo *cum singula de prebendis* libro sexto despicit

---

58 fratres² fol. 19r

---

37 patrem²...me Ier 3:19.   41 cham...erit Gn 9:25–27.   57 odit...59 discordias Prv 6:19.

42 ex hiis C.2, q.7, c.27.   44 cauete C.23, q.5, c.20.   46 si uos C.23, q.5, c.35.   48 heresis C.24, q.3, c.27.   50 inter scisma C.24, q.3, c.26.   52 hereticus C.24, q.3, c.28.   54 qui...ecclesia C.24, q.3, c.31.   56 dixit apostolus C.24, q.3, c.29.   59 ad mensam C.11, q.3, c.24.   60 fine Clem 5.3.3.   63 cum singula VI 3.4.33.

tornadizos and similar things by writing on the walls what is contained in the aforementioned letters. And: *he who despises his neighbour sins, but he who shows mercy to the poor shall be blessed* (Prv 14:21). And: *a foolish man despises his mother* (Prv 15:20).

The *ravens of the brooks* that have to *pick out the eye* are the prelates of the church, most of all you, friars of the Dominican Order who have to be black like ravens on account of the severity of life. Hence: *black am I, but beautiful* (Ct 1:4). Or else they are called black like ravens because they preach the blackness and darkness of sins to better the habits of men. Hence Is 1:18: *if your sins were like scarlet, they shall be made white as snow, and if they were red like crimson, they shall become like white wool.* Or else they are called ravens and black also like you friars of the Dominican Order who are as much of black color in the habit of your honesty.

Of the brooks, that is: the raillery of the malign and those who err in the faith. For just like water runs quickly through a brook and is not native to it and does not originate in it but comes from somewhere else, so they who err in the faith and want division pretend to carry pure water which they do not have. And they hide under the cunning schemes of their vengeful flow not pure but cloudy waters. For they are founts without water and clouds stirred up by whirlwinds by which the darkness of ignorance is preserved (D.2, c.40 de poen.; C.2, q.7, c.31).

The *young of the eagle* are the Christian princes [and] kings, for a certain powerful Nebuchadnezzar was called *an eagle with mighty wings* (Ez 17:3). So the princes who are the young of the eagle that gaze directly at the true sun – one may know: Jesus Christ – are held to devour the erring eyes that mock the father against his law by introducing a division between legitimate faithful children and despise the birth – one may see: the Christians begotten now and before by the holy mother Church; they must do this by

enim uocando confesos tornadizos et quid simile ut in parietibus describendo ut in predictis literis continetur ʳ nam qui despicit proximum suum pecat qui autem miseretur pauperi beatus erit prouerbiorum ·XIIII⁰· ʳ et stultus homo despicit matrem suam proverbiorum ·XV⁰·

ʳ corui qui tenentur subfodere oculum de torrentibus sunt prelati ecclesie premaxime uos fratres ordinis predicatorum ʳ qui debent esse nigri ut corui propter asteritatem uite · vnde nigra sunt sed formosa canticorum ·I⁰· capitulo ʳ uel dicuntur nigri ut corui quia predicant nigredinem et obscuritatem pecatorum ut mores hominum emendent · ʳ vnde ysaie capitulo ·I⁰· si fuerint pecata vestra ut coccinum uelut nix dealbabuntur et si fuerint rubra quasi vermiculus uelut lana alba erunt ʳ uel dicuntur corui et nigri sicut et vos fratres ordinis predicatorum qui nigri talis coloris estis in habitu vestre honestatis

ʳ de torrentibus que est cauilacio malignancium et in fide errancium · nam sicut per torrentem transit aqua velociter et non est naturalis nec inde oritur sed extraordinarie orta · sic in fide errantes et diuisionem querentes simulant mundam aquam gestare quam non habent ʳ et latent sub calidis machinacionibus fluctuum sibi uendicancium non munde sed turbidinis aque ʳ hii enim sunt fontes sine aqua et nebule turbinibus exagitate quibus caligo tenebrarum reseruatur *de penitencia* distincione ·II· capite *sic enim inquid* et ·II· quescione ·VII· capite *secuti*

ʳ filii aquile sunt principes reges xpistiani quidam enim uocabant potentem nabuchodonosor aquilam magnarum alarum ut ezechiel ·XVII⁰· capitulo ʳ sic principes qui ut filii aquile qui verum solem scilicet ihesum xpistum directo respiciunt tenentur oculos erroneos qui subsanant patrem contra legem suam diuisionem inter legitimos fideles filios inducendo et despiciunt partum videlicet xpistianos nunc et ante genitos a santa matre ecclesia tenentur comedere vastando

---

71 sunt Vulgate: sum   **88** ut...**91** capitulo *marginalia*.

65 qui...**68** erit Prv 14:21.   **67** stultus...suam Prv 15:20.   **71** nigra... formosa Ct 1:4.   **74** si...**78** erunt Is 1:18.   **88** aquilam...alarum Ez 17:3.

85 sic...inquid D.2, c.40 de poen.   **86** secuti C.2, q.7, c.31.

laying waste to their life and goods, removed and torn out first by the ravens – that is to say: the prelates of the church and you yourselves, friars of the Dominican Order.

Because an ambiguity such as this *between blood and blood, leprosy and leprosy* [Dt 17:8] concerns at first you churchmen (X 4.17.13; VI 5.2.11). And: the names of the witnesses and the accuser must be made known if there is no danger (VI 5.2.20; X 5.1.24). And: blind errors must be exposed and explained by the prelates and their advisors (X 5.7.9; VI 5.2.4).

For the confiscation and execution of heretics must be carried out by virtue of an edict by a leading churchman and of the Church (VI 5.2.19) in a way that they do not seem to be signed out of greed or vengeance more than justice and obedience (C.23, q.1, c.4; C.23, q.2, c.1), and a declaration beforehand by a judge ruling them to be such [persons] allowed to be seized by the laws (VI 5.2.19). For [otherwise] many could falsely claim those to be heretics that are not in order to take away their goods, as Giovanni d'Andrea[55] and Dominic[56] [of San Gimignano] note about VI 5.2.6.

Therefore they were wrong who rashly asserted that anyone could in his own right plunder and kill whom he believed or thought to be a heretic.[57] For that way, the power of the church and of the prelates and of the royal

---

[55] Giovanni d'Andrea, see note 33, above. The work referenced here is Giovanni's *In Sextum Decretalium librum Novella Commentaria*.

[56] Dominic of San Gimignano (c. 1375–1424) was an Italian jurist and canonist born near Siena who commented both Roman and church law. As such he was influential in the deposition of rivalling popes Benedict XIII and Gregory XII at the council of Pisa. The reference here is to his *Lectura super Sexto Decretalium*.

[57] The author of course alludes here to the insurrection of 1449 and the anti-*converso* violence that followed. The perpetrators then had tried to justify their crimes by framing them as legitimate persecution of alleged heretics whom they charged with the secret practice of the Jewish faith. Much of the accusations against the rebels rested on the affirmation that they had indeed not acted within the law and according to due process. Most prominently, Juan de Torquemada in the first chapter of his *Tractatus contra madianitas* gives a painstaking analysis of their outrageous pseudo-legal proceedings.

eorum vitam et bona extractis et euulsis prius per coruos scilicet
prelatos ecclesie et uos metipsos predicatorum ordinis fratres ·   95
ʳ cum talis ambiguitas inter sanguinem et sanguinem lepram et
lepram prius ad uos ecclesiasticos pertineat in capitulo *per uenerabilem
qui filii sint legitimi* et in capitulo *ut inquisicionis* § *prohibemus de
hereticis* libro sexto ʳ et testium et acusatoris nomina cessante periculo
debent publicari ut in capitulo finale eodem titulo § *sic tamen* iunto   100
capitulo *qualiter et quando* elemento secundo § *debet de accus-
sacionibus* ʳ et per prelatos suosque consultores errores debent ab
oculis detegi et lucidari ut in capitulo *ab abolendam de hereticis* in §
illos et capitulo *super eo* eodem titulo libro sexto

ʳ nam spoliacio et occisio hereticorum debet fieri edicto principis   105
ecclesiastici et ecclesie capitulo *cum secundum de hereticis* libro sexto ʳ
ne ex cupiditate uel ulcione pocius quam iusticia et obediancia signare
videantur ·XXIII· quescione ·VI· capite *quid culpatur* et quescione ·II·
capite ·I· ʳ et declaracio prius per iudicem iudicans illos esse tales
contra quos iura permictunt ocupacionem per dictum capitulum *cum*   110
sucundum ʳ quia possent multi fingere eos esse hereticos qui tamen
non essent ut eorum bona auferent notant iohannes andree et
dominicus in capitulo *presidentes* circa finem *de hereticis* libro sexto

ʳ errabant ergo qui calide aserbant quemquam posse sua auctoritate
spoliare et interficere quem credebat uel sciebat esse hereticum ʳ quia   115
per hoc detrahebantur potestati ecclesie et prelatorum et rregie
magestati quod absit ʳ vnde regem honorificate ·Iᵃ· petri ·II· VIIIº·
distincione *quo iure* ʳ quia per deum rreges regnant et legum
conditores recta discernunt proverbiorum ·IIIIº· ʳ et qui non obedierit

---

96 fol. 19v **98** et...**101** accus-sacionibus *marginalia.*

---

96 ambiguitas...**99** lepram Dt 17:8.   **117** regem honorificate I Pt 2:17.
118 per...**121** discernunt Prv 8:15.   **119** qui...**122** moriatur Ios 1:18, II
Re 3:39.

---

97 per uenerabilem X 4.17.13.   **98** ut inquisicionis VI 5.2.11.   **100** sic
tamen VI 5.2.20.   **101** qualiter...quando X 5.1.24.   **103** ab abolendam X
5.7.9.   **104** super eo VI 5.2.4.   **106** cum secundum VI 5.2.19.   **108** quid
culpatur C.23, q.1, c.4.   **109** capite ·I· C.23, q.2, c.1.   **113** presidentes VI
5.2.6.   **118** quo iure D.8, c.1.

majesty were lessened, what God may forbid! Hence: *honour the king!* (I Pt 2:17; D.8, c.1). For *by [the wisdom of] God kings rule and lawgivers see what is right* (Prv 8:15). And: *he who does not obey the king shall die* (Ios 1:18, II Re 3:39; X 1,33,2). Most of all since otherwise the diminishing of the nation would be to the king's dismay, for *a people restored is the king's glory, [but] its diminishing a prince's dismay* (Prv 14:28; C.1, q.4, c.11).
And our Lord Jesus Christ kept honouring the high priests until the day of the Passion (Io 18:19-24; D.93, c.25). And he ordered the lepers to show themselves to the priests (Lc 17:14; D.1, c.34). For *just as in the waters there shines the face of the ones looking therein, so the hearts of men are laid open to the wise* (Prv 27:19).

I conclude therefore, that on account of the official duty of [your] Order and habit you must put an end to the leprosy of said wall, of which I warn you for the third and last time, so that you may be willing to finally give in and write some other, devout words to praise Christ on the same spot, after the example of the holy apostles who nominated in the place of the thief Judas Saint Matthias (Act 1:15-26; C.26, q.2, c.2), the eve of whose feast is even a fast day (X 3.46.1).

And it is not new that said words are a leprosy found on the wall. For one reads in Lv 13, that the Lord ordered Moses that leprosy appearing on the skin or on a house or on a garment had to be shown to a priest and according to his judgment one was polluted or vindicated (D.1, c.60 de poen.). For that reason, since they are corrupted words, they are to be loathed. Hence Prv 8:13: *the fear of the Lord hates evil. I loath arrogance and pride and a wicked way and a treacherous mouth.* And in that very place the same wise man says: *for it is better to be humbled with the meek than to divide spoils with the proud* (Prv 16:19). Therefore said words about spoils must be

principi · morte moriatur ·II°· regum ·III°· capitulo et capitulo *si quis de maioritate et obediencia* ʳ maxime quia aliter regi fieret in diminucionem plebis contricio quia relata gente gloria regis a diminucione contricio principis prouerbiorum ·XIIII°· I· quescione ·III· § *ex hiis*

ʳ et dominus noster ihesus xpistus usque ad pasionis diem seruauit honorem pontificibus iohannis ·XVIII°· XXIII· distincione *dominus* ʳ et precepit leprosis ut hostenderent se sacerdotibus luce ·XVII°· *de penitencia* distincione ·I· § *hinc idem* ʳ nam quomodo in aquis splendet vultus prospiciencium sic corda hominum manifesta sunt prudentibus prouerbiorum ·XXVII°·

ʳ concludo igitur quod ex debito oficii ordinis et habitus lepram dicte parietis abolere debetis ad quod finaliter et tercio vos moneo ut uelitis mox efectui mancipare ʳ et alia deuota verba loco eadem ad laudem xpisti describere ʳ exemplo santorum apostolorum qui loco iude furis santum mathiam colocarunt actuum ·I°· et capite *non statim* ·IX· quescione ·II· ʳ cuius vigilia eciam ieiunatur ut in capitulo ·I· *de obseruacione ieiunorum*

ʳ nec est nouum dicta verba esse lepram in pariete repertam ʳ quia legitur leuitici ·XIII°· quod dominus precepit moisi ut lepra siue in cute siue in domo siue in veste appararet sacerdoti ostenderet et iuxta eius iudicio contaminaretur uel uendicetur *de penitencia* distincione ·I· § *denique* ʳ ideo cum sint praua verba detestanda sunt vnde proverbiorum ·VIII°· timor domini odit malum aroganciam et superbiam et viam prauam et os bilingue detestor ʳ et ibidem idem sapiens ait quia melius est humiliari cum mitibus quam diuidere spolia cum

---

139 fol. 20r

---

122 relata...**125** principis Prv 14:28.   **125** dominus...**128** pontificibus Io 18:19–24.   **127** precepit...sacerdotibus Lc 17:14.   **128** quomodo...**132** prudentibus Prv 27:19.   **134** santorum...**137** colocarunt Act 1:15–26   **139** dominus...**143** uendicetur Lv 13.   **143** timor...**144** detestor Prv 8:13.   **145** quia...**148** superbis Prv 16:19.

---

120 si quis X 1.33.2.   **124** ex hiis C.1, q.4, c.11.   **126** dominus D.93, c.25.   **128** hinc idem D.1, c.34. de poen.   **135** non statim C.26, q.2, c.2.   **136** capitulo ·I· X 3.46.1.   **142** denique D.1, c.60 de poen.

rooted out, which I urge you to do. In order for me at least not to have worked in vain, may these words do good in the hearts of you who love Jesus. He himself who is resurrection and life may guide you on the way of peace so that you may be able to ascend to the summit of the heavenly choir, and I likewise.

Amen.

superbis · igitur dicta spolii verba ut lepra abrradicantur ʳ ad quod ortor vos · saltim ne in vanum laborauerim proficiant verba ista in cordibus vestris qui ihesum diligitis ʳ ipse qui est resurreccio et vita vos dirigat in viam pacis ut ad culmen celestis scole scandere valeatis similiter et ego 150

⁓·: Amen :·⁓

BIBLIOGRAPHY

Accorsi, Federica, *Estudio del 'Espejo de verdadera nobleza' de Diego de Valera con edición crítica de la obra* (Pisa, 2011).
Albaric, Michel, 'Hugues de Saint-Cher et les concordances bibliques latines (XIIIe-XVIIIe siècles)', in *Hugues de Saint-Cher († 1263), bibliste et théologien: études réunies*, ed. Louis-Jacques Bataillon *et al.* (Turnhout, 2004), 467–79.
Altamura, Antonio, *Antonio de Ferrariis Galateo: Epistole. Edizione critica* (Lecce, 1959).
Amador de los Ríos, José, *Historia social, política y religiosa de los judíos en España y Portugal* (Madrid, 1875).
Baer, Yitzhak (Fritz), *Die Juden im mittelalterlichen Spanien* (Berlin, 1936).
Barriendos, Mariano, & Barriendos, Josep, 'Los inicios de la Pequeña Edad del Hielo en España: aportaciones de la climatología histórica al clima del siglo XIV', *Geographicalia*, 73 (2021), 55–79.
Bautista, Francisco, 'Predicación anticonversa, inquisición y tolerancia en un discurso de 1461–1462: en torno a Alonso de Oropesa y Alonso de Espina', *Medieval Encounters*, 28 (2022), 377–446.
Beinart, Haim, *Los conversos ante el tribunal de la Inquisición* (Barcelona, 1983).
Benito Ruano, Eloy, 'Del problema judío al problema converso', in his *Los orígines del problema converso* (Madrid, 2001), 15–38.
Brocato, Linde M., 'Toledo 1449: the complex political space(s) and dynamics of civil violence', in *A Companion to Medieval Toledo*, ed. Yasmine Beale-Rivaya and Jason Busic (Leiden, 2018), 164–94.
Cantera Burgos, Francisco, *Álvar García de Santa María y su familia de conversos: historia de la judería de Burgos y de sus conversos más egregios* (Madrid, 1952).
Castán Lanaspa, Guillermo, 'La gran mortandad de 1348: sobre el mito y la realidad (conocida) de la Peste Negra en España', *Nuestra Historia*, 9 (2020), 73–94.
Castro, Américo, *España en su historia: cristianos, moros y judíos* (Buenos Aires, 1948).

Cerno, Marianna, 'Jesus' New Face: a newly discovered version of the "Epistula Lentuli"', *Apocrypha*, 32 (2022), 9–49.
Cohen, Jeremy, *The Friars and the Jews: the evolution of medieval anti-Judaism* (Ithaca, 1982).
Conde Salazar, Matilde, et al., *Alonso Díaz de Montalvo: la causa conversa* (Madrid, 2008).
de Azcona, Tarsicio, 'Dictamen en defensa de los judíos conversos de la Orden de San Jerónimo a principios del siglo XVI', in *Studia Hieronymiana*, Vol. II, ed. Pedro Sainz Rodríguez (Madrid, 1973), 347–80.
Díaz Ibáñez, Jorge, 'Alonso de Cartagena y la defensa de la exención del obispado burgalés frente al primado toledano', *En la España medieval*, 34 (2011), 325–42.
Domínguez Bordona, Jesús, *Fernando del Pulgar: Letras* (Madrid, 1929).
Escudero de la Peña, J. M., *Divina retribución sobre la caida de España en tiempo del noble rey Don Juan el primero. Compuesta por el Bachiller Palma* (Madrid, 1879).
Formentín Ibáñez, Justo and Villegas Sanz, María José, *Jaime Pérez de Valencia: Tratado contra los judíos* (Madrid, 1998).
Franco Silva, Alfonso, 'La esclavitud en Andalucía a fines de la Edad Media: problemas metodológicos y perspectivas de investigación', *Studia*, 47 (1989), 147–67.
García Cárcel, Ricardo and Moreno Martínez, Doris, *Inquisición: historia crítica* (Madrid, 2000).
García-Serrano, Francisco, 'Ambiguity, Friendship and Pragmatism: medieval friars in Iberia and beyond' in *Conflict and Collaboration in Medieval Iberia*, ed. Kim Bergqvist, Kurt Villads Jensen, & Anthony John Lappin (Newcastle, 2020), 181–206.
Gilly, Carlos, 'The Council of Basel's "De Neophytis" Decree as Immediate Cause of and Permanent Antidote to the Racial Purity Statutes', in *The Conversos and Moriscos in Late Medieval Spain and Beyond*, vol. IV: *Resistance and Reform* (Leiden, 2021), 13–44.
Gil Ortega, Carmen, 'Alfonso Carrillo de Acuña: un arzobispo proconverso en el siglo XV castellano', *eHumanista/conversos*, 3 (2015), 139–41.

Giordano, Maria L., *Apologetas de la fe: elites conversas entre inquisición y patronazgo en Espana (siglos XV y XVI)* (Madrid, 2004).
Gitlitz, David M., *Secrecy and Deceit: the religion of the Crypto-Jews* (Albuquerque, 2002).
Gómez Llauger, Núria, 'Radicalism and Pauline Thought in Pedro de la Cavallería's *Zelus Christi contra judeos, sarracenos et infideles*' in *Propaganda and (Un)Covered Identities in Treatises and Sermons: Christians, Jews, and Muslims in the premodern Mediterranean*, ed. Cándida Ferrero Hernández & Linda G. Jones (Barcelona, 2020), 71–82.
González Rolán, Tomás, & Saquero Suárez-Somonte, Pilar, *De la sentencia-estatuto de Pero Sarmiento a la Instrucción del Relator: estudio introductorio, edición crítica y notas de los textos contrarios y favorables a los judeoconversos a raíz de la rebelión de Toledo de 1449* (Madrid, 2012).
Gonzálvez Ruiz, Ramón, 'El Bachiller Palma y su obra de polémica proconversa', in *"Qu'un sang impur...": les conversos et le pouvoir en Espagne à la fin du moyen âge*, ed. Jeanne Battesti Pelegrin (Aix-en-Provence, 1997), 47–59.
—, 'El bachiller Palma, autor de una obra desconocida en favor de los conversos', in *Simposio "Toledo Judaico"*, vol. II (Toledo, 1973), 31–48.
Gordon, James D., 'The Articles of the Creed and the Apostles', *Speculum*, 40 (1965), 634–40.
Gramsch-Stehfest, Robert, *Bildung, Schule und Universität im Mittelalter* (Berlin, 2019).
Harris, Jennifer, 'Enduring Covenant in the Christian Middle Ages', *Journal of Ecumenical Studies*, 44 (2009), 563–86.
Hernández Franco, Juan, 'Construcción y deconstrucción del converso a través de los memoriales de limpieza de sangre durante el reinado de Felipe III', *Sefarad*, 72 (2012), 325–50.
—, 'El pecado de los padres: construcción de la identidad conversa en Castilla a partir de los discursos sobre limpieza de sangre', *Hispania*, 64 (2004), 515–42.
Holl, Bernhard, *Die Conversos: christliche Gegner und Verteidiger der iberischen Neuchristen in den Jahren vor 1492* (Baden-Baden, 2022).

—, 'Antijüdische Polemik unter falscher Flagge: das vorgebliche Pamphlet eines anonymen Judaisierers 1480 in Sevilla', *Zeitschrift für Religions- und Geistesgeschichte*, 72 (2020), 412–24.

Izquierdo Benito, Ricardo, 'Edad Media', in *Historia de Toledo*, ed. Julio de la Cruz Muñoz (Toledo, 1997), 115–256.

Kamerick, Kathleen, *Popular Piety and Art in the Late Middle Ages: Image Worship and Idolatry in England 1350–1500* (New York, 2002).

Kämmerer, Carmen, *Codeswitching in Predigten des 15. Jahrhvnderts. Mittellatein – Frühneuhochdeutsch, Mittellatein – Altitalienisch/Altspanisch* (Berlin, 2006).

Kohut, Karl, 'Der Beitrag der Theologie zum Literaturbegriff in der Zeit Juans II. von Kastilien. Alonso de Cartagena (1384–1456) und Alonso de Madrigal, genannt El Tostado (1400?–1455)', *Romanische Forschungen*, 89 (1977): 183–226.

Lacave, José L., 'Los estudios hebraicos y judaicos en España, desde Amador de los Ríos hasta nuestros días', in *Los judíos en la España contemporánea: historia y visiones, 1898–1998*, ed. Ricardo Izquierdo Benito *et al.* (Ciudad Real, 2000), 115–20.

Linde, Cornelia, *How to Correct the Sacra Scriptura? Textual criticism of the Latin Bible between the twelfth and fifteenth century* (Oxford, 2012).

López Martínez, Nicolás, 'El Arzobispo Carrillo y la política de su tiempo', in *Miscelánea José Zunzunegui* (Vitoria, 1975), I, 247–67.

Lutz, Cora E., 'The Letter of Lentulus Describing Christ', *The Yale University Library Gazette*, 50 (1975), 91–97.

Menny, Anna L., *Spanien und Sepharad: über den offiziellen Umgang mit dem Judentum im Franquismus und in der Demokratie* (Göttingen, 2013).

Miguel, Jerónimo, *Juan de Lucena: Diálogo sobre la vida feliz; Epístola exhortatoria a las letras. Edición, estudio y notas* (Madrid, 2014).

Miquel Juan, Matilde, 'Sentimientos pintados y contemplaciones mentales: espiritualidad visual y literatura medieval hispana a finales del siglo XV', in *Isabel de Villena i l'espiritualitat europea tardomedieval*, ed. Anna Isabel Peirats Navarro (Valencia, 2022), 357–86.

Monsalvo Antón, José M., 'Mentalidad antijudía en la Castilla medieval (ss. XII–XV)', in *Xudeus e Conversos na Historia*, vol. 1: *Mentalidades e Cultura*, ed. Carlos Barros (Santiago de Compostela, 1994), 21–84.

—, *Teoría y evolución de un conflicto social: el antisemitismo en la corona de Castilla en la Baja Edad Media* (Madrid, 1985).

Netanyahu, Benzion, *The Marranos of Spain: from the late 14th to the early 16th Century, according to contemporary Hebrew sources* (Ithaca and London, 1966).

Nirenberg, David, *Anti-Judaism: the western tradition* (New York, 2013).

—, 'Poetics and Politics in an Age of Mass Conversion', in *Cultures of Conversions*, ed. by Jan N. Bremmer et.al. (Leuven, 2006), 31–51.

—, 'Figures of Thought and Figures of Flesh: "Jews" and "Judaism" in late-medieval Spanish poetry and politics', *Speculum*, 81 (2006), 398–426.

Pastore, Stefania, 'Doubt in Fifteenth-Century Iberia', in *After Conversion: Iberia and the emergence of modernity*, ed. Mercedes García-Arenal (Leiden, 2016), 283–303.

Paz y Melia, Antonio, *Opúsculos literarios de las siglos XIV á XVI* (Madrid, 1892).

Perea Rodríguez, Óscar, '"Quebrantar la jura de mis abuelos": los conversos en los cancioneros castellanos del tardío medievo (1454–1504)', *La Corónica*, 40 (2011), 183–225.

—, 'Enrique IV de Castilla y los conversos: testimonios poéticos de una evolución histórica', *Revista de poética medieval*, 19 (2007), 131–75.

Pertusi, Agostino, *La caduta di Costantinopoli*, vol. II: *L'eco nel mondo* (Milan, 1976).

Phillips, William D., *Slavery in Medieval and Early Modern Iberia* (Philadelphia, 2014).

—, 'La historia de la esclavitud y la historia medieval de la Península Ibérica', *Espacio, Tiempo y Forma*, 23 (2010), 149–65.

Plotke, Seraina, *Die Stimme des Erzählens: mittelalterliche Buchkultur und moderne Narratologie* (Göttingen, 2017).

Prudlo, Donald, *Thomas Agni da Lentini: Vita sancti Petri Martiris* (Oxford, 2022).

Rosenstock, Bruce, *New Men: conversos, Christian theology and society in fifteenth-century Castile* (London, 2002).

Roth, Norman, *Conversos, Inquisition and the Expulsion of the Jews from Spain* (Madison WI, ²2002).

Round, Nicholas G., '"Perdóneme Séneca": the translational practices of Alonso de Cartagena', *Bulletin of Hispanic Studies*, 75 (1998), 17–29.

Sánchez Herrero, José, *Concilios provinciales y sínodos toledanos de los siglos XIV y XV: la religiosidad cristiana del clero y pueblo* (La Laguna, 1976).

Schuster, Peter, 'Die Krise des Spätmittelalters. Zur Evidenz eines sozial- und wirtschaftsgeschichtlichen Paradigmas in der Geschichts-schreibung des 20. Jahrhunderts', *Historische Zeitschrift*, 269 (2001), 19–55.

Serrano Rodríguez, Eugenio, '"Laudare, benedicere, praedicare": Toledo y la Orden de Predicadores', *Anuario de historia de la Iglesia*, 30 (2021), 65-102.

Sicroff, Albert A., *Les Controverses des statuts de "pureté de sang" en Espagne du 15ᵉ au 17ᵉ siècle* (Paris, 1960).

Suárez Fernández, Luis, *Enrique IV de Castilla: la difamación como arma política* (Barcelona, 2001).

—, *Monarquía hispana y revolución trastámara* (Madrid, 1994).

Valdeón Baruque, Julio, *Cristianos, judíos y musulmanes* (Barcelona, 2006).

Townsend, Gertrude, 'Prophets and Apostles in the Creed Tapestry', *Bulletin of the Museum of Fine Arts*, 26, (1928), 64–70.

Vidal Doval, Rosa, *Misera Hispania: Jews and conversos in Alonso de Espina's 'Fortalitium fidei'* (Oxford, 2013).

Ward, Scott, *Historiography, Prophecy, and Literature: 'Divina retribucion' and its underlying ideological agenda* (Bloomington IN, 2009).

Wolff, Philippe, 'The 1391 Pogrom in Spain: social crisis or not?', *Past and Present*, 50 (1971), 4–18.